Early Man
in Britain
and Ireland

CROOM HELM STUDIES IN ARCHAEOLOGY

General Editor: Leslie Alcock, University of Glasgow

SURVEYING FOR ARCHAEOLOGISTS AND OTHER FIELDWORKERS
A. H. A. Hogg

CELTIC CRAFTSMANSHIP IN BRONZE
H. E. Kilbride-Jones

Pointed hand-axe, similar to forms from Lower Middle gravels, Swanscombe, England, provenance unknown. Dept. of Archaeology, University of Glasgow.

Early Man in Britain and Ireland

An Introduction to Palaeolithic and Mesolithic Cultures

Alex Morrison

CROOM HELM LONDON

Croom Helm Ltd, 2–10 St John's Road, London SW11

British Library Cataloguing in Publication Data

Morrison, Alex
   Early man in Britain and Ireland.–
   (Croom Helm studies in archaeology).
   1. Paleolithic period – Great Britain
   2. Mesolithic period – Great Britain
   3. Great Britain – Antiquities
   I. Title
   936.1'01   GN772.22.G7

   ISBN 0-85664-084-0
   ISBN 0-85664-089-1 Pbk

Printed in Great Britain by Biddles Ltd, Guildford, Surrey

CONTENTS

List of Plates

List of Figures

List of Tables

Introduction

1. The Pleistocene Period   15

    Pleistocene Glaciations   15
    Pleistocene Environment   21
    Dating the Pleistocene   26
    Pleistocene Chronology   32

2. Human Biological Development   39

    Australopithecus   41
    Homo erectus   43
    Transitional Forms of Man   45
    The Neanderthaloids   47
    Homo sapiens sapiens   49

3. The Evidence for Man's Presence in Britain in Earlier Palaeolithic Times   54

    The Hand-axe Groups   60
    Clactonian Industries   70
    Interpretation of Human Activity   72
    Later Developments   75

4. The Upper Palaeolithic in Britain   82

    The Earlier Upper Palaeolithic Period   85
    The Later Upper Palaeolithic Period   91

5. Post-glacial Environmental Changes   101

    Land- and Sea-level Changes   101
    Vegetational and Climatic Development   106
    Human Influence on the Environment   112

6. The Earlier Mesolithic Period   114

    The Concept of a 'Middle Stone Age'   114
    The Eighth–Seventh Millennia bc   115
    Star Carr   118
    Southern England   122

Wales   126
The Pennines and Northern England   126
Ireland   130
Barbed Points   132
Conclusions   132

7. The Later Mesolithic Period   134

England and Wales   136
Ireland   146
Scotland   154
Mesolithic to Neolithic   171

Bibliography   174

Index   204

PLATES

Frontispiece The hand-axe – used over a longer period of time than any other artifact in the history of human culture in Britain

Plate I	Examples of 'eoliths'	55
Plate II	Pointed hand-axes, Swanscombe	63
Plate III	Cordate hand-axe with tranchet point	67
Plate IV	Clactonian core and flake	71
Plate V	Levalloisian 'tortoise core'	75
Plate VI	Levalloisian core and flakes	78
Plate VII	Later Mesolithic flints, Surrey	139
Plate VIII	Small tranchet axe, Surrey	139
Plate IX	Mesolithic barbed points, Scotland and north-east England	155
Plate X	Mesolithic hammer-stones and bone points, Oronsay	159
Plate XI	Antler 'mattocks', Oronsay	159
Plate XII	Parts of barbed points, Oronsay	160
Plate XIII	Perforated cowrie shells, Oronsay	160
Plate XIV	Barbed points and 'fish hook', Risga	162
Plate XV	Uniserially barbed point, Glenavon, Banffshire	165
Plate XVI	Antler 'axe' or 'mattock', Stirlingshire	169

FIGURES

1.1	Geological Time Scale	14
1.2	Limits of north-west European glaciations	16
1.3	Pleistocene sea-level fluctuations	19
1.4	Formation of river terraces	20
1.5	Representative Pleistocene environments, with some associated faunas	23
1.6	The interglacial environmental stages	25
1.7	The C^{14} cycle	28
1.8	The Pliocene/Pleistocene boundary	33
1.9	Some tentative Pleistocene correlations	36–7
2.1	Man's place in the animal kingdom	40
2.2	Some major Australopithecine remains	42
2.3	Sites with remains of *Homo erectus*	44
2.4	Transitional forms of man	46
2.5	Some Neanderthaloid discoveries	48
2.6	Some important fossil remains of modern man	50
2.7	The major developments and possible relationships of early man	51
2.8	Examples of hominid skulls	52
3.1	Pebble tools and the earliest hand-axes	57
3.2	Generalised stratification at Westbury-sub-Mendip, Somerset	58
3.3	Hand-axes and scrapers from Swanscombe and Hoxne	62
3.4	The Hoxnian environmental sequence and cultural associations at Swanscombe, Hoxne and Clacton-on-Sea	64–5
3.5	Size and shape variation in hand-axes	68
3.6	Cores and flakes of the Clactonian industries	69
3.7	Map of British Earlier Palaeolithic sites and glaciation limits	73
3.8	Examples of Levalloisian and Mousterian artifacts	76
3.9	Suggested chronological sequence of some earlier Palaeolithic sites	80
4.1	Late Pleistocene glaciation, climatic fluctuation and cultural developments in Britain	84
4.2	Earlier Upper Palaeolithic artifacts	86
4.3	Map of Earlier Upper Palaeolithic sites, the Devensian glaciation limits and possible sea-level	88
4.4	Late-glacial and Later Upper Palaeolithic environmental and cultural chronology	92
4.5	Later Upper Palaeolithic artifacts	94

4.6   Map of Later Upper Palaeolithic sites, retreat stages of   98
      Devensian glaciation and possible sea-level

5.1   Map of raised beach regions and sites with transgression   103
      deposits
5.2   Table of sites with radiocarbon-dated transgression deposits   104
5.3   Pollen diagrams from Hockham Mere, Scaleby Moss, Drymen   107–8
5.4   Table summarising Post-glacial (Flandrian) environmental   109
      changes

6.1   Map of the North Sea area during the eighth millennium bc   117
6.2   Map of Earlier Mesolithic sites in England, Wales and Ireland   119
6.3   Flint, bone and wood artifacts from Star Carr   121
6.4   Artifacts from the Colne Valley and Broxbourne   123
6.5   Artifacts from Thatcham, Dozemare and Middlezoy   125
6.6   Earlier Mesolithic artifacts from the Pennines   128
6.7   Barbed antler and bone points from Earlier Mesolithic sites in   131
      Eastern England
6.8   Radiocarbon chronology of Earlier Mesolithic sites in England,   133
      Wales and Ireland

7.1   Map of Later Mesolithic sites in England and Wales   135
7.2   Artifacts from the Pennines and south-east England, with   137
      techniques of microlith production
7.3   Later Mesolithic artifacts from England and Wales   142
7.4   Radiocarbon chronology of Later Mesolithic sites in England   145
      and Wales
7.5   Map of Later Mesolithic sites in Ireland   147
7.6   Later Mesolithic artifacts from Ireland   150
7.7   Radiocarbon chronology of Later Mesolithic sites in Ireland   153
7.8   Map of Later Mesolithic sites in Scotland   156
7.9   Mesolithic stone and flint artifacts from Scotland   163
7.10 Barbed antler and bone points from Later Mesolithic sites in   166
      Scotland
7.11 Radiocarbon chronology of Mesolithic sites in Scotland   170

TABLES

1.1   Western European Temperatures during Last Glaciation   21
3.1   Classification of Hand-axes   60
5.1   Factors Determining Habitat and Vegetation   111

INTRODUCTION

The span of man's existence as a Stone Age hunter and gatherer – the Palaeolithic and Mesolithic periods of this book – was the longest in his whole history of physical and cultural development. In contrast to this, the surviving material evidence for that existence is minimal compared with later periods, and consists of little more than stone artifacts. The influence of climate and environment on man's activities and distribution during these early phases of technological development was strong, and the study of the changing Pleistocene and early Holocene climate, flora and fauna as a background to cultural evolution has required the close co-operation of the archaeologist with the geologist, zoologist, botanist, physicist and others. This is demonstrated in Chapter 1, where it has been necessary to range widely beyond the British Isles and the strictly archaeological evidence in order to emphasise the multi-disciplinary approach to the problems of the Quaternary environment and chronology. The brief review of human physical evolution in Chapter 2 is also a 'world-view', calling attention to the scarcity of early human remains in the British Isles, perhaps not surprising in view of the open locations and destructive effects of the sequence of ice advance and retreat.

It was usual, in many earlier studies of Palaeolithic and Mesolithic culture, to regard British developments as a simple extension of Continental culture, constructing typological and cultural sequences based, often arbitrarily, on European terminology. The situation of Britain and Ireland in relation to the Continent must be borne in mind: islands where periodically the sea-levels would be higher than at present, particularly during the Palaeolithic period. The physical separation was thus intensified, inhibiting the spread of culture at precisely those times when the climate would have favoured the movement of human groups into more northerly temperate regions. A major exception is the comparatively short period during the eighth millennium bc, when the isostatic recovery of the land outstripped the rising sea-level long enough to allow the development of similar cultural equipment among communities around a diminished North Sea basin (Chapter 6). Isolation, however, was never complete, and Continental 'affinities' did exist, but the trend is increasingly towards the interpretation of the British evidence in terms of its own local developments, varying according to functional, seasonal and environmental differences.

No attempt has been made to be definitive, but it is hoped that some indication has been given of the rate of progress in recent years in Palaeolithic and Mesolithic research. Despite this progress, many regions still need intensive investigation (for example the Mesolithic of inland Wales, south-west and north-west England, much of Scotland, and Ireland outside the north-east), so that any attempt at a complete or comprehensive study would soon be superseded by the results of work in progress – a positive and encouraging state of affairs.

I have been aided and encouraged by many friends and colleagues in the preparation of this book. In particular, I would like to thank the late Dr John Corcoran, who started me off on the study, Dr G. Jardine, who read and made useful comments on Chapters 1 and 5, Dr E. W. MacKie for help and discussion in the selection of artifacts for illustration from the Hunterian Museum; for helpful discussion of many matters beyond my direct knowledge I thank Dr R. Price, Dr J. Dickson and Dr E. Slater, but opinions, conclusions and any errors or omissions are my own responsibility. I am grateful also to Miss S. Leek for her patience and skill in drawing the figures, and to the University Court of the University of Glasgow for permission to use photographs of artifacts in the University's Hunterian Museum.

A. Morrison
Glasgow

TIME (10⁶ yrs)	SYSTEM	ERA		ANIMAL LIFE	PLANT LIFE	EARTH MOVEMENTS
0.01	Holocene	Quaternary	C			Changes due to ice action eustasy and isostasy
3	Pleistocene		A	Man		
12	Pliocene		I			Alpine orogeny, producing Alps, Pyrenees, Carpathians, Himalayas etc.
			N		Modern forms of vegetation, tropical in the earlier stages but becoming more temperate	
25	Miocene	Tertiary	O	Primitive anthropoids		
40	Oligocene		Z			
			O			
60	Eocene		I			
70	Palaeocene		C	Mammals		
			M			
	Cretaceous		E	True birds		
			S			
135		Secondary	O		Flowering plants	
	Jurassic		Z			
			O	Dinosaurs		
190			I			
225	Triassic		C	Reptiles		
	Permian		P		Conifers	Hercynian (Armorican / Variscan) orogeny. Harz, Black Forest, Vosges, Auvergne, Ardennes, mountains of south of Ireland, Devon, Cornwall.
270						
	Carboniferous		A	Amphibians	Seed – bearing plants	
340			L			
	Devonian		A	Insects	Spore – bearing ferns	
400		Primary	E			Caledonian orogeny remains of mountains in N. Ireland Scottish Highlands and Scandinavia.
	Silurian			Jawless fish	Land plants	
430			O			
	Ordovician		N	Molluscs	Algae	
500			O		and	
	Cambrian		I	Marine arthropods	Fungi	
600			C			
4000 +	Precambrian	Proterozoic		Algae and primitive forms of life		Many ancient mountain systems

Figure 1.1: Geological Time Scale.

Chapter 1

THE PLEISTOCENE PERIOD

Compared with the geological time scale (Figure 1.1), the period which has elapsed since man's appearance as a tool-making creature is brief, although it can now be numbered in millions of years. Natural changes in landscape occurred during the geological eras due to earth movements, volcanic activity, deposition, erosion, glaciation and changes in sea-level. By comparison, the impact of early man's activities on the landscape was minimal, becoming important only in recent, historical time, although its beginnings can be traced to a period when man was still an unspecialised hunter and food collector. Analysis of fossil pollen samples from strata dated to periods when modern species of man had not yet appeared suggests some destruction of forest cover, perhaps due to uncontrolled use of fire in driving animals during hunting. In later periods, selective hunting and 'overkill' affected the distribution and numbers of certain species of animals.

The slow evolution of man himself, his tool-making ability and way of life, took place in the most recent period of earth history, the Quaternary, which included several ice ages and the Recent or Post-glacial epoch. The earlier part of this Quaternary period, known as the Pleistocene epoch in geological, biological and climatological contexts, or the Palaeolithic period (Old Stone Age) from the point of view of man's cultural development, began perhaps two to three million years ago. The later subdivision of the Quaternary, the Holocene epoch, began with the retreat of the last ice-sheet some 10,000 years ago and is known culturally in its early phase in the British Isles and north-western Europe as the Mesolithic period.

Pleistocene Glaciations

Several times during the Pleistocene epoch the glaciers and ice-caps in the mountain regions developed and expanded over the foothills and lowlands as piedmont glaciers to unite as gigantic inland ice-sheets. On such occasions, the Alps had an ice cover many hundreds of metres in thickness which spread into southern Germany and northern Italy. Scandinavian ice, which in some areas may have been more than 2,500 metres in thickness, extended westwards to the proximity of the British Isles and southwards to the Netherlands and north Germany. In Britain, during one glaciation, the local ice-sheet extended south as far as the Thames Valley (Figure 1.2). Smaller local ice-masses occurred in the Massif Central, Vosges, Black Forest, Harz, Bohemian Forest, Erzgebirge, etc., contemporaneously with the Scandinavian and British ice-sheets.

It is now known that temperatures declined gradually during the Tertiary period and glaciers may have existed in several parts of the globe before the

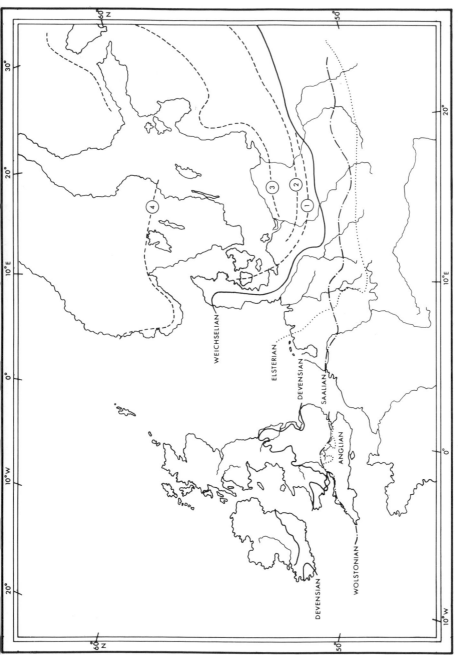

Figure 1.2: Limits of north-west European glaciations. Simplified lines of end moraines of Anglian/Elster, Wolstonian/Saalian and Devensian/Weichselian glaciations. The equation of British with Continental terminology is highly tentative. The retreat stages of the Weichselian glaciation are: 1, Pomeranian; 2, Frankfurt-Posen; 3, Riga; 4, Salpausselkä/Fenno-Scandian/Finiglacial moraines. After Woldstedt, 1958; West, 1968.

end of the Miocene epoch (Flint, 1971). The stratigraphical position of the Pliocene/Pleistocene boundary in north-western Europe, which is believed to coincide with the onset of cooler conditions, has now been set at a level where the Coralline Crag gives way to the Red Crag deposits in East Anglia, and where the Reuver clays are succeeded by the Praetiglian deposits in the Netherlands. Selection of the boundary between the Pliocene and Pleistocene at this horizon of lithological change is supported by evidence of a decrease in southern species of marine mollusca and an increase in cold-preferring species at the same horizon (West, 1968). This change was accompanied by the appearance of forms of true elephant (*Elephas (Archidiskodon) meridionalis*) and horse (*Equus stenonis*) in the East Anglian Red and Icenian Crags, elements of a Villafranchian fauna, including many Tertiary survivals, which had largely disappeared by the end of the Lower Pleistocene.

The repeated advances and retreats of the European ice-sheets have left their mark on the terrain crossed by the ice. Interpreting the evidence for the glacial sequence and stratigraphy is complicated as the result of later ice-sheets obliterating the traces of earlier, with the partial exception of the last (Devensian/Weichselian/Würm) glaciation, which did not reach the southern limits of preceding ice-sheets (Figure 1.2). The most extensive and severe of the northern glaciations appears to have been the second advance of the Elsterian ice-sheet, Elsterian II or Anglian II (Lowestoft stade).

Evidence for glaciations, ice advance and retreat and periglacial phenomena can still be traced in many parts of the British Isles and north-western Europe. Corries, cwms or cirques, hollowed out by freeze/thaw abrasion, show the collecting-places of perennial snow and their present location can indicate the height of the former snow line. Rock debris, carried as morainic material by the ice and dumped during melting, remains intermittently along the sides of valleys as lateral moraines; at the confluence of two valley glaciers, the inner lateral moraines converged to form a medial moraine, and where the melting front of a glacier had been stationary for some time a terminal moraine was formed. The retreat stages of the last glaciation in northern Europe have been defined to a great extent by the successive series of end moraines found between north Germany and central Scandinavia (Figure 1.2). Morainic material, boulder clay or glacial till, normally consisting of an unstratified mixture of finely ground soil, clay and stones, forming the roughly crescentic end moraines or deposited as drumlins – elongated, rounded hillocks with long axes parallel to the direction of ice movement – give the characteristic hummocky appearance to formerly glaciated regions. Such features are common in northern England, southern and central Scotland, and northern Ireland. Rounded and polished rock exposures (*roches moutonnées*) and approximately parallel scratching or striation of rock surfaces indicate the abrasive power and general direction of ice-flow. Erratic boulders and smaller rock fragments (granite from Ailsa Craig found in England, Wales and eastern Ireland; Scandinavian rocks present in south-east England and on the North German Plain) testify to the distances covered by expanding ice-sheets and to their transporting power. The U-shaped valley is a glaciated form and deepening of valleys by ice action has produced many of the fjords of Norway and sea-lochs of western Scotland; where the ice in the main valley cut below the erosion level of smaller tributary valleys, hanging valleys were created and streams now fall, often from a considerable height, into the lowered main valley. Sediments deposited in sinuous ridges (eskers) show the courses of former melt-water streams which flowed within or under wasting ice-sheets. From the glacier front, pro-glacial streams carried sands and gravels which formed outwash fans or deltas of fluvio-glacial material against the ice mass, or were carried well beyond the ice margins. Lakes have been formed where outflow from glaciers has been dammed by moraines or where the ice hollowed out the surface over which it moved. Of a more transitory nature were ice-dammed lakes which did, however, survive long enough in some places to leave their imprint on the present landscape. An example of this can be seen at the 'Parallel Roads' of Glenroy in Inverness-shire, where a glacial lake existed long enough for successive shorelines to be cut into the side of the valley. Wide melt-water channels, the *Urstromtäler* or 'ancient stream valleys' of the North European Plain, show where outwash streams from the Scandinavian ice-sheets were dammed between it and the Central Uplands of Europe and were forced into mainly east–west courses. The finer outwash materials – sands and silts – were dried out and carried by drying winds coming off the ice-sheet, to be redeposited in periglacial regions, often hundreds of miles from the ice front. These aeolian materials formed the widespread loess deposits of central Europe and the Ukraine. The limon of north-eastern France and some of the brickearths of south-east England are probably attenuated forms of loess. In central and western Europe, two layers, the Older and Younger Loess, have been recognised, the former probably laid down during the Saalian/Riss glaciation (although the lower layers may date to an earlier glaciation) and the latter during the Weichselian/Würm. A thick soil profile, developed on the Older Loess in many areas, was formed at the time of the Eemian (Riss-Würm) interglacial and thinner soil profiles within the main loess deposits indicate phases of climatic amelioration or interstadials within a glaciation. Studies of such fossil soils and their contained mollusca, and of other organic material such as pollen grains, have greatly extended the knowledge of Pleistocene environments.

It is known that, during the Pleistocene epoch, world-wide sea-levels fell and rose due to the formation and melting of the ice-sheets. In glaciated regions, these eustatic changes were accompanied by isostatic depression of the earth's surface under the weight of ice during glaciations and recovery in interglacial periods. The overall drop in sea-level in relation to the land during the Pleistocene epoch was more than 200 metres, but the pattern is believed to be complicated by a general slow uplift of the land in relation to sea-level which has been in progress since late Tertiary times (Butzer, 1972, p. 216). Remnants of a well preserved series of Pleistocene raised beaches, identified in the western Mediterranean area (Butzer, 1972, p. 25), approximate in height and age to shorelines in other regions, suggesting eustatic movements of sea-level (Figure 1.3), often to well below present levels during times of ice advance. Most of the raised shorelines of northern Britain are of more recent age, formed towards the end of the last glaciation and subsequently uplifted by isostatic recovery of the land after the melting of the last ice-sheet.

Changes of sea level and climatic factors are also responsible for the formation of river terraces. In the lower reaches of rivers such as the Somme and Thames, the terraces are *thalassostatic*, their formation being due largely to

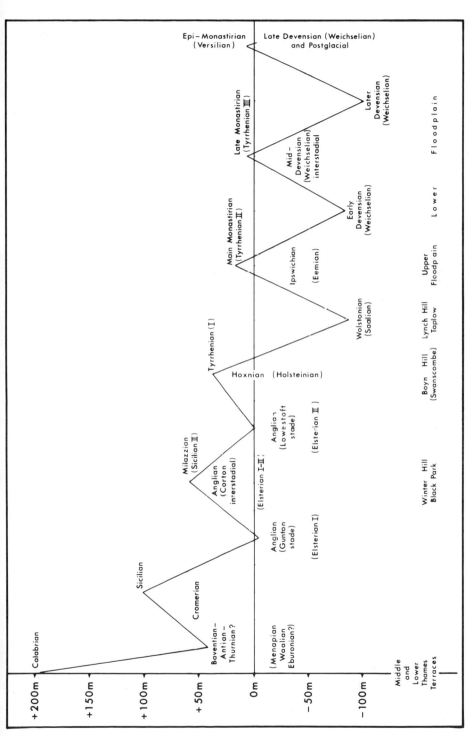

Figure 1.3: Pleistocene glacio-eustatic sea-level fluctuations, with Mediterranean shorelines (Calabrian, Sicilian, etc.) and tentative correlation with north-west European cold, glacial and interglacial periods and Thames river terraces. The fluctuation curve is greatly simplifed and does not show minor oscillations. The period divisions are not time-proportionate.

changes of sea level (Figure 1.4). The terraces are the remains of former flood-plains incised by the eroding river and left above later flood levels. In inland rivers, or in the upper reaches of rivers flowing directly into the sea, terrace formation is controlled by the climatic cycle rather than by fluctuations in sea-level. In such cases, in interglacial times, the river cut down into its bed. In cold periods, however, due to climatic deterioration, loss of forest cover, greater solifluction and frost erosion, inland rivers carried a greater load of sediment and in places this was deposited along their courses. Such aggradation during glacial phases is the reverse of processes occurring in the seaward sections of river valleys (Zeuner, 1958, pp. 124–31; 1959, pp. 42–9). Attempts to assign river terraces to particular glacial or interglacial phases are complicated by many factors and detailed sequences have been achieved only where additional evidence, for example of cold or temperate fauna, is available. Where such sequences are reasonably well known, it has been possible to give a relative dating to human remains or artifacts contained within the terraces – as at

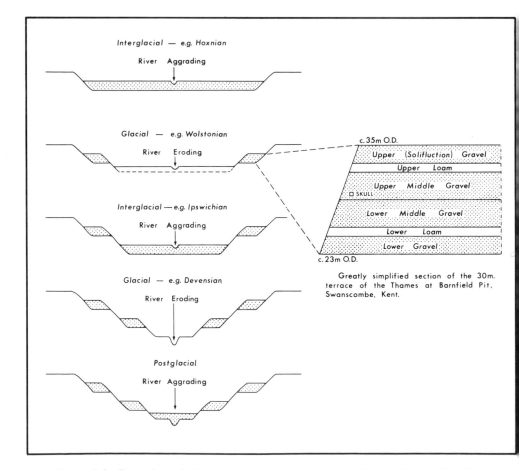

Figure 1.4: Formation of river terraces under 'thalassostatic' conditions. Simplified diagram of lower Thames terraces. Not to scale.

Barnfield Pit, Swanscombe, on the lower reaches of the Thames (Figure 1.4). It must be emphasised, however, that location of artifacts or faunal remains in river terraces does not necessarily mean contemporaneity. The contained materials may not be in a primary context and could have been derived from earlier deposits by fluvio-glacial action (Wymer, 1974).

Pleistocene Environment

In the higher latitudes of the northern hemisphere, in the present 'temperate' regions, Pleistocene environmental development was dominated mainly by the extreme climatic fluctuations of alternating glacial and interglacial periods. While there is little evidence before the Upper Pleistocene for man's presence or activities in these regions during periods of actual ice-advance, it cannot be doubted that, in general, Palaeolithic man's biological and cultural development was greatly affected by the physical background of changing Pleistocene environment.

Temperature is a major parameter in most biological processes, so that fluctuations between arctic and temperate conditions must have had drastic effects on the form and distribution of plant and animal life. Estimates of temperature change have been made, based mainly on evidence from the last glaciation, and it seems likely that, for the British Isles, the differences between average temperatures for cold periods and those for temperate periods were of the order of 5° to 8° C (West, 1968). Manley (1951) shows the 10° C isotherm for January during the final cold phase (Pollen Zone III) of the last glaciation as drawn across the south of England between the Fenland and the Bristol Channel, and even in the Allerød (Pollen Zone II) interval of temporary climatic improvement this isotherm was no further north than the central Lowlands of Scotland; its present location is beyond the north coast of Scotland. Klute (1951) listed temperatures for western Europe during the last glaciation; these are reproduced in Table 1.1. In a reconstruction of the climate of Europe during the Quaternary period, Kaiser (1969) suggested that the maximum drop in temperature for central Europe during the Pleistocene glacial periods was 15° to 16° C. Shotton (1960) suggested that the formation of fossil tundra-polygons (polygonal-shaped cracks in the soil formed by the freeze/thaw cycle during former permafrost conditions) in the Avon Valley, Worcestershire, would have required a drop in temperature of more than 12.5° C below present annual average.

Table 1.1: Western European Temperatures during Last Glaciation

	Jan. Temp.	July Temp.
Near the southern edge of the ice-sheet	−22° C	5° C
Vicinity of Paris	−16° C	10° C
Southern France	−10° C	12° C

Source: Klute (1951).

As already suggested, vegetation growth depends on temperature and, allowing for differences in latitude and longitude, changes in vegetation type and distribution, as revealed by pollen analysis and macroscopic studies (see Chapter 5), can indicate climatic fluctuations. If time and climatic improvement allow the development of a temperate deciduous forest similar to the mixed oak forest of the Post-glacial climatic optimum, then the period of time involved may be classed as an *interglacial*. During a glaciation, where the period of temporary climatic improvement was too short or temperatures too low to allow more than a type of boreal forest (for example birch, pine, hazel) to develop, the period is termed an *interstadial* (the Allerød (Pollen Zone II) interstadial occurred between the Pollen Zones I and III *stadials* of the last glaciation) (West, 1968, 1970a).

In higher latitudes, vegetation of the glacial episodes was characterised by a dominant non-tree assemblage, particularly of herbaceous plants, sedges and grasses. A high percentage of arctic-alpine and northern-montane phytogeographic forms was present and trees were represented only by a few dwarf or arctic types. A representative list, mainly from Devensian sites, would include:

Dwarf birch (*Betula nana*)
Least willow (*Salix herbacea*)
Aspen (*Populus tremula*)
Juniper (*Juniperus communis*)
Purple saxifrage (*Saxifraga oppisitifolia*)
Silverweed (*Potentilla onserina*)
Alpine meadow rue (*Thalictrum alpinum*)
Mountain sorrel (*Oxyria digyna*)
Cotton grasses (*Eriophorum* spp.)
Polar willow (*Salix polaris*)
Reticulate willow (*Salix reticulata*)
Sea buckthorn (*Hippophaë rhamnoides*)
Crowberry (*Empetrum nigrum*)
Dock (*Rumex* spp.)
Sedges (*Carex* spp.)
Curled pondweed (*Potamogeton crispus*)
Mountain avens (*Dryas octopetala*)
Alpine poppy (*Papaver alpinum*)

This open, park-tundra habitat with its permafrost conditions and solifluction soils gave way gradually to cold steppe, park steppe, sub-arctic or boreal forest with increasing distance from the periglacial regions (Figure 1.5).

The vegetation of interglacial times is best represented in Britain by evidence from the Hoxnian, Ipswichian and present Post-glacial (Flandrian) periods. Each of these interglacials can be represented by four environmental zones (Turner and West, 1968; West, 1968, 1970; Sparks and West, 1972). The first zone covers the climatic improvement at the end of a glacial period with the gradual change from an open habitat with light-tolerant species to closed forest conditions early in the second zone. Humus-enriched soils mature to mulls, brown earths, etc., according to geographical location. During the second and

Summer temperature low

Continental

Oceanic

T U N D R A

Vulpes (Alopex) lagopus (arctic fox), Gulo gulo (glutton or wolverine), Lepus timidus (arctic hare), Dicrostonyx sp. (arctic lemming), Coelodonta (Tichorhinus) antiquitatis (woolly rhinoceros), Rangifer tarandus (steppe reindeer), Ov-bos moschatus (musk-ox), Elephas (Mammuthus) primigenius (woolly mammoth).

L O E S S   S T E P P E

Vulpes (Alopex) lagopus, Lepus timidus, Coelodonta (Tichorhinus) antiquitatis, Rangifer tarandus, Bison cf. priscus (bison), Ovibos moschatus, Elephas (Mammuthus) primigenius, plus some Sub-Arctic Forest forms.

S U B - A R C T I C   F O R E S T

Ursus arctos (brown bear), Gulo gulo, Lynx lynx (European lynx), Cervus elaphus (red deer), Alces alces (elk), Rangifer tarandus (forest form), Bos primigenius (aurochs).

W A R M   C O N T I N E N T A L   F O R E S T - S T E P P E

A fauna consisting of both Temperate Forest and Warm Continental Steppe forms.

W A R M   C O N T I N E N T A L   S T E P P E

Lagomys spp., Alactaga jaculus (jerboa), Citellus spp., Marmota bobac (steppe marmot), Equus caballus przewalski (Mongolian steppe horse), Equus hemionus (onager), Saiga tarica (saiga antelope).

T E M P E R A T E   F O R E S T

Ursus arctos, Lynx lynx, Hippopotamus (mild winters only), Dicerorhinus kirchbergensis (mercki) (woodland rhinoceros), Cervus elaphus, Alces alces, Bos primigenius, Bison cf. bonasus (forest bison), Elephas (Palaeoloxodon) antiquus (forest elephant).

Summer temperature high

Figure 1.5: Representative Pleistocene environments ('biotopes') with some associated faunas. After Zeuner, 1958, 1959; Cornwall, 1968; Butzer, 1972.

third zones, the mixed oak forest of the 'climatic optimum' is infiltrated by late-arriving or expanding forms such as hornbeam (*Carpinus*), fir (*Abies*) or spruce (*Picea*), contributing to soil deterioration already under way. The leaching and acidification of soils encourage the expansion of conifers and heathland, a process accelerated in the fourth zone by climatic deterioration leading to periglacial conditions and a return to open tundra environments. The cycle is summarised in Figure 1.6 and in Chapter 5 (Figure 5.4) for the Flandrian.

Form and distribution of vegetation are therefore controlled by soil and climate, and animal life, being dependent directly or indirectly on plant food, is closely associated with the various forms of vegetation-habitat. Zeuner (1958, pp. 131–2; 1959, p. 309) saw Pleistocene faunal types as adaptations to broad vegetational environments rather than simply to climate alone – a classification into 'cold' and 'warm' faunas which makes no allowance for the many discoveries of the two forms in association. Some of the most important mammal forms show developments in the Middle and Upper Pleistocene towards environmental adaptation. The southern elephant, *Elephas (Archidiskodon) meridionalis*, a surviving Villafranchian form, disappeared early in the Middle Pleistocene, but the line continued in Europe through a diversification of species. *Elephas (Palaeoloxodon) antiquus*, the straight-tusked elephant, appeared during the Cromerian interglacial and was the temperate woodland species of the Hoxnian and Ipswichian interglacials, surviving to the beginning of the last glacial period. The second line of development was through the steppe-elephant, *Elephas (Mammuthus) trogontherii*, culminating in the woolly mammoth, *Elephas (Mammuthus) primigenius*, particularly adapted to the cold steppe and tundra of the last glaciation. *Dicerorhinus etruscus*, a Lower Pleistocene (Villafranchian) rhinoceros, was extinct before the end of the Anglian (Elster, Mindel) glaciation, but it was probably ancestral in Europe to *Dicerorhinus kirchbergensis (merckii)*, a temperate-forest rhinoceros, and also to *Dicerorhinus hemitoechus*, a steppe-adapted rhinoceros. By the Wolstonian (Saalian, Riss) glaciation, *Coelodonta (Tichorhinus) antiquitatis*, the woolly rhinoceros of cold steppe and tundra regions, had arrived in Europe from the east. These fossil forms of elephant and rhinoceros are important in Pleistocene stratigraphy as environmental indicators. The types of Pleistocene environment and their associated faunas are shown in Figure 1.5.

Faunas of the glacial periods are best represented in Britain by remains from the last two glaciations. These include: *Elephas (Mammuthus) primigenius* (mammoth); *Coelodonta (Tichorhinus) antiquitatus* (woolly rhinoceros); *Megaceros giganteus* (giant deer); *Rangifer tarandus* (reindeer, both steppe and forest forms); *Ovibos moschatus* (musk-ox); *Bison* species; *Equus caballus* (wild horse); *Microtus nivalis* (snow vole); *Lemmus lemmus* (Norway lemming); *Dicrostonyx henseli* (arctic lemming); and *Alopex lagopus* (arctic fox). An excellent example of cold-environment conditions was revealed by excavations at Salzgitter-Lebenstedt, near Hanover, West Germany (Tode *et al.*, 1953), a summer camp-site of the early Weichselian glacial period. The occupants may have been a form of Neanderthal man, the industry was Mousterian of Acheulian tradition. Animal remains reflect the environment and hunting preferences of the time: reindeer 72 per cent, mammoth 14 per cent, bison 5.4 per cent, wild horse 4.6 per cent, woolly rhinoceros 2 per cent,

Figure 1.6: Interglacial environmental stages. After Turner and West, 1968; West, 1970; Sparks and West, 1972.

ZONE	CLIMATE		SOILS	PLANT COVER	POLLEN	FAUNAL FORMS
EARLY GLACIAL	cold	Deteriorating	Skeletal–mineral soils / Solifluction	Steppe tundra	Shrubs grasses herbs — Increase in nonarboreal pollen	Lemmus sp.
IV	cool, post–temperate		Podsol–acidic mor soils (leaching →)	Steppe / Heath	Pinus Betula — Mixed oak forest Abies Carpinus	Equus caballus / Dama clactoniana / Bos primigenius / Megaceros giganteus
III	warm, late–temperate		Brown earth mull soils	Open forest	Mixed oak forest Taxus Corylus	Hippopotamus (Ipswichian only)
II	early–temperate			Closed forest	Betula	Bos primigenius / Cervus elaphus / Dama clactoniana (Hoxnian only) / Equus cf. caballus / Elephas antiquus / Dicerorhinus kirchbergensis (merckii) / Dicerorhinus hemitoechus / Sus cf. scrofa / Martes cf. martes / Canis cf. lupus
I	cool, pre–temperate	Ameliorating	Solifluction	Steppe tundra	Pinus — Decrease in nonarboreal pollen — Shrubs grasses herbs	
LATE GLACIAL	cold		Skeletal–mineral soils			

the remainder consisting of wolf, musk-rat, swan, duck, a type of vulture, perch, pike, crabs, molluscs and insects. Vegetation included arctic willow and least willow, cold forms of pondweed, thrift, ragged robin, mosses, docks and sedges. Soil evidence suggested permafrost and the site was near the contemporaneous northern tree-limit. A radiocarbon date of 55,600 years bp was obtained.

Some typical interglacial faunal forms have been mentioned above and a representative list is given in Figure 1.6.

Land and freshwater mollusca can be useful indicators of environment and environmental change and, to a lesser extent, climate (Sparks, 1961, 1964; Kerney, 1971; Evans, 1972). Marine mollusca have been used to interpret sea-level change and coastal environment in the Lower Pleistocene of East Anglia (Norton, 1967). Studies of fossil insects have also yielded information on environment and climatic fluctuation. Coleoptera, in particular, are fastidious as to environmental requirements, and have undergone so little morphological change since the Lower Pleistocene that their presence in faunal assemblages can be used as a sensitive indicator of change, particularly in the thermal environment (Coope, 1959, 1970, 1975; Coope *et al.*, 1961, 1971).

Dating the Pleistocene

Until fairly recent times, Pleistocene and early post-Pleistocene events had to be recorded in a chronology based on location of evidence in geological or archaeological strata. Artifacts or human remains were dated by correlation with known successions of prehistoric cultures based on typology and stratigraphy, or by reference to the particular glacial or interglacial deposits in which they were found. This did not allow a dating in terms of years other than in a very generalised sense, but cultures and their artifacts could be placed in sequence and to some extent interrelated. Such forms of *relative dating*, as applied to human remains, have been classified and graded by Oakley (1969, pp. 1–10) into first, second and third order forms according to whether the find can be related directly to the deposit within which it occurs or to some wider scheme of stratigraphical or archaeological succession. It is important that the find be established as contemporaneous with its containing deposit, particularly where some method of absolute dating is to be applied. Contemporaneity of human or animal remains in a deposit has been determined in some cases by analysis of the *fluorine content* of the bones. Fluorine in ground water is absorbed by buried bones as part of the process of fossilisation, and bones which have been in the ground for the same length of time should have approximately the same concentration of fluorine. This method and the similar *uranium* and *nitrogen* analysis techniques will only date relatively and approximately, but they have been invaluable in contributing, for example, to the exposure of the 'Piltdown Man' forgery, where skull, jaw and accompanying animal remains were revealed as belonging to widely differing periods of time; fluorine tests of the *Homo erectus* remains from Trinil in Java showed the primitive skull and seemingly more modern femur to be contemporary.

Dates in years can now be applied to Pleistocene and later remains by various techniques. Such methods of *absolute dating* have also been classified by Oakley (1969, loc. cit.) and his various orders of dating may be mentioned briefly here.

A.1 Direct dating of the find itself. This order of dating is confined at present to materials dated by the radiocarbon method (bone, wood, leather, etc.); for example samples of collagen (structural protein) from the femur and tibia which dated the 'Red Lady' burial (in fact a young man of Cro-Magnon type, sprinkled with red ochre and accompanied by 'Proto-Solutrean' (Earlier Upper Palaeolithic) artifacts and animal remains) in Paviland Cave, Gower, south Wales (Oakley, 1968).

A.2 Direct dating of the deposit within which the find occurs; for example the potassium-argon (K/Ar) dating of volcanic rocks in Bed I of Olduvai Gorge, Tanzania, bracketing the level at which occurred remains of '*Zinjanthropus*' (*Australopithecus boisei*) and primitive stone tools (Evernden and Curtis, 1965).

A.3 Dating of the deposit within which the find occurs by inference from a deposit of the same type which has been directly dated elsewhere, for example the age of '*Pithecanthropus*' remains from the faunal bed at Trinil, Java, was obtained by correlation with a volcanic deposit containing Trinil fauna dated by the potassium-argon method in another region of Java (von Koenigswald, 1962).

A.4 Dating by inference from some theoretical consideration, for example where Pleistocene climatic fluctuations on land have been related to palaeotemperature changes seemingly recorded in foraminiferal layers of sea-bed cores dated by sub-stages in the uranium decay series (Emiliani, 1955; Rosholt *et al.*, 1961).

It is not intended to give a complete list of dating methods for Palaeolithic and Mesolithic sites and remains. Most methods have been adequately covered in recent studies by Oakley (1969), Michael and Ralph (1971) and Bishop and Miller (1972). A brief outline of three of the more important radiometric techniques will give some indication of the complexities involved in dating material from the periods covered.

Radiocarbon (C^{14}) Dating

This is perhaps the most potentially useful dating method so far discovered. This technique makes use of the decay of the unstable radioactive isotope of carbon, Carbon-14 or C^{14} and its known half-life. The C^{14} cycle is shown diagrammatically at Figure 1.7. Dates are determined by calculating the amount of radiocarbon surviving in a sample of organic material now, as against the quantity at death, the date obtained thus being the time of death of the organism. Among the materials suitable for dating by this technique are: wood, charcoal, plant remains (including seeds), peat, leather, skin, antler and bone.

The number of disintegrations per minute of C^{14} decreases with age and is related to the amount of C^{14} remaining. In organic samples used for dating purposes, the amount of radioactivity is very small, even in new material. Background radiation in laboratories, particularly cosmic radiation, is sufficient to 'drown out' the weak activity of a prehistoric sample. Even with

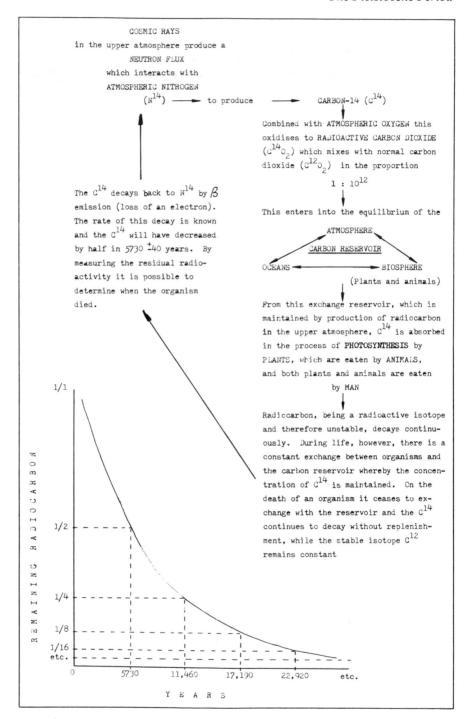

Figure 1.7: The C^{14} cycle in diagrammatic form.

shielding and anti-coincidence counting, sufficient outside radiation gets through to affect the disintegration-count of the sample. To compensate for this and also for errors of measurement, repeat-counts have to be made and this makes it necessary for radiocarbon dates to be published with a standard deviation (1σ), for example 8000 ± 100 bp. This is a statement of statistical probability, and indicates that 8000 bp is the mean date, with a 68 per cent chance that the correct date lies within the range 7900 to 8100 bp. With two (2σ) standard deviations (8000 ± 200 bp) there is a 95 per cent probability of the correct date lying within the range 7800 to 8200 bp, and with three (3σ) standard deviations (8000 ± 300 bp) there is a 99.7 per cent probability that the date will lie between 7700 and 8300 bp. It has been suggested that these three ranges be regarded as 'fairly probable', 'probable' and 'highly probable' (Barker, 1958; Burleigh, 1974). The letters bp mean *before present*, the conventional 'present' being internationally accepted as AD 1950 (Godwin, 1962). Dates can be converted to bc by subtracting 1950 from the bp date.

The radioactivity of very old material becomes increasingly difficult to detect and a limit of about 40,000 years has been set. It has been possible to increase the range to about 70,000 years by laboratory treatment of specimens but determinations of dates older than 50,000 years are rare.

Errors in determination can be caused by the properties of the sample or its condition. There may be exchange between the C^{14} and C^{12} in marine shells, enriching the C^{14} and giving dates which are 'too young'. Isotopic fractionation takes place in some plants so that they absorb a smaller proportion of radiocarbon; the ratio of C^{12} to C^{13} (the two stable isotopes of carbon) is known and can be measured by mass spectrometry; if a sample shows a variation from this ratio, it is possible to apply a correction to the date determined for the sample, thus compensating for the fractionation which has taken place (Burleigh, 1974). Dates which are 'too old' may be obtained from marine shells or plants absorbing radioactively dead carbonates in solution (Shotton, 1967, pp. 360–3). Contamination of samples by older or younger organic material in the ground or in contact with the sample after excavation can also produce over- or under-assessment of age. In addition, wood used in prehistoric structures may be from the heart of a tree and therefore much older than the date of felling, particularly in the case of long-lived specimens, and fossil wood has often been used for artifacts.

Until recently, a major assumption in radiocarbon dating has been that the production and quantity of C^{14} in the atmosphere was constant in time. Dendrochronological techniques combined with radiocarbon dating have disproved this.

Dendrochronology

This method is based on the assumption that growth-rings in trees represent calendar years, and that it is possible to determine absolute dates by counting back through the rings of modern trees, cross-matching with successively older trees and linking with growth-rings in timbers of ancient structures, etc. Systematic radiocarbon dating of tree-ring samples of known age has shown serious discrepancies between tree-ring and radiocarbon dates increasing backwards in time, so that by around 5000 BC the radiocarbon dates may be more than 700 years too young. The gap does not necessarily continue to widen back in time beyond this period and there are suggestions of a reversal of the trend (Broecker, 1965; Damon, 1968). It has been suggested that periods of greater C^{14} concentration coincide with warmer climatic phases and lesser concentration with colder. As well as changes in planetary temperature, fluctuations in solar and cosmic ray activity or in the intensity of the earth's magnetic field, the latter of which affects the concentration of cosmic radiation reaching the atmosphere, have also been suggested as responsible for variations in the production of atmospheric radiocarbon. The problems are well discussed in Olsson (1970). Calibration curves for radiocarbon dates based on the dendrochronology of the oldest known tree, bristlecone pine (*Pinus aristata*), have been produced by Suess (1970) and, more recently, Ralph, Michael and Han (1973), but final agreement on cause and correlation is not yet in sight.

From the above, it is evident that radiocarbon years are not equivalent to calendar years and there seems to be no point, at this stage of development, in attempting to calibrate against any published curve (cf. Waterbolk, 1971). Dates in this book, therefore, are expressed in conventional radiocarbon years by use of lower-case letters, for example 12,378 bp, or for later, post-Palaeolithic dates 7538 bc. The most recent assessment of the half-life of radiocarbon is 5730 ± 40 years but, by international agreement and to avoid confusion, radiocarbon dates are still calculated and published in the journal *Radiocarbon*, as here, on the basis of the earlier calculated half-life of 5568 ± 30 years (Godwin, 1962). Radiocarbon dates in years bp may be converted to the new half-life date by multiplying by 1.03. Many dates in the text are shown without the standard deviation for convenience, but Mesolithic dates are expressed at one standard deviation in the chronological tables at Figure 6.8, Figure 7.4, Figure 7.7 and Figure 7.11.

Protoactinium/Thorium (Pa²³¹/Th²³⁰) Dating

The radioactive isotopes of uranium, U^{238} and U^{235}, produce respectively, in a sub-stage of their decay series to lead, the isotopes Thorium^{230} (Th^{230}) and Protoactinium^{231} (Pa^{231}). The half-life of Pa^{231} is 32,000 years and that of Th^{230} is 75,000 years. These elements are present in ocean floor sediments and since the U^{238}/U^{235} ratio is constant whereas the Pa^{231}/Th^{230} ratio changes through time because of the differing half-lives, it is possible to date these marine sediments or cores taken from them. The limiting factor is the more rapidly declining quantity of Pa^{231} as against Th^{230}, and the effective limit backwards in time is about 150,000 years. This dating technique would theoretically help to bridge the gap between the short-term radiocarbon method and the much longer-term potassium-argon method, but it has been used almost exclusively on marine sediments. Recently a form of uranium-series dating (Th^{230}/U^{234}) has been applied with some success to fossil bones from Hoxnian and Ipswichian sites in south-east England (Szabo and Collins, 1975).

Potassium-argon (K/Ar) Dating

Yet another technique involving radioactive decay but with a range extending back to the beginnings of geological time. The radioactive isotope of potassium

(K^{40}) decays to the inert gas argon (Ar^{40}) with a half-life of 1.3×10^9 (1300 million) years. In the formation of igneous rocks containing potassium, the free argon is driven off so that any argon thereafter occurring in the rock after cooling will be a product of the disintegration of K^{40}, unless further metamorphism takes place, when the existing argon will disappear and the process begin again. The ratio of Ar^{40} to K^{40} therefore provides the dating evidence. The technique is limited to rocks such as lavas and some types of volcanic ash. Errors due to the loss of some of the radiogenic argon, giving 'too young' dates, or absorption of atmospheric argon, are possible and there is also the risk that older, unaltered material has been included in a reconstituted lava. Such hazards mean that potassium-argon dating can involve a much greater percentage error than the radiocarbon technique, thus limiting its usefulness to archaeology where dates of less than 300,000–400,000 years are concerned. It is to be hoped that refinements in the technique will produce more accurate dates for the Middle and Early Upper Pleistocene. By the potassium-argon method, the age of archaeological material is determined by its stratigraphical position in relation to the dated rocks, as in the case of the hominid remains and primitive stone tools in Bed I at Olduvai Gorge, Tanzania (Evernden and Curtis, 1965).

Potassium-argon dating has made possible the construction of a *palaeomagnetic time-scale*. Detailed study of magnetism in ancient volcanic rocks has shown that there were long periods in the past when the polarity of the earth's magnetic field was reversed in relation to present polarity. These periods of reversed polarity and the periods of normal polarity which separated them (assuming that present polarity is 'normal') are known as polarity epochs. The present, Brunhes, normal epoch was preceded by the Matuyama reversed epoch and the earlier Gauss normal and Gilbert reversed epochs (Figures 1.8 and 1.9). Shorter polarity reversal 'events' have been traced within the longer epochs. The application of potassium argon dating to rocks with known polarity has allowed the construction of a time-scale which is gradually being checked against volcanic stratigraphy in widely separated regions (Cox, 1972; Dalrymple, 1972). There is still some disagreement as to existence, location and duration of some events, and it has been recently suggested that the Gilsa event should be omitted from the stratigraphy (Grommé and Hay, 1971). The name has been retained here because of references in books and papers published prior to 1971. Attempts have also been made, with some success, to correlate palaeomagnetic evidence from deep-sea cores with continental occurrences, for example Glass *et al.* (1967) and Ericson and Wollin (1968). Palaeomagnetic chronology has made it possible to date rocks unsuitable for direct dating by the potassium-argon method by correlation of their palaeomagnetism with K/Ar-dated stratigraphy elsewhere. The major limitation of potassium-argon dating is, of course, that it is confined to those areas where recent volcanic activity has provided suitable dating material.

An isolated determination by any method of absolute dating cannot be accepted as sufficient to date a level or object with any degree of confidence. More suitable is a group or network of such dates as, for example, is now available for Bed I at Olduvai Gorge (Isaac, 1972), or, where possible, a cross-checking of dates by using different methods.

Pleistocene Chronology

Any attempt to correlate Pleistocene stratigraphy with absolute chronology is complicated by the lack of agreement among the authorities and disciplines involved. Stratigraphical terminology is still to a great extent unstandardised and often no clear distinction is made as to whether the classification system in use is lithostratigraphic (rock or sediment stratification), biostratigraphic (based on the occurrence of fossil fauna, pollen or foraminifera from deep-sea sediments), climatostratigraphic (for example the succession of glaciations, interglacials, interstadials), chronostratigraphic, or a stratigraphic unit based on some combination of these (West, 1968; Flint, 1971; Isaac, 1972). The application of the terminology of the Alpine glacial sequence beyond the strictly limited type-region has caused much controversy and inaccuracy in the past, but it is increasingly being replaced by divisions based on local sequences of deposits. There is, for example, no evidence to suggest a period of glacial ice in the British Isles equivalent to the Günz stage in the Alps, and it may be that major glaciations in north-western Europe were confined to the Middle and Upper Pleistocene.

A major point of contention in attempts to construct a framework for dating subdivisions of the Pleistocene is the location, both chronological and stratigraphical, of the Pliocene/Pleistocene boundary and, as a corollary, the duration of the Pleistocene itself. Estimates for the age of the boundary have ranged from around 600,000 to more than 4 million years. The variations appear in the main to be due to differing forms of evidence and their interpretation, and to the differences in geographical location (for example continental as against marine sediments) of the materials used for chronological or climatological determinations.

Lithostratigraphical criteria such as the transition from the Coralline Crag to the Red Crag in East Anglia and corresponding biostratigraphical evidence of decrease of warmth-loving marine mollusca in temperate waters have been mentioned. Changes in fauna from Upper Pliocene Astian forms to Lower Pleistocene Villafranchian forms (both names from sites at Villafranca d'Asti, Piedmont, north Italy) have been noted, particularly the first appearance of true horse, elephant and ox (Kurtén, 1968, pp. 8–17), but such changes are not necessarily contemporaneous and, being time-transgressive, should be accepted only as indicators of a broad zone of change. Zagwijn (1973) has suggested that model Pliocene/Pleistocene boundaries might be constructed taking parameters already used to define the *end* of the Pleistocene (the surpassing of the 5° C, 10° C and 14° C mean summer isotherms). These, however, would give a Pleistocene threshold varying between about 700,000 and about 10 million years ago!

At a site at Tjörnes in north-east Iceland, intercalated marine, non-marine and glacial sediments and lavas occur. It has been possible to detect differing palaeomagnetic layers in the sequence and to correlate them with known dated palaeomagnetic activity (Einarsson, Hopkins and Doell, 1967). Referring to this site, Zagwijn (1973, p. 4) suggested that a possible parameter for use in constructing a model Pliocene/Pleistocene boundary might be the point in time at which an ice-sheet just covered the whole area within the present coastline of Iceland, a stage reached again in the ice *retreat* about 10,000 years ago. The

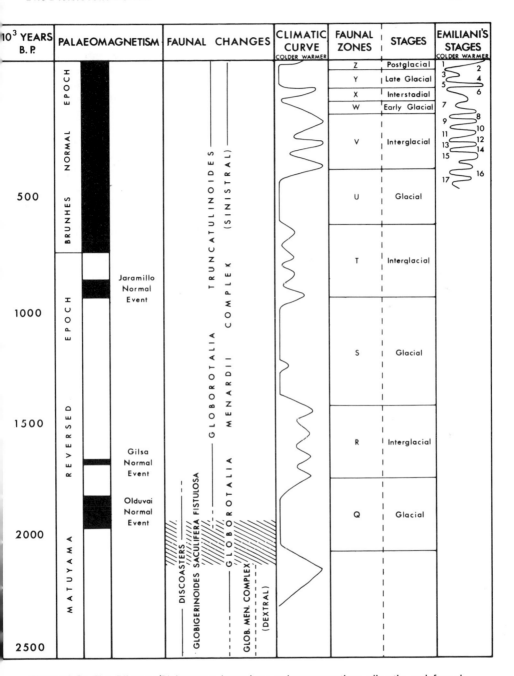

Figure 1.8: The Pliocene/Pleistocene boundary, palaeomagnetism, climatic and faunal changes, based on the work of Emiliani, Ericson, Ewing, Glass and Wollin. The hatched area is the Pliocene/Pleistocene 'boundary-zone' suggested by the micropalaeontological studies of deep-sea cores.

first expansion of the ice to this stage seems to be recorded in the Furuvik tillite beds at Tjörnes and dated, on two differing interpretations of the palaeomagnetic stratigraphy, to either around 1.9 million years ago or between 2.4 and 3.0 million years ago. The later date, according to Zagwijn, is near the beginning of the Praetiglian cold phase at the base of Netherlands Pleistocene sedimentary sequence, but again there is a wide range rather than a marked boundary. A summary of this and other evidence has been published by Zagwijn (1974).

Potassium-argon dating of rocks containing early Villafranchian fauna (in North America, Blancan) gives a range of 2.5 to 3.5 million years for the beginning of the Pleistocene (Evernden *et al.*, 1964; Curtis, 1965; Savage and Curtis, 1970). If, however, the Lower Villafranchian is regarded as Pliocene and only the Upper Villafranchian is taken to be Pleistocene, then dates for the base of the Mediterranean Calabrian marine series (= Upper Villafranchian) place the Pliocene/Pleistocene boundary at 1.6 to 1.8 million years ago (Emiliani, Mayeda and Selli, 1961; Shotton, 1967, p. 371; Selli, 1967; Suggate, 1973).

Micropalaeontological studies of deep-sea cores (Ericson, Ewing and Wollin, 1963 and 1964; Glass *et al.*, 1967; Ericson and Wollin, 1968) from the floors of the Atlantic and Pacific oceans have shown significant changes in the occurrence of certain forms of planktonic foraminifera across a proposed Pliocene/Pleistocene boundary zone of about 250,000–300,000 years duration (Figure 1.8). Warm-water forms such as discoasters and *Globigerinoides sacculifera fistulosa* disappear above the boundary zone, *Globorotalia truncatulinoides* appears above the boundary zone, *Globorotalia menardii* tests (the calcareous skeletons) coil to the right (dextral = warmer water) below the boundary zone, to the left (sinistral = cooler water) above it. There is also an increase in size and thickness of the tests of *Globorotalia menardii* above the boundary zone. By measurement of the magnetism in deep-sea cores, attempts have been made to relate these changes in marine sediments to continental palaeomagnetic stratigraphy (Glass *et al.*, 1967), and to suggest that the zone of change began about the base of the Olduvai normal magnetic event within the Matuyama reversed polarity epoch, or about 2 million years ago (Figures 1.8 and 1.9). More recently, a date of about 1.6 million years for the boundary has been suggested, again from studies of calcareous plankton in deep-sea cores (Bilal *et al.*, 1977). Oakley (1969, p. 46; 1970, p. 307) has proposed an arbitrary placing of the Pliocene/Pleistocene boundary at 2 million years ago.

Chronology is further complicated by the scarcity of reliable absolute dates for the period between the latest potassium-argon dates and the earliest possible range of radiocarbon dating. Climatic variations within this period have been detected by analysis of foraminiferal remains from deep-sea cores. The isotopes of oxygen, O^{18} and O^{16}, are present in sea water. The ratio O^{18} to O^{16} is higher in cold water than in warm. Certain planktonic foraminifera use these oxygen isotopes in building their skeletons or tests and the O^{18}/O^{16} ratio is preserved in these tests, indicating whether they formed in cold or warm water. Mass-spectrometric analysis of foraminifera, particularly *Globigerina* forms, has yielded evidence of the isotopic temperature of the water in which they were formed and from this a palaeotemperature curve has been obtained

(Emiliani, 1955, 1961, 1964, 1966). The curve shows a succession of warm and cold cycles for the Pleistocene epoch, beginning about 425,000 years ago (Emiliani, 1966), with estimates for the basal Pleistocene deposits at 600,000 to 800,000 years ago (Emiliani, 1961). The cores were dated by radiocarbon in the uppermost layers, the deeper layers being dated by extrapolation of the radiocarbon dates and uranium-series methods such as Pa^{231}/Th^{230} (Rosholt *et al.*, 1961).

Using the study of foraminifera in deep-sea cores, as mentioned already in the study of the Pliocene/Pleistocene boundary, geologists at the Lamont Geological Observatory (Ericson *et al.*, 1961; Ericson, Ewing and Wollin, 1963, 1964; Glass *et al.*, 1967; Ericson and Wollin, 1968) produced a quite different set of results. Instead of the O^{18}/O^{16} ratio, measurements of the varying abundance of temperature-sensitive *Globorotalia menardii* and of the changes in coiling direction of the tests of *Globorotalia truncatulinoides* (left = colder, right = warmer) were taken from a large number of cores. From this evidence, ten palaeontological (faunal) zones were proposed and equated with continental climatic fluctuations. Dating in the upper levels by radiocarbon and Pa^{231}/Th^{230} was extrapolated and magnetism in the cores correlated with palaeomagnetic epochs. This method produced a climatic/time scale for the Pleistocene, beginning about 2 million years ago and having four major glacial periods, four interglacial intervals, including the present, and a warmer interstadial phase (Zone X) during the last glaciation, thus differing widely from Emiliani's cycles (Figure 1.8).

Both schemes have been criticised to some extent. In the case of the O^{18}/O^{16} technique, it has been questioned whether or not the correct allowance was made for the changing isotopic composition and salinity of the oceans during the Pleistocene climatic fluctuations (Shackleton, 1967; Broecker, 1965). Broecker and van Donk (1970) suggested that Emiliani's time-scale should be increased by 25 per cent. Criticism has also been levelled at the Lamont sequence on the grounds that there is lack of detail and over-generalisation of curves compared with Emiliani's cycles, that only four glaciations are shown, that the Mindel (Elsterian, Anglian) glaciation is given four times the length suggested by radiometric dating, and that it is suggested that the Pleistocene began with a glaciation rather than a period of slowly cooling climate. The Lamont stages are well reviewed in Evans (1971, pp. 193–214), and marine-core analysis is discussed in general by Laporte (1968, pp. 81–91) and Vita-Finzi (1973, pp. 68–77). The techniques discussed above are on the whole for marine deposits and there is as yet no correlation with continental events that has received unqualified acceptance, although Evans (1971) has produced an interesting attempt at a Pleistocene time-scale on the basis of Emiliani's sea-core stages, insolation curves and radiometric dates.

The value of Emiliani's evidence for palaeotemperature cycles cannot be overrated and their concept must surely be a major contribution in breaking down the classical idea of four or five long glacial periods separated by interglacial episodes. The work of Ericson and his associates has provided important faunal zonation for the past 2 million years and a set of useful criteria for estimating the Pliocene/Pleistocene boundary.

The table at Figure 1.9 can therefore be no more than a tentative correlation of time and glacial/interglacial stratigraphy, particularly in the Lower and in

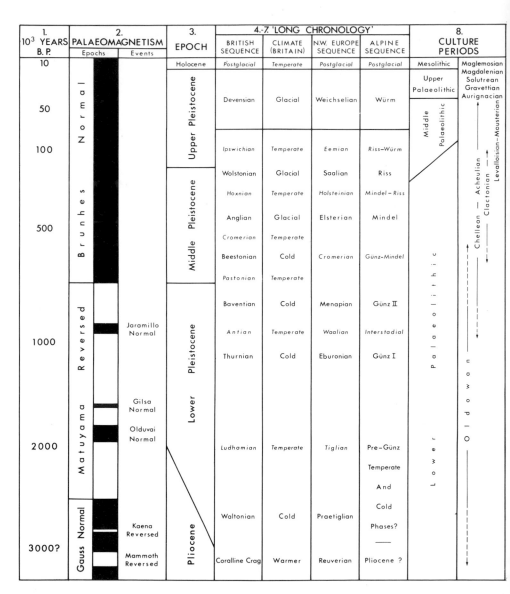

Figure 1.9: Some tentative correlations of Pleistocene chronology, glacial stratigraphy, human and cultural development. See explanatory notes in text.

9. CULTURE SITES	10. HOMINID FORMS	11.-14.'SHORT CHRONOLOGY'				15. 10³ YEARS B.P.
		BRITISH SEQUENCE	CLIMATE (BRITAIN)	NW. EUROPE SEQUENCE	ALPINE SEQUENCE	
Star Carr (C14) Paviland Cave (C14)		Postglacial	Temperate	Postglacial	Postglacial	10
Willendorf (C14)		Devensian	Glacial	Weichselian	Würm	
La Cotte de St. Brelade (C14)						50
Salzgitter-Lebenstedt (C14)						
		Ipswichian	Temperate	Eemian	Riss-Würm	100
Fontéchevade (L,B)		Wolstonian	Glacial	Saalian	Riss	
Swanscombe (L,B)		Hoxnian	Temperate	Holsteinian	Mindel-Riss	
		Anglian	Glacial	Elsterian	Mindel	
		Cromerian	Temperate			
		Beestonian	Cold	Cromerian	Gunz-Mindel	
Torralba (L,B)		Pastonian	Temperate			
Torre in Pietra (K/Ar)		Baventian	Cold	Menapian	Günz I	
Vértesszöllös (I,B)		Antian	Temperate	Waalian	Interstadial	
Westbury Sub Mendip(L,B)?		Thurnian	Cold	Eburonian	Günz I	500
Mauer (Heidelberg) (L,B)		Ludhamian	Temperate	Tiglian	Donau-Günz?	
					Donau	
					And	
					Earlier	1000
		Waltonian?	Cold	Praetiglian ?	Cold	
Olduvai I (K/Ar)					And	
						2000
					Temperate	
Koobi Fora (K/Ar)					Phases	
					———	3000?
		Coralline Crag	Warmer	Reuverian	Pliocene ?	

Column 10 (HOMINID FORMS), read vertically: HOMO SAPIENS SAPIENS / NEANDERTHALOIDS / HOMO SAPIENS / HOMO ERECTUS / AUSTRALOPITHECINES – HOMO

most of the Middle Pleistocene, and especially in attempting to relate north-west European to Alpine events much before the last glaciation. It is intended to give a synoptic view of Pleistocene successions and developments rather than to suggest an absolute chronology.

Columns 1 and 15	Dating by potassium-argon for the earlier stages and by radiocarbon for the last 60,000 years.
Column 2	Shaded sections of the column show normal polarity.
Column 3	The Middle Pleistocene is taken as beginning with the Cromerian complex, by which stage the Villafranchian fauna, which defines the Lower Pleistocene, had been greatly reduced.
Columns 4 to 7 and 11 to 14	Examples of both 'long' and 'short' chronologies are given. The long chronology is after Flint, 1971 (Tables 24-A and 29-F) but without the expanded stages of Ericson *et al.* (1964) and Ericson and Wollin (1968). The short chronology is after West (1968) and Evans (1971 and 1972), avoiding the extreme compression of Emiliani (1961, 1966). An example of long versus short chronology is provided by the Hoxnian (Holsteinian, Mindel-Riss, 'Great') Interglacial. This interval was calculated by Penck and Brückner (1909) and Penck (1908) as having lasted about 240,000 years, based on soil formation and the thickness and weathering of deposits from the preceding glaciation. Holmes (1965, pp. 701–2) suggested that these processes could not be compressed into a period of less than 300,000 years. Counting of possibly annual laminated sediments in an interglacial lake bed of Hoxnian age at Marks Tey in Essex (Shackleton and Turner, 1967; Turner, 1970), however, revealed a seemingly much shorter period of time for this interglacial of the order of 30,000 to 50,000 years, a duration which agrees well with the interglacial cycles of Emiliani (1966). The British and north-west European glacial and interglacial sequences are after Shotton (1971), Sparks and West (1972) and Mitchell *et al.* (1973).
Column 8	Only the major culture trends are shown. The term 'Middle Palaeolithic' is used here as a cultural subdivision rather than in any chronological sense.
Column 9	Selected culture sites are dated as follows: (C^{14}) – radiocarbon absolute dating (K/Ar) – potassium-argon absolute dating (L) – lithostratigraphic relative dating (B) – biostratigraphic relative dating The column emphasises the scarcity of absolute dates in the Later Lower Pleistocene and Middle Pleistocene.

Chapter 2

HUMAN BIOLOGICAL DEVELOPMENT

Finds of early man's remains are rare in the British Isles and, so far, nothing older than about a quarter of a million years has been discovered. In a book of this length, detailed study of human evolution is not possible, but, since it is necessary to set cultural evolution against man's biological development, a brief outline of the stages of that development is included here.

Human skeletal remains do not survive well and the record of fossil man is inevitably patchy, with many large gaps which may never be filled. The fragmentary nature of the evidence and earlier preoccupation with the search for a 'Missing Link' – the ape–human transitional stage – resulted in a confusing multiplication of terms, where each discovery became a new species or even genus as anthropologists, palaeontologists or geologists sought to establish the priority and future status of their finds. Many missing links have been supplied, for all levels of evolutionary development, but the gaps are still unfilled. This is mainly due to difficulty in agreeing where a 'link' belongs: at the upper end of a lower evolutionary stage, in the lower level of the next stage, or as a separate entity establishing a 'new form'. However, in the 1960s, the 'lumping' or combining of fossil forms into existing nomenclature reduced the multiplicity of names and created a more manageable and understandable scheme (Harrison and Weiner, 1963; Campbell, 1965; Howells, 1966; Garn, 1971).

Man's place in the animal kingdom (Figure 2.1) is within the hominid family, a family which has been expanded both materially and chronologically in recent decades with the discoveries and classification of *Ramapithecus* and *Australopithecus*. Our nearest living relations are in the pongid family, the great apes; but it is no longer necessary to seek our ancestry along the line of purely ape evolution. Evidence is now available to suggest the occurrence of some 'proto-hominid' features early enough in the evolutionary sequence to pre-date the divergence of the pongid branch of development. There is a possibility that a common ancestor to both pongids and hominids existed in the form of such primitive Oligocene primates as *Aegyptopithecus* (Simons, 1967) or *Propliopithecus* (Pilbeam, 1967, 1969).

Developments towards the hominids may have taken place against a background of changing environmental conditions, such as a fluctuation of forest cover. Some forms, probably in savannah regions, adapted to successively longer periods of existence on the ground, acquiring characteristics which gradually set them apart from the mainly forest-dwellers. A representative of this stage of development is *Ramapithecus*, a Miocene form now regarded by some authorities as the earliest hominid (Simons, 1961, 1964b, 1968, 1977). The jaw-bones and teeth of this creature show features which are more hominid than ape-like – reduction of canine teeth, teeth smaller in general than in the pongids, the rounded and divergent dental arch of hominid form. There

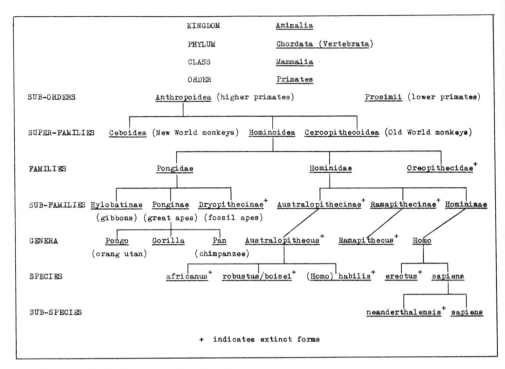

Figure 2.1: Man's place in the animal kingdom.

are suggestions that *Ramapithecus* might have developed a more upright stance, but this can only be inference. The shorter face and reduction in the size of the canines suggest the loss of the 'fighting teeth' of the apes and, as compensation, perhaps greater use of the hands for holding sticks and stones for offensive and defensive purposes. Proving *Ramapithecus* a tool-user, however, is almost an impossibility. If broken sticks or stones were picked up and used, they would be extremely difficult to identify. The problem of archaeological context is much more difficult than in the case of the 'eoliths' (Chapter 3), since there is no question of *Ramapithecus* having used fire or artificial shelter. Leakey (1968) has suggested, from finds at Fort Ternan, Kenya, that *Ramapithecus* may have used lumps of stone to break up the skulls and limb-bones of animals, but there is no great amount of evidence as yet. Remains of *Ramapithecus* have been found in India, China, Africa, France, Germany, and perhaps Spain and Greece. The evidence is so far confined to teeth and jaw-bones, so that finds of postcranial remains could alter the present classification. A major gap in the evidence exists between the Late Miocene/Early Pliocene finds and the earliest remains of *Australopithecus*, which are some millions of years younger. It is possible that fragmentary finds from Ngorora, Kenya (Bishop and Chapman, 1970), dated to about 9 million years ago, and Lothagam, Kenya (Patterson, Behrensmeyer and Sill, 1970), dated 5 to 5.5 million years ago, both tentatively classified as *Australopithecus*, may yet prove to be late surviving forms of *Ramapithecus* or some intermediate development.

Australopithecus

On present evidence, the first undoubted hominids are of the genus *Australopithecus*, discovered by Dart at Taung, South Africa, in 1924 (Dart, 1925). The first finds were in South Africa, but the focus of discovery has more recently shifted to East Africa; there are as yet no certain finds of *Australopithecus* outside Africa. An outline of distribution and chronology is given in Table 2.2.

Remains show that *Australopithecus* had an upright stance and bipedal gait, though perhaps not so advanced in walking ability as later forms of man, and had teeth essentially human in form. Height ranged from about 1.2 to over 1.5 metres and cranial capacity from around 450 to almost 700 cc, overlapping with the great apes at the lower end of the range and with early forms of *Homo erectus* at the upper end. The Australopithecines have been subdivided specifically into at least two major forms. A smaller, gracile form, *Australopithecus africanus* (Figure 2.8b), and a larger, more heavily built form, *Australopithecus robustus* or *boisei* (Figure 2.8a), have been distinguished. The division has been attributed by some authorities to dietary differences due to evolution in, and adaptation to, environments altering with climatic change. The *robustus/boisei* types with specialised dentition and sagittal crest associated with massive chewing muscles are suggested as mainly vegetarian, existing perhaps in a more forested environment and dying out without contributing to the main line of human evolution. The smaller, less specialised *africanus* is seen as an omnivorous form, developing in a more open, savannah type of environment (Robinson, 1965).

There is no undoubted evidence linking *africanus* or *robustus/boisei* with tool-making and, where direct association with stone implements does occur as with the Oldowan artifacts (pebbles or small boulders flaked crudely in one or two directions to produce an implement for cutting, chopping or scraping) in Bed I at Olduvai Gorge, the evidence suggests *Australopithecus (Homo) habilis* – a third species or probably an advanced form of *africanus* – as the most likely maker. There seems little doubt that all species *made use of* stones, bones, sticks and tree branches; Dart (1957), on the basis of finds from Makapansgat, Transvaal, has suggested an 'osteodontokeratic' culture for *Australopithecus africanus*, consisting of animal bones, teeth and horn showing signs of adaptation and use, but this is not completely accepted by other authorities (Kurtén, 1973). More important is the evidence for 'culturally patterned behaviour' (Butzer, 1972) – tool-making associated with a range of animal remains in a primitive 'home base' with indications of simple group activities. Such evidence, from Olduvai Gorge (Leakey, 1971), again points to *habilis* and suggests he was already an accomplished hunter and scavenger almost 2 million years ago.

At East Rudolf, Kenya (Leakey, 1973a), a cranium (KNM-ER 1470) with a capacity of around 800 cc and, according to Leakey, showing clear affinities with the genus *Homo*, was recovered from a level 37 metres below a horizon dated by the potassium–argon method to 2.61 million years ago. Detailed studies have not yet been published.

The evolution towards the later *Homo erectus* forms may have been through the more advanced *habilis* species (Howells, 1966), linking, perhaps, with the

SITE	TYPE	DATING	DATING METHOD	CULTURE
Ngorora, Baringo District, Kenya	Australopithecus?	9 + m.yrs	K/Ar.	
Lothagam, Kenya	Australopithecus cf. africanus?	5 - 5½ m.yrs	Faunal assoc.	
Kanapoi, Kenya	Australopithecus?	4 - 4½ m.yrs	Faunal assoc.	
Chemeron, Baringo District, Kenya	Australopithecus?	2 - 3 m.yrs	Faunal assoc.	
	Australopithecus africanus			
	FORMER NAMES			
Omo Valley, Ethiopia		1.84 - 3.75 m.yrs	K/Ar.	cf. Oldowan?
Taung, Cape Province	Australopithecus africanus	Lower Pleistocene	Faunal assoc.	None
Sterkfontein, Transvaal (Fig. 2.8b).	Plesianthropus transvaalensis	" "	" "	?
Makapansgat, Transvaal	Australopithecus prometheus	" "	" "	'Osteodontokeratic culture'?
Garusi, Lake Eyasi, Tanzania	Meganthropus africanus	" "	" "	?
	Australopithecus robustus/boisei			
	FORMER NAMES			
Omo Valley, Ethiopia		1.84 - 3.75 m.yrs	K/Ar.	?
East Rudolf, Kenya		2.61 m.yrs	K/Ar.	?
Bed I, Olduvai Gorge, Tanzania	Zinjanthropus boisei	c. 1.7 m.yrs	K/Ar.	?
Peninj, Lake Natron, Tanzania		1.4 - 1.6 m.yrs	K/Ar.	None
Chesowanja, Baringo District, Kenya		c. 1 m.yrs	Faunal assoc.	None
Kromdraai, Transvaal	Paranthropus robustus	Middle Pleistocene?	" "	?
Swartkrans, Transvaal (Fig. 2.8a).	Paranthropus crassidens	Middle Pleistocene?	" "	?
	Australopithecus (Homo) habilis			
	FORMER NAMES			
East Rudolf, Kenya	'Pre-Zinjanthropus' or	2.61 m.yrs	K/Ar.	cf. Oldowan?
Bed I, Olduvai Gorge, Tanzania	Homo habilis	1.6 - 1.85 m.yrs	K/Ar.	Oldowan
Bed II, Olduvai Gorge, Tanzania		1.0 m.yrs	K/Ar.	Oldowan?
Koro Toro, Chad	Tchadanthropus uxoris	Lower Pleistocene?	Faunal assoc.	None

Figure 2.2: Some major Australopithecine remains from African sites.

earlier forms of *erectus* (for example *modjokertensis, lantianensis, capensis*). Unfortunately, no undoubted evidence for this advanced form of *Australopithecus* has yet been found outside Africa. The only remains from other parts of the world which have been suggested as belonging to the genus are the mandibles and teeth of *Meganthropus palaeojavanicus* from the Djetis beds at Sangiran, Java, compared to the *robustus/boisei* forms by Robinson (1955), or to *habilis* by Tobias and von Koenigswald (1964), and the fragments from Tell Ubeidiya, Israel, which were associated with simple pebble tools resembling those from Bed I, Olduvai Gorge (Tobias, 1966).

Homo erectus

The next major advances in human development were in overall body size as well as in brain capacity. The top of the skull of the 'upright ape-man' *Pithecanthropus erectus* (the type fossil, now known as *Homo erectus erectus*), discovered at Trinil, Java, in 1891 (Dubois, 1894), was associated with a femur (found nearby in 1892) of modern size and appearance. Tests of the fluorine content of the skull and femur have shown them to be contemporaneous (Bergman and Karsten, 1952). The brain capacity has been estimated at 900–1,000 cc. The small and primitive skull associated with a body of approximately modern proportions emphasises the different rates of development of the human physical system. The cranial capacity of *Homo erectus* ranges between 750 and about 1,200 cc, approaching the lower range of modern man. There is a heavy bony ridge or torus above the eyes behind which an almost flat receding forehead blends into a very low-vaulted, thick-walled skull. The lower part of the face is projecting and the jaw musculature must still have been very heavy.

From the quantity of remains now known (Table 2.3), it has been claimed (Howells, 1966) that stages of development or progressiveness can be discerned within the *erectus* grouping. The earliest finds from Java, China (Figure 2.8c), and Africa (Modjokerto, Sangiran, Lantian and Swartkrans) are more primitive and the cranial capacities well below those of the more advanced Middle Pleistocene types. The find from Vértesszöllös has been classified as *sapiens* by some authorities (Howells, 1966; Thoma, 1966) despite its early date and primitive tools. The direction of *Homo erectus* development is as yet little known and it is still impossible to show direct links with later forms of men. Late survivors have been seen in the remains from Ngandong, Java (Weidenreich, 1951; Coon, 1962; Howells, 1966; Heberer, 1973), Broken Hill, Zambia (Coon, 1962; Heberer, 1973) and Morocco (McBurney, 1958; Briggs, 1968), although these have also been classed as Neanderthaloids.

In technology and social organisation, *Homo erectus* had advanced far beyond the Australopithecine stage. Even where actual traces of artifacts are missing from sites of human remains (for example in Java), there is enough indirect evidence to suggest that *erectus* was everywhere a skilled tool-maker. His industries varied from the simple pebble or chopper tools at Vértesszöllös or Choukoutien to a range of hand-axes and associated equipment from Ternifine and Beds II and IV at Olduvai Gorge. His distribution shows a spread away from the mainly sub-tropical areas and an adaptation to a much wider

SITE	TYPE	FORMER NAMES	AGE	DATING METHOD	CULTURE
Modjokerto (Djetis beds), Java	Homo erectus modjokertensis	Pithecanthropus modjokertensis	Lower Pleistocene c. 1.0 x 10³ yrs?	Faunal association and K/Ar	None
Sangiran (Djetis beds), Java	Homo erectus modjokertensis	Pithecanthropus modjokertensis	"	"	None
Lantian, Shensi, China	Homo erectus lantianensis	Sinanthropus lantianensis	Lower Pleistocene	Faunal association	None
Swartkrans, Transvaal	Homo erectus capensis	Telanthropus capensis	Low.-Mid. Pleistocene	Faunal association	cf. Oldowan?
Trinil, Java	Homo erectus erectus	Pithecanthropus erectus	Middle Pleistocene 0.5 x 10⁶ yrs	Faunal association and K/Ar	None
Sangiran (Trinil beds), Java	"	"			
Mauer, Heidelberg, W. Germany	Homo erectus heidelbergensis	Euranthropus	Middle Pleistocene	Faunal association	None
Vértesszöllös, Hungary	Homo erectus palaeohungaricus		Middle Pleistocene	Faunal association	Buda pebble/choppers
Ternifine, Algeria	Homo erectus mauritanicus	Atlanthropus mauritanicus	Middle Pleistocene	Faunal association	Acheulian
Sidi Abderrahman, Morocco	"	"	"	"	"
Choukoutien, China (Fig. 2.8c).	Homo erectus pekinensis	Sinanthropus pekinensis	Middle Pleistocene	Faunal association	Choukoutienian
Bed II, Olduvai Gorge, Tanzania	Homo erectus leakeyi	'Chellean Man'	c. 0.5 x 10³ yrs	K/Ar	Acheulian
Bed IV, Olduvai Gorge, Tanzania	"		Middle Pleistocene	Stratig., palaeomag.	Acheulian
Přezletice, Czechoslovakia	Homo erectus?		Lower Pleistocene	Faunal association	Stone and bone implements
LATE DEVELOPED SURVIVORS OF HOMO ERECTUS GROUP?					
Témara, Morocco	Homo erectus?		late Middle/Upper Pleistocene	Faunal association	Acheulian
Rabat, Morocco	Homo erectus?	'Rabat Man'	late Middle/Upper Pleistocene	Stratigraphy	None
Tangier, Morocco	Homo erectus?		late Middle/Upper Pleistocene	Stratigraphy	Aterian
Broken Hill, Zambia	Homo erectus?	Homo rhodesiensis	Upper Pleistocene	Faunal association	Stillbay
Ngandong, Solo River, Java	Homo erectus?	Homo soloensis	Upper Pleistocene	Faunal association	Stone and bone implements

Figure 2.3: Sites with remains of *Homo erectus*.

range of climate and environment than earlier hominids. For some regions, and for cave occupation generally, fire would have been necessary; there is evidence for this at Vértesszöllös and Choukoutien, but none in Africa until Upper Pleistocene times. Sites with traces of fire and artifacts but no human remains are known at Torralba and Ambrona, Spain (Howell, 1966, 1970), and at Terra Amata, Nice (de Lumley, 1967, 1969b). The variety and size of the animals killed and eaten by the occupants of the Choukoutien caves show an already competent system of co-operation in hunting and trapping. At Torralba, during late Mindel (Elsterian, Anglian) times, long-tusked elephant, *Elephas (Palaeoloxodon) antiquus*, was hunted, trapped and butchered on a site which also had Acheulian hand-axes and implements of wood and bone. Artificial structures are known from another Acheulian site at Terra Amata, Nice, and also nearby at Lazaret (de Lumley, 1969a), where human remains might be late *erectus* or transitional forms. Little is known of burial or ritual, if such existed at this stage, but the condition of some of the human skulls and long bones at Choukoutien suggests some form of ritual cannibalism.

Transitional Forms of Man

The period of time from the latest definitely known finds of *Homo erectus* to the earliest appearance of undoubted forms of Neanderthal man is a long one, with only a handful of rather tantalising and fragmentary remains. The controversy over the possible existence of a separate and direct line of development leading to modern man from early Pleistocene times has often focused on these few remains (Figure 2.4). A 'Preneanderthal' line is seen as developing from the Steinheim remains by way of the Saccopastore early Neanderthalers to both 'specialised' and 'unspecialised' Neanderthal forms of the last glaciation. The 'Presapiens' view sees the Swanscombe remains as part of a sequence leading to Fontéchevade and modern man (Boule and Vallois, 1957). There is not enough evidence, however, to prove these theories either way, and the existing material could all be ancestral to Neanderthal man, particularly if the Steinheim skull could be regarded as providing a face for the parietals and occipital from Swanscombe.

The earliest remains, and the oldest known in the British Isles, are the three skull bones from Swanscombe, Kent (Figure 2.8d), associated with a terrace of the Thames of later Hoxnian date (see Figure 1.4 above), perhaps about 250,000 years ago (Ovey, 1964; Szabo and Collins, 1975). Fluorine analysis has shown the bones to be contemporary with Hoxnian faunal remains from the same levels and a Middle Acheulian hand-axe industry was associated. No artifacts were found in association with the Steinheim skull, but it would appear also to be of Hoxnian (Mindel-Riss, Holsteinian) date (Adam, 1954).

The Montmaurin (I) mandible is less securely dated and the associated flakes offer no real cultural association (Vallois, 1955). The material from Tautavel (Oakley, Campbell and Molleson, 1971; McKern, 1974) was associated with a cold fauna of Riss I date, perhaps about 200,000 years ago, and the parts of two human skulls from Fontéchevade were stratified with interglacial animal remains of the Riss-Würm period (Vallois, 1949). Little can be said of the life-styles of these poorly represented human beings, and there is certainly no

SITE	NAMES	AGE	DATING METHOD	CULTURE
Barnfield Pit, Swanscombe, Kent (Fig. 2.8d).	Swanscombe man Homo cf. sapiens Homo cf. steinheimensis	Middle Pleistocene (Hoxnian)	Faunal association, Stratigraphy	Middle Acheulian
Steinheim an der Murr, W. Germany	Homo steinheimensis Homo cf. sapiens Homo sapiens steinheimensis	Middle Pleistocene (Mindel-Riss)	Faunal association	None found
La Niche, Montmaurin, Haute-Garonne, France.	Homo aff. neanderthalensis	Mindel-Riss or Riss-Würm?	Faunal association	Stone flakes
Caune de l'Arago, Tautavel, Pyrénées-Orientales, France.		Middle Pleistocene (Early Riss)	Faunal association	Tayacian?
Fontéchevade, Charente, France.	Fontechevade man Homo 'praesapiens'	Upper Pleistocene (Riss-Würm)	Faunal association	Tayacian

Figure 2.4: Transitional forms of man, or early *Homo sapiens*.

uniformity in the few cultural remains found. It may, however, be reasonable to compare the evidence for activity at Hoxne, Suffolk, with the finds at Swanscombe (Chapter 3 below).

Most authorities, in dealing with these remains, are in reasonable agreement as to their position between the *erectus* and Neanderthal groups, but find little common ground in discussing their various lines of development. Brace (1967) would see the Swanscombe, Steinheim and Fontéchevade remains as being unequivocally ancestral to Neanderthal man. A basic layer of early *sapiens* in the Mindel-Riss/Hoxnian interglacial, branching into *sapiens neanderthalensis* and *sapiens sapiens* at a later date is suggested by Heberer (1973). The more complex view envisages a wide range of types of early *Homo* existing in the Middle Pleistocene, from non-sapient forms up to and including the Swanscombe and Steinheim remains (Weiner, 1958; Napier and Weiner, 1962; Day, 1965), but the evidence is still insufficient to bridge the gap to Neanderthal man.

The Neanderthaloids

Forms of Neanderthal man probably existed more than 100,000 years ago, with some roots perhaps in late *Homo erectus* and in Middle Pleistocene 'transitional' forms. The 'Neanderthal problem', in simple terms, is the difficulty encountered in trying to accept that the somewhat primitive-looking and specialised Neanderthal man could possibly be the direct ancestor of *Homo sapiens sapiens*. The problem is further complicated by the fact that the Neanderthals were modern man's immediate predecessors and, for a short time, probably his contemporaries as well. Although early descriptions, for example of the remains from La Chapelle-aux-Saints (Figure 2.8c) (Boule, 1911–13), tended to over-emphasise the primitive features, some of which were in fact pathological, there is no doubt that the 'Classic' Neanderthals of the early stages of the last glaciation – the only forms strictly entitled to the designation *Homo sapiens neanderthalensis* – were highly specialised in appearance by comparison with Neanderthaloids of the previous interglacial period and with some later Near Eastern forms (Table 2.5). The extreme specialisation has been suggested as a response to biological isolation and perhaps adaptation to the extreme environments of western Europe in the early Würm (Weichselian) glaciation. This theory must be modified by the appearance of strong 'Classical' features in some of the remains from Shanidar and other Near Eastern sites (McKern, 1974).

It is possible that many of the Neanderthaloids of the last interglacial period (Riss-Würm or Eemian) did not develop the specialised features of the later west European early glacial forms – heavy, continuous bony ridge above the eyes, wide nasal aperture, large bun-shaped skull projecting in the occipital region, short but strong stature with long bones more robust and slightly more bent than in modern man – but rather evolved more towards the 'progressive' forms of the Near East. An intermediate form of this development might be represented by the finds from Mugharet et-Tabūn. Some, particularly those resembling the Mugharet es-Skhūl V (Figure 2.8f) remains, have been suggested as 'proto-Cro Magnon' (Brothwell, 1961) and compared with early

SITE	AGE	DATING METHOD	CULTURE	TYPE
Ehringsdorf, Weimar, E. Germany	Last Interglacial (Eemian)	Faunal association and Pa/Th dating	Mousterian	Mixture of primitive and progressive features
Krapina, Croatia, Yugoslavia	Last Interglacial (Riss-Würm)	Faunal association	Mousterian	Mixture of primitive and progressive features
Gánovce, Czechoslovakia	Last Interglacial (Eemian)	Faunal association	Mousterian	'A primitive progressive'
Saccopastore, nr. Rome, Italy	Last Interglacial (Riss-Würm)	Faunal association	Mousterian	Transitional to Classic Neanderthal forms
La Cotte de St. Brelade, Jersey	Last Glaciation < 47,000 ±1500 bp	Faunal association and C14 dating	Levalloiso-Mousterian	Teeth only
La Ferrassie, Dordogne, France	Last Glaciation (Würm)	Faunal association	Mousterian	Classic Neanderthal
La Chapelle-aux-Saints, Corrèze, France (Fig. 2. 8e).	Last Glaciation (Würm)	Faunal association	Mousterian	Classic Neanderthal
Mugharet-es-Skhūl, Israel (Fig. 2. 8f).	Last Glaciation or equivalent	Faunal association	Levalloiso-Mousterian	'Progressive' Neanderthal (esp. Skhūl V)
Mugharet et-Tabūn, Israel	Last Glaciation 40,900 ±1000 bp	Faunal association and C14 dating	Levalloiso-Mousterian	Mixture of Classic and more advanced features
Shanidar, Iraq.	Last Glaciation > 30,000 -c. 46,000 bp	Faunal association and C14 dating	Mousterian	Mixture of Classic and more advanced features

Figure 2.5: Some major discoveries of Neanderthaloid remains.

Upper Palaeolithic remains from Czechoslovakia and Russia (Brothwell, 1961; Jelínek, 1969). These 'progressive' Neanderthaloids are the most likely forerunners of modern man, but their dates are late and they do not completely fulfil the requirements for direct ancestry. Some authorities, particularly Brace (1964, 1967; Brace *et al.*, 1971), would see no difficulty in accepting the evolution of Neanderthal man from the *erectus* species and his eventual development into modern man, with no particular 'sidelines' or divergences, but rather the extremes of a range of variability within any species, including present-day populations.

The Neanderthaloids employed a range of stone industries from Final Acheulian to forms overlapping with Upper Palaeolithic industries. The use of bone is also recorded at a number of sites. Their major advances were in the flake-tool cultures, particularly the Mousterian, and their use of the Levalloisian prepared-core technique, indicating the beginnings of specialisation and adaptation to varied environments. They spread further north and into colder regions than any previous groups, suggesting the possession of adequate clothing and artificial shelters where cave formations were not available. The range of their activities and hunting abilities can be seen at such sites as Salzgitter-Lebenstedt (Tode *et al.*, 1953) and Molodova (Klein, 1969). Some possibly Neanderthaloid teeth have been recovered during excavations on Jersey, in the Channel Islands (Oakley, Campbell and Molleson, 1971), but the occurrence of Mousterian artifacts on the mainland (Chapter 3) suggests the existence of a few communities in southern England.

Perhaps more important are Neanderthal man's advances in non-material culture. The careful and deliberate burial of the dead, often with grave-goods, at La Chapelle, La Ferrassie, Le Moustier, Mugharet es-Skhūl, Shanidar, Teshik-Tash and many other sites suggests the beginnings of a belief in some form of after-life, or at least a response to the problems of life and death. Artificially arranged groups of bones and skulls of the cave-bear, *Ursus spelaeus*, in caves at high altitudes in France, Germany, Switzerland and Austria indicate a cult of some complexity, perhaps foreshadowing some Upper Palaeolithic rituals.

Homo sapiens sapiens

Fossil remains of modern man first appear in the archaeological record between 30,000 and 40,000 years ago (Figure 2.6). Body structure and skull shape differ little from present-day human populations (Figure 2.8g), although some individuals from early Upper Palaeolithic sites (for example Předmosti, Kostenki) show, in still-prominent eyebrow ridges or a degree of prognathism, vestiges of preceding stages of development (Jelínek, 1969). The distribution range of *Homo sapiens sapiens* covered most regions of the world, including Australia and America, before the end of the Pleistocene. The Upper (or Advanced) Palaeolithic industries of this sub-species were based in the main on the production of blades from which a wide range of highly specialised tools was manufactured, including 'tool-making tools' such as the burin. The working of bone and antler reached a peak of craftmanship in cultures such as the Magdalenian, seldom achieved in post-Pleistocene times. Evidence for burial

SITE	AGE	DATING METHOD	CULTURE	COMMENTS
Cro-Magnon, Dordogne, France (Fig. 2.8g),	Last Glaciation (Würm III)	Faunal association	Aurignacian	
Oberkassel, W. Germany	Last Glaciation	Faunal association	Magdalenian	
Pavlov, Moravia, Czechoslovakia	Last Glaciation c. 25,000 bp	Faunal association and C14 dating	E. Gravettian (Pavlovian)	Occupation site
Paviland, Gower, S. Wales	Last Glaciation 18,460 ±340 bp	Faunal association and C14 dating	"Proto-Solutrean" (Earlier Upper Palaeolithic).	The 'Red Lady' of Paviland
Sun Hole, Mendip Hills, Somerset	Last Glaciation 12,378 ±150 bp	Faunal association and C14 dating	Cheddarian (Creswellian) (Later Upper Palaeolithic).	
Robin Hood's Cave, Creswell Crags, Derbyshire	Last Glaciation 10,390 ±90 bp	Faunal association and C14 dating	Creswellian (Later Upper Palaeolithic).	
Gough's Cave, Cheddar Gorge, Somerset	Late Glacial/Early Post-Glacial 9080 ±150 bp, 7130 bc	Faunal association and C14 dating	Cheddarian (Creswellian) (Later Upper Palaeolithic).	'Cheddar Man'
Thatcham, Newbury, Berkshire	Holocene (Boreal) 9490 ±150 bp, 7540 bc	Pollen analysis, fauna, and C14 dating	"Maglemosean" (Earlier Mesolithic).	

Figure 2.6: Some important fossil remains of modern man.

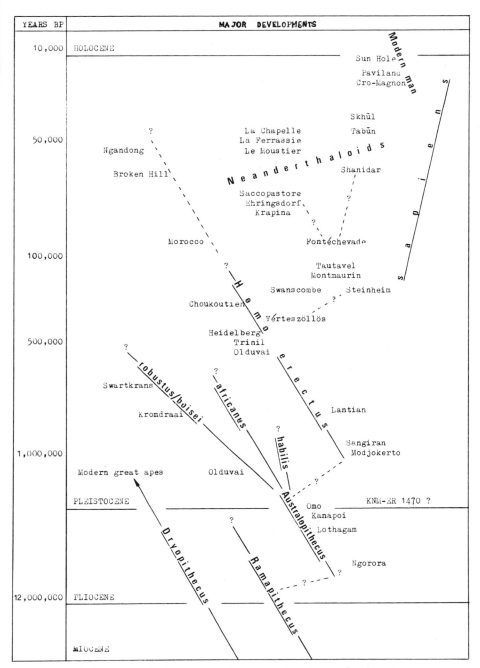

Figure 2.7: The major developments and possible relationships of early man.

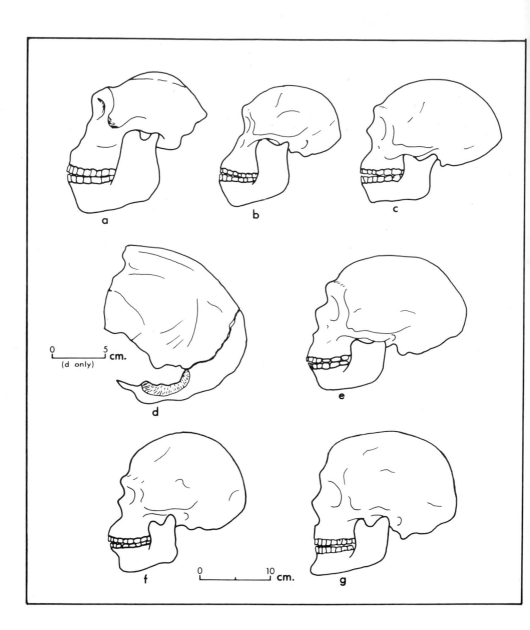

0 ‖—————‖ 5 cm.
(d only)

0 ‖—————‖ 10 cm.

Figure 2.8: Examples of hominid skulls: (a) *Australopithecus robustus/boisei*, Swartkrans, Transvaal; (b) *Australopithecus africanus*, Sterkfontein, Transvaal; (c) *Homo erectus pekinensis*, Choukoutien, China; (d) Early *Homo sapiens*, Barnfield Pit, Swanscombe, Kent; (e) *Homo sapiens neanderthalensis*, La Chapelle-aux-Saints, Corrèze, France; (f) 'Progressive' Neanderthaloid, (Skhūl V), Mugharet-es-Skhūl, Israel; (g) *Homo sapiens sapiens*, Cro-Magnon, Dordogne, France.

of the dead is much more widespread than in earlier periods and a complex system of hunting and fertility rituals is suggested by much of the cave art and portable carvings, though these are poorly represented in the British Isles.

This summary of human development has been greatly abbreviated and selective. No attempt has been made to reinterpret evidence or answer many long-standing questions. Material is still accumulating and many recent discoveries from Olduvai Gorge, Lake Rudolf and Ethiopia have yet to be fully analysed and evaluated. Figure 2.7 is therefore more of an attempt to show the fossil species in some sort of chronological order than to indicate any hard and fast phylogenetic links.

Chapter 3

THE EVIDENCE FOR MAN'S PRESENCE IN BRITAIN IN EARLIER PALAEOLITHIC TIMES

The use of the term Palaeolithic or Old Stone Age for man's earliest technological stage gives perhaps undue emphasis to a single durable aspect of this extended period of human physical and cultural evolution. The material most commonly used for tools and weapons was probably stone, and although wood and bone must also have been important, the full extent of their use is unknown for most of the Palaeolithic period due to low survival rate and man's occupation of mainly open sites, where exposure would accelerate the decay of organic material.

Early stone-chipping gradually revealed the characteristics and suitability of different rock-types. A hard siliceous rock will give a sharp cutting edge and can be shaped relatively easily by flaking or chipping once the properties of fracture are appreciated. Flint, like glass, will fracture conchoidally, producing a very sharp-edged flake and, where available, it was used more than any other stone, but chert, chalcedony, jadeite, jasper, opal and mudstone were also used. In regions where flint was unobtainable, quartzes, granites, lavas, indurated shales and even fossilised wood were utilised (Oakley, 1972; Watson, 1968). Where non-siliceous rocks have been used, implements often have a crudeness suggestive of a low level of workmanship; this, however, may be due entirely to the quality of the raw material available and the impossibility of controlled flaking.

The earliest deliberate working of stone probably consisted of hammering two rocks together to achieve a broken edge, developing to the use of a stone hammer or anvil. This 'stone-on-stone' technique produced deep, rough flake-scars and a rather zig-zag cutting edge. With the later use of a more resilient wood or bone hammer, better control was possible, with shallower flakes and a straighter cutting edge. Further refinements included indirect percussion, using a pointed wooden or bone punch between hammer and core, and pressure-flaking, a retouching technique seen at its best in the Solutrean leaf-shaped blades of the Upper Palaeolithic.

Some early implements, from the simple Oldowan chopper to the evolved Acheulian hand-axe, were core tools – a basic core from which flakes were struck until the desired shape was achieved. With flake tools, including the simple Clactonian flakes as well as the more refined products of the Levalloisian and Mousterian industries, the core was the source of raw material from which flakes were produced. There were, however, no simple or mutually exclusive 'core industries' and 'flake industries'; flakes had been utilised since the Oldowan culture, flake tools were made and used throughout the long-surviving Acheulian hand-axe tradition and many Clactonian cores were 'chopper-cores'.

The concepts of 'Man the Toolmaker' and the appearance of deliberate tool-making as a major criterion for humanity have become widely accepted (Le Gros Clark, 1958; Oakley, 1969, 1970). Some animals may be classified as tool-*users* by their ability to utilise stones, broken sticks or other convenient materials for simple purposes, and by implication the early hominids must have passed through a similar stage of development. The period when early man ceased to rely on whatever available broken stones could be picked up, and began to copy and improve upon nature, is obviously the most difficult to identify in the archaeological record of cultural evolution. The issue is further complicated by the many ways in which 'worked' stones can be produced naturally – by thermal action, solifluction, the effects of waves on coastal deposits, etc. Attempts to recover and identify man's earliest tools reached an intensity in the later nineteenth and early twentieth century in the south-east of England with the many finds of 'eoliths' – weathered and chipped flints and other stones – from the Kent plateau and beneath the Crags (Lower Pleistocene shelly deposits on the East Anglian coasts) of Norfolk and Suffolk (Plate I). The term 'eolithic', which was once used as a label for a theoretical

Plate I: Examples of 'eoliths'. Left, from the Benjamin Harrison Collection, marked 'Kent Plateau'. Right, from East Anglia, marked 'Low water on chalk, Cromer' and 'hand axe'. Hunterian Museum, University of Glasgow.

culture of early Pleistocene and even later Pliocene times based on these discoveries, is now descriptive of the problem of the stones and their status as artifacts or products of nature. In a recent useful and succinct summary of the situation (Coles, 1968, pp. 22–30), the criteria for any object's acceptance as an artifact are re-emphasised: undoubted association with other evidence of man's activities – for example stone-working, hearths, food remains, burial, etc; some standardisation of shape; in the case of a stone tool, signs of flaking from two or three directions. Although some of these English finds are probably not accidents of nature, many of them must be seen as such (Barnes, 1939a,b) and no entirely satisfactory solution has been proposed; but the 'eolith problem' can perhaps be safely shelved in the light of abundant evidence for early physical and cultural evolution in Africa (see Chapter 2 above).

The first recognisable standardised tools are the pebble choppers of the Oldowan culture which were already in existence, in Bed I of Olduvai Gorge, Tanzania, and in the Lake Rudolf Basin, Kenya, between 1.5 and 2.5 million years ago (Leakey, 1976; Coppens *et al.*, 1976). These consist of a heavier tool, probably used for chopping, pounding or digging, produced by flaking the ends or sides of water-worn pebbles or small boulders in two directions to make a rough working edge (Figure 3.1/1–2); and a smaller range of utilised flakes. The raw materials were lavas, quartz, quartzite and chert. In north-west Africa (Morocco, Algeria, Tunisia) industries designated 'Pebble Culture' or 'Pre-Acheulian', and consisting of choppers, chopping-tools and polyhedral cores, evolving through unidirectional, bidirectional and multidirectional flaking (Figure 3.1/3), have been associated with fossil Mediterranean beaches and faunal remains of the Lower Pleistocene (Biberson, 1976).

Spatial and chronological gaps still inhibit attempts to demonstrate a uniform spread of pebble/chopper industries beyond Africa, although a number of sites with similar early tools have already been recorded in parts of Europe (Valoch, 1976b). In the small cave of Grotte du Vallonet (Roquebrune-Cap-Martin, Alpes Maritimes) in the south of France, pebble-choppers, flakes (Figure 3.1/4–6) and possibly worked bones were found associated with an Upper Villafranchian fauna which included bear, deer, rhinoceros (*Dicerorhinus etruscus*), horse (*Equus stenonis*) and elephant (*Elephas meridionalis*). Palaeomagnetic evidence suggests a dating to the Jaramillo Normal Event (Figures 1.8 and 1.9) about 900,000 to 950,000 years ago (Lumley, 1976). Vallonet and similar sites have been suggested as representing pioneer stages in the extension of man's ecological range from the tropics to the boreal zones (Isaac, 1974).

Until recently, little definite evidence existed for man's presence in Britain before the Hoxnian interglacial, apart from the probability that some Clactonian assemblages (see below) can be dated to a late stage of the Anglian (Lowestoft) glaciation (Wymer, 1974, 1977). However, discoveries of worked flints associated with a mainly Cromerian faunal assemblage in a carboniferous limestone quarry near Westbury-sub-Mendip, Somerset (Bishop, 1974, 1975), suggest an even earlier date for human activity and allow a reassessment of other 'early' assemblages. The work at Westbury is a good example of the techniques involved in the study of Palaeolithic material, particularly cave sites. The interpretation of lithostratigraphical and biostratigraphical evidence can indicate changing climatic or environmental

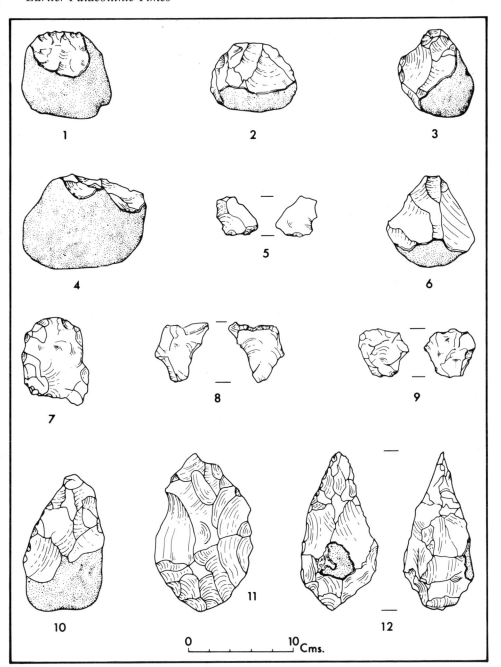

Figure 3.1: Some pebble tools and early hand-axes. Pebble or chopper tools: 1, 2, Bed I, Olduvai Gorge, Tanzania; 3, Ain Hanech, Algeria; 4–6, Grotte du Vallonet, S. France; 7–9, Westbury-sub-Mendip, Somerset. Early British hand-axes: 10, 11, Kent's Cavern, Torquay, Devon; 12, Fordwich, Kent. After Leakey, 1951; Lumley, 1976; Balout, 1955; Bishop, 1975; Garrod, 1925; Roe, 1976a; Smith, 1933.

conditions, and can also be used for relative dating by the presence or absence of particular faunal forms whose appearance or extinction in the Pleistocene record is known with some accuracy from evidence at various other sites.

The Westbury deposits are in two groups (Figure 3.2), a lower Siliceous Group consisting of sands and gravels, and an upper Calcareous Group of mainly limestone breccias and conglomerates. The Rodent Earth bed was separated from the main layered sequence (it is shown at the top of this sequence in Figure 3.2 for convenience), but its contained fauna suggests contemporaneity with the Calcareous Group. Most of the faunas appear to correspond to remains found on European sites at Mosbach, Mauer, Hundsheim and Tärko, dating to a period from the Cromerian to the Elsterian (Anglian) (Koenigswald, 1973). The faunas in the Siliceous Group (sands and gravels redeposited from pre-existing materials and not contemporary with the faunas) are regarded as no earlier than late Lower Pleistocene and no later than Cromerian *sensu stricto*. The bear remains, at all levels in the Calcareous Group, are of *Ursus deningeri* which survived in Europe until the Elsterian (Anglian) and by the Holsteinian (Hoxnian) had evolved into *Ursus spelaeus*, the cave bear. Among the vole remains in the Rodent Earth bed, the absence of *Mimomys* and the occurrence of *Arvicola cantiana*, which probably replaced *Mimomys savini* at about the boundary between the Late-temperate and Post-temperate zones of the Cromerian Interglacial (Cr III–Cr IV), plus the pre-

Layers			Faunas	Flints	Age
	10	Rodent Earth	Sorex sp., Neomys sp., Desmana moschata, Talpa europaea, Mustela sp., Arvicola cantiana, Pitymys gregaloides, Microtus arvalis, Ursus deningeri, Pisces, Aves.		Anglian ?
	9	Upper Breccia	Ursus deningeri		
	8	Upper Breccia	Ursus deningeri	Flints	
	7	Stalagmitic Breccia	Ursus deningeri	Flints	
	6	Upper Conglomerate	Ursus deningeri		
	5	Red and Yellow Bone Conglomerate	Ursus deningeri, Equus mosbachensis, Pitymys gregaloides, Homotherium latidens, Bison sp.	Flints Flints Flints	
	4	Black and Brown Conglomerate	Ursus deningeri, Homotherium latidens, Equus mosbachensis.		
	3	Yellow Silty Layer	Canis lupus mosbachensis, Ursus deningeri.		
	2	Lower Breccia	Ursus deningeri, Felis gombaszoegensis, Canis lupus mosbachensis.		
Siliceous Group	1	Sands and Gravels	Hyaena brevirostris, Dicerorhinus sp., Bison sp., Felis sp.		Late Lower Pleistocene

Figure 3.2: Generalised stratification at Westbury-sub-Mendip, Somerset. Adapted from Bishop (1974, 1975).

sence of other undoubted Cromerian faunas, suggest an age of Cr IV for much of the Westbury material. There are also similarities to a faunal and floral assemblage from Ostend, Norfolk, which pollen analysis has placed in Cr IV (Stuart and West, 1976; Stuart, 1977). Interpretation of the Westbury stratification is not straightforward, however, and there are complications such as the pollen analysis of a sample from Bed 4 which indicates Zone II of an interglacial or perhaps the existence of an as yet unspecified temperate phase between the Cromerian and the Hoxnian (Bishop, 1975, p. 96).

The flints are mainly flakes and what might be a small broken hand-axe of crude appearance (Figure 3.1/7–9). Suggestions of early Acheulian have been made but there is insufficient evidence to seek industrial affinities. Roe (1975, p. 7) has noted that some of the implements are within the range of so-called bifacial choppers. The occurrence of minute fragments of charcoal in the sediments of Bed 4 coupled with the preservation of the flints might indicate actual occupation of the former cave system.

At Kent's Cavern, Torquay, Devonshire, a breccia (B1) layer near the bottom of the cave deposits contained faunal remains, principally *Ursus spelaeus*, but also *Homotherium latidens* (a sabre-tooth cat), *Pitymys gregaloides* and *Arvicola greeni* (voles) attributable to a late Cromerian or intra-Anglian phase and possibly contemporary with the Calcareous Group faunas at Westbury-sub-Mendip (Campbell and Sampson, 1971). An early hand-axe industry, which may be contemporary with the B1 breccia deposits, includes crude hand-axes (Figure 3.1/10–11), chopping-tools and flakes, all indicative of a stone-on-stone flaking technique. This industry, the 'Chellean' of Garrod (1926), has been designated Early Acheulian and, if the dating is at all accurate, the site could be of major importance to any study of the earliest hand-axe industries in Europe (Campbell and Sampson, 1971, pp. 22–3). Preliminary investigation of the cave-bear remains suggests the possibility of some specialised hunting activity in the killing of some of these animals during hibernation.

The discoveries at these early sites indicate the importance of caves in the preservation of stratigraphy and *in situ* material culture – a rare occurrence before Upper Palaeolithic times. Most Lower Palaeolithic finds are from open sites, in deposits which are fluviatile, lacustrine or aeolian, and particularly in the gravels of river terraces. The bulk of the materials is therefore not contemporary with its containing deposits and has probably been *derived* from a primary, usually earlier, location by fluvio-glacial action (Wymer, 1976). The extent of transportation by such natural processes can often be related to the degree of abrasion on flint implements (sharp, slightly rolled, very rolled, etc.). Wymer (1977, p. 100) has noted the relationship between the distribution of deposits of the Wolstonian Glaciation and the scarcity of Lower Palaeolithic finds in the same area, suggesting obliteration by Wolstonian ice of any evidence for human occupation during the preceding interglacial in the regions covered by that ice (Figure 3.7).

Even beyond the southern limits of the most extensive glaciation, finds of Lower Palaeolithic artifacts in non-derived deposits are rare. A pre-Hoxnian age has been suggested for material from other sites, mostly in river gravels (Roe, 1976a). Hand-axes from a 40-metre terrace of the River Stour at Fordwich, Kent, apparently *in situ* (Smith, 1933), have been subjected to metrical analysis (Roe, 1968a). They are in general thicker and clumsier than those of Hoxnian age, showing signs of a stone-on-stone flaking technique (Figure 3.1/12). Hand-axes from a lower (30-metre) terrace of the Stour are much closer in size and appearance to those from sites of established Hoxnian age, suggesting an earlier dating for the higher terrace and its artifacts. Elsewhere, hand-axes described as 'morphologically and technologically archaic' (Roe, 1976a) are known from Terrace A, Farnham, Surrey, at Warren Hill, Suffolk (Oakley, 1939; Solomon, 1933) and also at St Catherine's Hill, Christchurch, Dorset, and Corfe Mullen, Dorset (Calkin and Green, 1949; Roe, 1975). These have been tentatively labelled 'Earlier Acheulian', but the geological chronology is uncertain.

The Hand-axe Groups

Hand-axes have been found in quantity and somewhat more securely dated in deposits of the Hoxnian Interglacial period and later, though rarely in primary contexts. A descriptive classification of hand-axes has been attempted (Wymer, 1968), based mainly on general shape, butt and edge form, and type of point (Table 3.1).

There are intermediate forms indicated by double letters, for example FG or JK. Thus, for example, a full description of the cordate/ovate hand-axe with tranchet point and reversed S edge from Reculver, Kent (Wymer, 1968, Figure 40), would be JK f/vi. A more objective form of classification (Roe,

Table 3.1: Classification of Hand-axes

Shape	Butt and Edge	Point
D pointed hand-axes, stone-flaked, longer than 20 cm	(a) over 50% cortex or natural fracture on butt[a]	(i) rounded, lingulate or irregular point[a]
E pointed hand-axes, stone-flaked, 20 cm or less	(b) trimmed butt[a]	(ii) acute point[a]
F pointed hand-axes, developed flaking technique	(c) trimmed butt, chamfered corners[a]	(iii) ogee point[a]
	(d) flat-based butt[a]	(iv) basil point[a]
G sub-cordate hand-axes	(e) straight-edged[b]	(v) without tranchet edge[b]
H cleavers	(f) twisted edge, usually reversed S[b]	(vi) with tranchet edge[b]
J cordate hand-axes		
K ovate hand-axes		
L segmental chopping tool		
M ficron hand-axes		
N flat-butted cordate hand-axes		

Notes: a. Mainly applicable to F hand-axes.
            b. Mainly applicable to J and K hand-axes.
Source: Wymer, 1968, pp. 46–61.

1964, 1968a) has demonstrated the existence of at least three groups of hand-axes and involves a statement of size (length, breadth and thickness plus weight), refinement (thickness over breadth as a degree of coarseness) and shape (breadth, measured at fixed points along the length of the implement, related to length).

The most prolific areas for hand-axe industries are the Thames Valley, East Anglia, North Kent and the Hampshire Basin. In the Thames Valley, perhaps the best-studied stratified site is the Barnfield Pit at Swanscombe, in Kent. The hand-axes first occur in the Middle Gravels, which appear to represent a span of time from the late Hoxnian Interglacial into an early phase of the Wolstonian Glaciation (Figure 3.4). The collections from these levels are dominated by hand-axes of pointed form, many of small size and unrefined workmanship (Figure 3.3/2), but including some fine examples of more developed technique (Figure 3.3/1, Plate II) using wood or bone hammers. The three pieces of the Swanscombe Skull were discovered near the base of the Upper Middle Gravels (Ovey, 1964) in association with these forms of hand-axe. Fossil bones from just below the skull level have yielded a uranium series date of >272,000 years bp (Szabo and Collins, 1975). The Swanscombe Upper Loam and Upper Gravels have an assemblage combining pointed hand-axes with more refined cordate and ovate forms (Figure 3.3/3). The implements in the soliflucted Upper Gravels were probably derived from the Upper Loam.

At Hoxne, Suffolk, type-site for the Interglacial, a basin in boulder clay of Anglian age became a lake in the earlier stages of the Hoxnian Interglacial, the banks of which were the environment for the users of the 'Lower Industry' (Figure 3.4). This assemblage, the earliest so far placed with any degree of certainty within the Hoxnian, consists mainly of flakes, including scrapers, but with some hand-axes of cordate and ovate forms (Figure 3.3/4–5) exhibiting a refined flaking technique which probably involved the use of a wood or bone hammer. At a later stage, with the filling-in of the lake basin, a river regime was imposed and to this period, possibly contemporary with the Upper Loam at Barnfield Pit, Swanscombe, the 'Upper Industry' belongs. Flakes were again dominant, including elegantly flaked side-scrapers, but the hand-axes were pointed (Figure 3.3/6–7).

The location of apparently more advanced hand-axe assemblages in an upper level at Barnfield Pitt is thus reversed at Hoxne, where the 'refined' ovate/cordate forms are in the lower industry. This may be due to varying stylistic traditions or perhaps differing functional features existing con-temporaneously, and is a warning against too-easy acceptance of evolutionary typologies. Roe (1968a) has recognised a 'Pointed Tradition' and an 'Ovate Tradition' in his survey of hand-axe groups; the Swanscombe Middle Gravels implements and the pointed hand-axes from Hoxne are included in his Group II Pointed Tradition, but the more recent discoveries of flake-tools associated with the Hoxne pointed hand-axes (Wymer, 1974; Singer and Wymer, 1976) and their absence from the Swanscombe Middle Gravels industries make direct comparison of the two assemblages more difficult (Roe, 1976b). This is perhaps a further argument for functional variation and possibly some degree of specialisation.

With reference to Figure 3.4, it should be noted that there are suggestions, based on pollen analysis, that the upper part of the Swanscombe Lower Loam

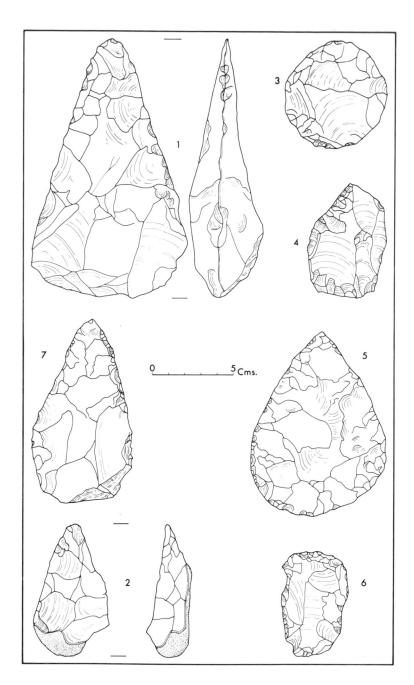

Figure 3.3: Hand-axes and scrapers from Swanscombe and Hoxne. 1, 2, hand-axes from Middle Gravels of Barnfield Pit, Swanscombe (1 found close to location of Swanscombe skull); 3, ovate hand-axe from Upper Loam, Swanscombe; 4, 5, scraper and cordate hand-axe from 'Lower Industry' at Hoxne; 6, 7, scraper and pointed hand-axe from 'Upper Industry' at Hoxne. After Swanscombe Committee, 1938; Wymer, 1968; Singer and Wymer, 1976.

Plate II: Two-pointed, pear-shaped hand-axes, Lower Middle Gravels, Barnfield Pit, Swanscombe, Kent. Hunterian Museum.

may be of Wolstonian age, with a consequently later, perhaps even post-Wolstonian, date for the upper levels (Wymer, 1974; Singer and Wymer, 1976). It has even been proposed, again on palynological evidence (Hubbard, 1977), that only the Lower Gravels and Lower Loam Clactonian industries are Hoxnian, that the hand-axe industries of the Lower and Upper Middle Gravels belong to a non-Hoxnian interglacial and that the Upper Loam and its industry are fully temperate and probably of Ipswichian age.

In the Middle Thames Valley, pointed hand-axe industries have been found in quantity in the gravels of the Lynch Hill Terrace (see Figure 1.3) on both sides of the Thames in the vicinity of Maidenhead, Berkshire. At Cannoncourt Farm, Furze Platt, and Baker's Farm, Farnham Royal (Lacaille, 1940), pointed hand-axes in sharp condition were associated with cordate and sub-cordate forms and also cleavers (Figure 3.5/3). The ficron shape is represented at both sites (Figure 3.5/2) and what is probably the largest hand-axe yet found in Britain was recovered from the Cannoncourt Farm gravel pit in 1919 (Figure 3.5/1). This large implement is well made and could hardly have had

POLLEN ZONES		GENERALISED VEGETATION	FAUNA
Temperate phase or Interstadial?			Horse, deer, bos/bison, elephant, giant beaver, beaver
			Voles, lemming, water-rat
early Wolstonian e Wo	Early-glacial	Park tundra?	
Ho IV b a	Post-temperate	Pine, birch, higher non-tree pollen	Wolf (Canis lupus), lion (Felis leo), straight-tusked elephant (Elephas antiquus), rhinoceros (Dicerorhinus kirchbergensis), horse (Equus caballus), fallow deer (Dama clactoniana), giant deer (Megaceros sp.), red deer (Cervus elaphus) aurochs (Bos primigenius), hare (Lepus sp.), lemming (Lemmus sp.), voles (Microtus sp.)
Ho III b a	Late-temperate	Mixed oak forest, fir, hornbeam, spruce	
Ho II c b a	Early-temperate	Mixed oak forest, yew, hazel, lime	Straight-tusked elephant, rhinoceros (Dicerorhinus kirchbergensis and D. hemitoechus), horse, fallow deer, red deer, giant deer, aurochs, wolf, marten (Martes sp.), cave bear (Ursus spelaeus), pig (Sus cf. scrofa), voles, beaver (Castor fiber), fish, birds
Ho I	Pre-temperate	Birch, pine	
1 A late Anglian (Lowestoftian)	Late-glacial	Park tundra?	

Figure 3.4: Attempted correlation of environmental and cultural sequences for three major Lower Palaeolithic sites in England, from late Anglian (IA) through Hoxnian (Ho) to early Wolstonian (eW). After Turner and West, 1968; Wymer, 1968, 1974; West, 1970; Kerney, 1971; Singer *et al.*, 1973; Singer and Wymer, 1976.

SWANSCOMBE (BARNFIELD PIT)	HOXNE	CLACTON-ON-SEA (GOLF COURSE)
Upper Gravels	**Fluviatile silts and gravels**	
Upper Loam — Cordate and ovate hand-axes. Riverside environment	'Upper Industry' side-scrapers and pointed hand-axes. Riverside or lakeside environment	
Upper Middle Gravels — Pointed hand-axe industry. Riverside environment. Skull: _Homo_ cf. _sapiens_. Uranium series date: ~272,000 years	**Resorted lake deposits**	
Lower Middle Gravels — 'Middle Acheulian' industry – mainly pointed hand-axes	**Peaty clay** — 'Lower Industry' refined cordate and ovate hand-axes with flake-tools in mint condition. Lakeside environment	
Lower Loam	Period of deforestation associated with arti-facts and charcoal. Lakeside environment	
Lower Gravels — Clactonian industry. Working floor? Animal bone midden? Riverside and marsh environment. Clactonian industry	**Lake sediments**	**Variegated marl** — Clactonian industry. Riverside and marsh environment. Cool climate
	Boulder clay	**Gravels** — Clactonian industry. Uranium series date: 245,000 years

the same function as more normal-sized hand-axes. In a recent study of hand-axes (Kleindienst and Keller, 1976), our present ignorance of the true function of these tools is stressed and ethnological evidence is quoted to show that hand-axes and cleavers could have been set upright in the ground as fixed tools rather than held in the hand. This interpretation is credible in terms of the large Cannoncourt Farm hand-axe, but there is a wide range of implements where shape and size are more indicative of hand-held tools for general butchering, skinning and chopping, with the cleaver as a mainly bone- or wood-splitting implement. At Whitlingham, Norfolk (Sainty, 1925), a possible flint-working site had pointed hand-axes associated with cleavers, as at Cannoncourt Farm and Baker's Farm.

A pointed hand-axe assemblage from Cuxton, Kent (Tester, 1965) contained numerous chopper-cores, identical to Clactonian forms, and similar cores were associated with mainly cordate hand-axes and flake-tools at Bowman's Lodge, Dartford, Kent (Tester, 1950, 1975). There seems to be no doubt as to the contemporaneity of hand-axes and cores showing Clactonian technique, but it is difficult to prove any direct cultural link since the Acheulian and Clactonian traditions are usually accepted as having been separated chronologically, though the possibility of a pre-Hoxnian 'Early Acheulian', as suggested above, could change the situation. At Highlands Farm, Rotherfield Peppard, Oxfordshire, in the gravels of the Ancient Channel of the Thames between Caversham and Henley, both Clactonian and Acheulian industries were recovered (Wymer, 1956, 1961), but it was not possible to separate them stratigraphically and they may have been derived from separate sources nearby. The hand-axes were mainly ovate/cordate, but there were quantities of cruder, stone-struck forms (Wymer's types D and E) (Plate III).

The phenomenon of the reversed S-twisted edge on some ovate/cordate hand-axes (Plate III). is probably explicable by a technique of flaking (Wymer, 1968, p. 56). This form is well represented by the industry from the site of what may have been a single occupation at Elveden, Suffolk (Paterson and Fagg, 1940), and examples have been recovered as far west as Broome, Devonshire (Moir, 1936) (Figure 3.5/4). A type of hand-axe suggested as a later development, partly on typological, partly on stratigraphical evidence, is the distinctive plano-convex series from Wolvercote, Oxfordshire, which may date to the Ipswichian Interglacial (Sandford, 1924; Wymer, 1968; Roe, 1976b). The artifacts were associated with a fauna including straight-tusked elephant, rhinoceros, horse and red deer. At High Lodge, Mildenhall, Suffolk, an assemblage of dominantly ovate/cordiform hand-axes stratified above two earlier flake industries is presumably of intra-Wolstonian date (Roe, 1968a).

Away from the river valleys and in a general north and west direction, the density of Acheulian find-sites diminishes (Figure 3.7). A prolific site in the west is Knowle Farm, Savernake, Wiltshire (Kendall, 1906) and nearby in the Hackpen Hill area are some of the highest finds (up to 290 metres above sea-level) of hand-axes in the southern English/north-eastern French Acheulian province (Lacaille, 1971). An industry of ovate hand-axes, choppers or cleavers, and flakes (Figure 3.5/5) has been recovered from the surface of raised beach deposits at Slindon, Sussex (Calkin, 1934; Pyddoke, 1950), indicating occupation at a time when relative sea-level was 30–35 metres higher than at present, probably during the Hoxnian Interglacial. In the north,

Plate III: Cordate hand-axe with tranchet point and twisted edge. England (provenance unknown). Dept. of Archaeology, University of Glasgow.

there are not many finds (less than 5 per cent of all known Lower and Middle Palaeolithic sites) beyond a line running roughly from the Wash to the Severn Estuary. The sites which have survived north of this line are possibly only a small proportion of a more intensive occupation, the evidence for which has been destroyed by glaciation and associated processes. Some hand-axe sites are known in the Midlands (Posnansky, 1963), particularly in the gravel pits at Hilton and Willington in Derbyshire, where the raw material for the artifacts was mainly a grey flint, probably from the Lincolnshire chalk, with a small quantity of quartzite. More recently, sub-cordate and pointed hand-axes have been recovered from silts, sands and gravels beneath a Wolstonian glacial till at Welton-le-Wold, Lincolnshire (Straw, 1976; Alabaster and Straw, 1976; Wymer and Straw, 1977). Associated with the artifacts and probably derived with them from a nearby location were remains of straight-tusked elephant (*Elephas (Palaeoloxodon) antiquus*) – including a complete tusk 2.2 metres in length – red deer (*Cervus elaphus*), horse (*Equus* sp.) and possibly Irish giant deer (*Megaceros* sp.). The fauna suggests a temperate, interglacial period, presumably Hoxnian.

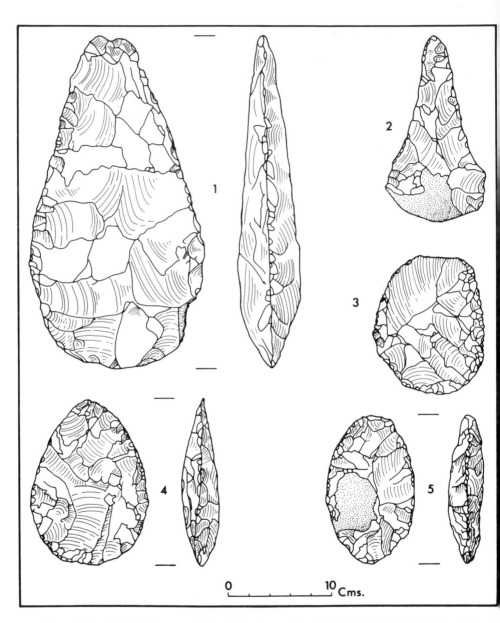

Figure 3.5: Size and shape variation in hand-axes. 1, pointed hand-axe, largest known in Britain, Cannoncourt Farm, Furze Platt, Maidenhead; 2, ficron hand-axe, Cannoncourt Farm; 3, cleaver from Cannoncourt Farm; 4, twisted ovate, Broome, Devon; 5, ovate hand-axe, Slindon, Sussex. After Lacaille, 1940; Reid Moir, 1936; Calkin, 1934.

Lacking finds of complete tool-kits in undisturbed primary contexts, there is little to be gained at present from constructing elaborate typologies for the Acheulian industries in Britain. Stages of development based on French evidence (Breuil and Koslowski, 1931–2; Breuil, 1939; Bordes, 1956) are really not applicable and any scheme would have to be based on the peculiar circumstances of the British evidence. A tentative framework for hand-axe evolution, but without implying a definite chronology, has been suggested recently (Roe, 1976b), in which four stages are outlined:

(1) thick archaic forms, unstandardised and showing evidence of stone-on-stone working, some of which are likely to be of pre-Hoxnian origin (Kent's Cavern, Fordwich, Warren Hill, Farnham, etc.);

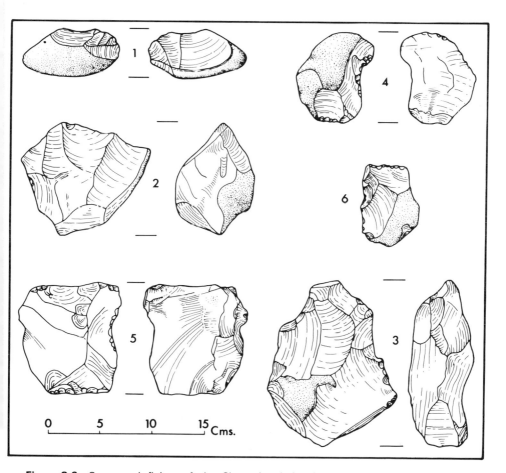

Figure 3.6: Cores and flakes of the Clactonian industries. 1, pebble chopper-core, Clacton-on-Sea; 2, biconical chopper-core, Highlands Farm Pit, Rotherfield Peppard, Oxfordshire; 3, proto hand-axe, Highlands Farm Pit; 4–6, flake-tools from Clacton-on-Sea. After Breuil, 1932; Wymer, 1961; Singer *et al.*, 1973.

(2) pointed hand-axes showing developed techniques of flaking with bone or wood hammers, of Hoxnian to Wolstonian age (Swanscombe Middle Gravels, Hoxne 'Upper Industry', Furze Platt, etc.);

(3) refined ovate/cordate forms, with or without flake-tools, of Hoxnian and Wolstonian age (Hoxne 'Lower Industry', Swanscombe Upper Loam, Elveden, etc.);

(4) finely finished pointed hand-axes, often of plano-convex shape, perhaps related to continental 'Late Acheulian' or 'Micoquian', of Wolstonian and Ipswichian age (Wolvercote, etc.).

Clactonian Industries

Apart from the Acheulian industries, dominated by various forms of hand-axe and sometimes associated with specialised or non-specialised flake-tools, the other major Lower Palaeolithic industry in Britain is the Clactonian. This is an industry which has no true hand-axes or standardised tool-forms, and consists mainly of chopper-cores and flakes with unspecialised flake-tools (Plate IV), taking its name from the site of Clacton-on-Sea, Essex, where the assemblage was first described as 'Mesvinian' by Warren (1922), and renamed by Breuil (1932). The most recent excavations have been at Clacton Golf Course (Singer *et al.*, 1973) and Barnfield Pit, Swanscombe (Waechter *et al.*, 1969, 1970, 1971, 1972).

Clactonian nodules or core-tools have been classified (Wymer, 1968, pp. 36–40) as A – pebble chopper-core, B – bi-conical chopper-core, and C – proto hand-axe (Figure 3.6/1–3). The associated unspecialised flakes could have been used for a number of purposes – as scrapers, knives, points, borers or piercers (Figure 3.6/4–6). Despite the apparent crudity of the artifacts, a wide range of functions was obviously possible with a minimum of working. Wymer (1974, p. 412) has compared the industry favourably with the more refined Acheulian implements, again raising the question of the hand-axe, its function, and why it was made at all.

The Clactonian industry was probably related to the widespread chopper-tool groups of the Lower Palaeolithic in Europe and Asia, which included the artifacts associated with 'Peking Man' (*Homo erectus pekinensis*) in the lower caves at Choukoutien, China, of intra-Mindel (Elsterian, Anglian) age, and the similarly dated 'Buda' industry from Vértesszöllös, Hungary, associated with another *Homo erectus* (or perhaps *Homo cf. sapiens*) type. In Britain, the industries are of the earlier Hoxnian Interglacial, for example at Clacton and Swanscombe (Figure 3.4), and perhaps as early as late Anglian (Lowestoftian). It has been suggested that the Clactonian was adapted to a mainly forested environment and therefore appeared earlier in the interglacial phase, during the period of thickening forest cover, than Acheulian assemblages which were associated with times of more open woodland, grassland and heath (Collins, 1969).

The most prolific site for Clactonian material has been Clacton itself (Warren, 1922, 1951; Oakley and Leakey, 1937; Singer *et al.*, 1973). The artifacts are stratified in gravels probably of late Anglian (Lowestoftian) age and above this in marl of the pre-temperate phase of the Hoxnian Interglacial

Plate IV: Clactonian core and flake. Lower Gravels, Barnfield Pit, Swanscombe, Kent. Hunterian Museum.

(Figure 3.4). Uranium series analysis of fossil bones from the gravels has given a date of 245,000 $^{+35,000}_{-25,000}$ years bp (Szabo and Collins, 1975). If the upper limit is taken, this date could come within the range of that obtained by the same method for the stratigraphically later base of the Upper Middle Gravels at Swanscombe (>272,000), mentioned above. The technique has not so far been widely applied terrestrially and greater accuracy may yet be possible (see also Chapter 1).

At Barnfield Pit, Swanscombe, the Clactonian industry is in the Lower Gravels and Lower Loam (Waechter *et al.*, 1969, 1970, 1971, 1972) of the pre-temperate and early temperate phases of the Hoxnian. A concentration of elephant, rhinoceros, deer and bear remains in the Lower Loam is thought to represent a midden, and groups of conjoinable flakes suggest a working or 'knapping' floor. Clactonian material has also been recovered from Rickson's Pit, Swanscombe, in deposits which are probably an extension of the Barnfield Pit Lower Gravels.

Some of the Clactonian material from East Farm, Barnham St Gregory, Suffolk (Paterson, 1937) was in gravels which may have been outwash from the late Anglian (Lowestoftian) Glaciation and therefore possibly of immediate pre-Hoxnian age; the gravels were overlain by a loam deposit containing a developed hand-axe assemblage. The only other unmixed Clactonian assemblage is that from the Globe Pit, Little Thurrock, Essex (Wymer, 1957; Snelling, 1964). Artifacts of Clactonian type have been found at Grovelands, Reading, Berkshire, and Southacre, Norfolk, but in presumed association with more standardised and finely worked flake-tools (Singer *et al.*, 1973), suggesting a later industry, perhaps comparable to High Lodge, Mildenhall, Suffolk (Roe, 1968a), where a non-Levalloisian flake industry could either be a continuation of some form of Clactonian, or a functional or evironmental adaptation by hand-axe groups during a Wolstonian temperate phase or interstadial.

Interpretation of Human Activity

The evidence for human occupation of Britain in earlier Palaeolithic times is not such as to allow a detailed discussion of 'man–land relationships'. Allowing for the removal of evidence by fluvio-glacial processes, there seems to have been a preference for locations in or near river valleys and on lake shores. These sites would have been sources of water and fish for early man and also drinking-places for the animals he hunted. At Torralba and Ambrona in Spain (Howell, 1966), groups using Acheulian hand-axes killed and butchered animals (mainly straight-tusked elephants) which had been trapped in boggy ground in the valley of the Ambrona river; similar techniques may have been used by the Thames-side or Hoxne lake-side hunters. The use of fire to hunt and stampede animals is suggested from a number of Palaeolithic sites, but little evidence exists in Britain. The pollen diagrams for Mark's Tey, Essex (Turner, 1970), and Hoxne, Suffolk (West, 1956, 1968), show a break in the mixed-oak forest development and a temporary reversion to grassland late in the early temperate (Ho IIc) phase of the Hoxnian Interglacial. At this level at Hoxne, some possible specks of charcoal and a few flint implements could

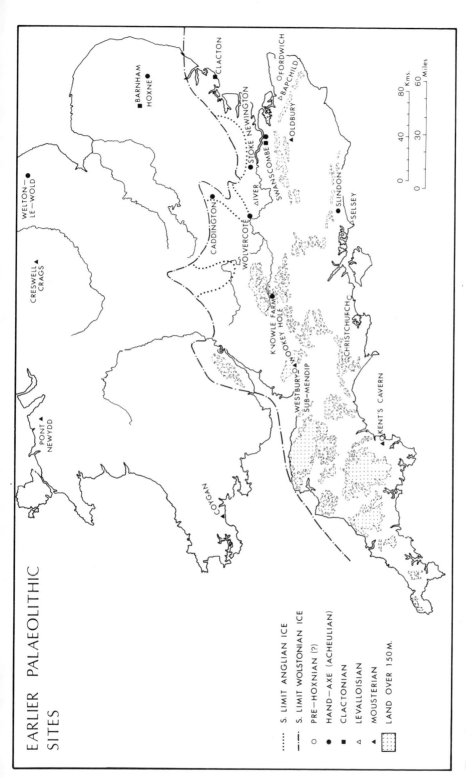

Figure 3.7: Map of some earlier Palaeolithic sites in England and Wales, with limits of Anglian and Wolstonian glaciations.

indicate human agency; but whether or not deliberate burning of vegetation in driving game, or accidental burning from camp fires, or even a completely natural fire, caused for example by lightning, was involved cannot be demonstrated with any certainty (Wymer and Singer, 1975).

Evidence of occupation sites is scarce, but a few undisturbed 'floors' include Round Green, Bedfordshire, and Gaddesden Row, Hertfordshire (Smith, 1916), Caddington, Bedfordshire (where heaps of flint nodules brought to the site could be identified), and Stoke Newington, London (Smith, 1894). Stoke Newington had a pointed hand-axe industry with cleavers, and the site has been tentatively dated (Wymer, 1968) to the Ipswichian Interglacial. The most interesting finds, however, were two stakes of birch, each about four feet in length, artificially sharpened at one end, possibly forming part of a wind-break or shelter, and a mass of fronds and rhizomes of ferns (*Osmunda regalis*) which may have been used as bedding (Smith, 1894). The scarcity of organic remains has already been stressed, but there is occasional rare evidence for the use of bone and wood. Apart from the Stoke Newington finds, mention should be made of the point of a thrusting spear made of yew wood and a few utilised bones from Clacton (Warren, 1911, 1951; Oakley *et al.*, 1977).

The main forms of animals hunted in the interglacial or temperate periods were straight-tusked elephant, temperate rhinoceros, deer and horse, as well as fish and birds. The role of hunting should not be over-emphasised; Mellars (1976) points out the potential importance of plant foods in 'hunting' societies, except in regions of extreme cold, and quotes evidence for a high percentage of vegetable materials in the food sources of recent and modern hunting/collecting cultures.

Evidence for the types of men associated with Lower Palaeolithic industries is also rare. The skull associated with the pointed hand-axes in the Upper Middle Gravels at Swanscombe has been classed as *Homo* cf. *sapiens* – a possible transition between *Homo erectus* and the Neanderthaloids or *Homo sapiens sapiens*. At Steinheim, in south-west Germany, a skull of similar age but with no associated artifacts is a possible predecessor of Neanderthal man. At Torralba/Ambrona in Spain, mentioned above, and Terra Amata in the south of France, there is plenty of evidence for hunting and other activities in intra-Mindel (Elsterian, Anglian) times by groups using hand-axes, but no human remains have been found in association. Elsewhere, Acheulian industries are closely linked with *Homo erectus*, as at Beds II and IV, Olduvai Gorge, at Sidi Abderrahman, Morocco, and Ternifine, Algeria (see Chapter 2 above). Industries similar to the Clactonian and of Mindel/Elsterian/Anglian age have been found with *Homo erectus* forms at Choukoutien, China and Vertesszöllös, Hungary, although the latter remains (part of an occipital) have also been suggested as *Homo* cf. *sapiens* (Thoma, 1966). It would thus seem that in the later Middle Pleistocene, as in earlier times, more than one stage of hominid evolution existed contemporaneously, using hand-axes or industries based on chopper-cores and unspecialised flakes; but the associations are not consistent and we should perhaps not assume too close a relationship between particular cultures and stages of human evolution at this time, when disparities may be due more to variations in function and environmental adaptation than to differences in chronology or human physical development.

Later Developments

Industries dominated by flakes struck from prepared cores (the 'Levalloisian technique') and sometimes associated with hand-axes are known from the time of the Wolstonian glaciation into the earlier stages of the last (Devensian) glaciation. Oakley (1969, p. 142) has described the technique as 'pre-fabricating flake-tools before detaching them from the core'. In these Levalloisian industries, the working of the core often produced a distinctive domed shape ('tortoise-core') and the preparation of the striking-platform can be traced in the facetting on the butt-end of flakes struck from such cores (Figure 3.8/1,2; Plate V). Wymer (1968) has noted the appearance of prepared cores in earlier Acheulian contexts and suggests the Levalloisian as a continuation and expansion of this technique to the exclusion of almost any other, apart from assemblages where hand-axes can be definitely associated. The implements produced would have functioned as knives, skinning-tools, scrapers and highly effective pointed spearheads (for example Figure 3.8/3–5; Plate VI).

The most prolific Levalloisian site is Baker's Hole, Northfleet, Kent (Smith, 1911). Most flakes are from broad tortoise-cores but there are some narrower examples (Figure 3.8/5; Plate VI) and there were ovate/cordate and pointed hand-axes in association. Animal remains included mammoth, temperate rhinoceros, deer and horse. To the south-east, the site of Bapchild, Kent (Dines, 1929), had an industry similar to that at Baker's Hole and, like the latter site, is probably of intra-Wolstonian age.

Plate V: Levalloisian 'tortoise core'. Provenance unknown. Hunterian Museum.

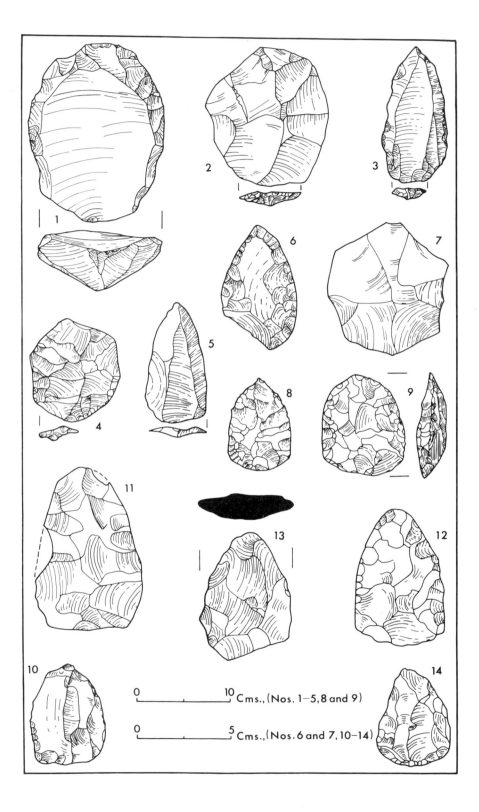

0 _____ 10 Cms., (Nos. 1–5, 8 and 9)

0 _____ 5 Cms., (Nos. 6 and 7, 10–14)

The Levalloisian industry from the brickearths (sands, silts, loams and clays deposited during a temperate or interglacial phase) at Crayford, Kent (Wymer, 1968), is probably of Ipswichian age and represents a later development of the flint-working technique, with blade-like flakes from prismatic cores resembling an Upper Palaeolithic industry (Mellars, 1974, p. 55). One of the sites was an occupation floor where evidence of flint-knapping was combined with the bones of animals which may have been butchered on the spot. The most common faunal remains were woolly rhinoceros (*Tichorhinus* (*Coelodonta*) *antiquitatis*), mammoth (*Elephas* (*Mammuthus*) *primigenius*), horse (*Equus caballus*), aurochs (*Bos primigenius*), red deer (*Cervus elaphus*), suslik (*Citellus eyrthrogenoides*) and various voles (*Microtus* sp.). A similar industry was recovered from a site at Creffield Road, Acton, London, and pointed Levalloisian flake-blades were found in contact with the apparently complete and articulated skeleton of a mammoth at Norwood Lane, Southall, London (Wymer, 1968). Further west, Levalloisian sites of probable Ipswichian age are known at West Drayton, London, and Iver, Buckinghamshire. At Brundon, Suffolk (Moir and Hopwood, 1939), Levalloisian flakes and flake-blades from tortoise-cores were associated with remains of mammoth, horse, red deer, aurochs, rhinoceros, cave-bear (*Ursus spelaeus*) and straight-tusked elephant (*Elephas antiquus*). A late site at Ebbsfleet, Kent, is presumably of early Devensian age (Wymer, 1968).

As with the Acheulian and Clactonian groups, there was a preference among users of Levalloisian industries for river-valleys, and this distribution probably coincided with those regions where good flint was readily available as exposures in valleys or transported by glacial action (Wymer, 1968). A wide range of animals has been associated with these sites and there may have been some specialisation, for example in the hunting of mammoth. No human remains have been recovered with Levalloisian assemblages, but contemporary continental finds include the Fontéchevade early *Homo sapiens* and the earlier Neanderthaloids (for example Ehringsdorf).

The term 'Middle Palaeolithic' has often been used, confusedly and confusingly, as a chronological subdivision including, in some cases, the early industries of Levalloisian technique. In the strict sense it is a cultural label and should perhaps be applied only to the various forms of the Mousterian culture of Neanderthal man. The Mousterian culture was a flake-tool industry characterised by flakes struck from discoidal cores (Figure 3.8/6,7), producing finely retouched side-scrapers and points, deriving probably from Lower Palaeolithic Clactonian and related cultures, with Acheulian and Levalloisian

Figure 3.8: Examples of Levalloisian and Mousterian artifacts. 1, tortoise-core, Baker's Hole, Northfleet, Kent; 2, broad flake, Baker's Hole; 3, narrow flake, Baker's Hole; 4, broad flake with secondary working, Baker's Hole; 5, narrow blade-flake from prismatic core, Baker's Hole. Mousterian implements: 6, Mousterian point, Pinhole Cave, Creswell Crags, Derbyshire; 7, discoidal core, Robin Hood's Cave, Creswell Crags, Derbyshire; 8, '*bout coupé*' hand-axe, Little Paxton, Huntingdonshire, and 9, a similar type from Mousehold Heath, Norfolk; 10–12, hand-axes of possible 'Mousterian of Acheulian tradition', Oldbury, Kent; 13, 14, 'bifaces' from Wookey Hole, Somerset. After Wymer, 1968; Armstrong, 1931; Mellars, 1974; Paterson and Tebbutt, 1947; Sainty, 1935; Collins, 1970; Tratman *et al.*, 1971.

Plate VI: Levalloisian prismatic core (top left), Baker's Hole, Northfleet, Kent, and three Levalloisian flakes, Biddenham, Bedfordshire. Hunterian Museum.

influences. It appears during the last interglacial, but the typical or 'cold' Mousterian is that of the early stages of the last glaciation, to which phase the British assemblages appear to belong. The assemblages have the basic flake-tools of Mousterian type, but associated with small and modified forms of hand-axe. The use of the term 'hand-axe' in reference to these late implements is perhaps unjustified, if such a definition were ever justified for any stage of their development, since the dimensions and shape of the tools have altered considerably. The degree of surface-working – particularly retouch, thinness and general appearance of some of the implements – appears to foreshadow the leaf-shaped, unifacially- and bifacially-worked points of the Early Upper Palaeolithic. They have been termed 'bifaces' (Tratman *et al.*, 1971), a description which avoids functional conjecture and which has been used by many archaeologists in reference to all hand-axes. A particular hand-axe form in Mousterian assemblages is the cordate '*bout coupé*' (Figure 3.8/8,9), in which the butt is squared or angled and the cutting edge usually runs completely around the implement (Roe, 1968a).

Many British Mousterian sites are of early Devensian age. At Little Paxton, St Neots, Huntingdonshire (Tebbutt *et al.*, 1927; Paterson and Tebbutt, 1947), on a terrace of the Great Ouse, Mousterian artifacts (Figure 3.8/8) were associated with a 'cold' fauna, including mammoth, woolly rhinoceros, horse and reindeer (*Rangifer tarandus*). In the A2 Cave Earth level at Kent's Cavern, Devonshire (Campbell and Sampson, 1971), a similar industry accompanied remains of horse (*Equus germanicus*), hyena (*Crocuta crocuta*), woolly rhinoceros, reindeer, giant deer (*Megaceros* sp.), brown bear (*Ursus arctos*), fox (*Vulpes vulpes*), mammoth and lion (*Felis leo*), a fauna indicating sub-arctic and boreal environments. Other finds of this period are known from Christchurch, Dorset (Calkin and Green, 1949), the Gipping Valley near Ipswich, Suffolk, and Mousehold Heath and other sites in Norfolk (Sainty, 1935) (Figure 3.8/9).

Little is known of what must have been intermittent occupation of southern Britain at this time, apart from the few stone artifacts and faunal remains. At a similar, if more continental, latitude, a Mousterian site with a wide range of material evidence at Salzgitter-Lebenstedt, near Brunswick, West Germany (Tode *et al.*, 1953), has been dated by the radiocarbon method to 55,600 bp (GrN-2083) (see also p. 24 above). This was a summer encampment (the July temperatures were probably about 5° to 7° C lower than at present) with large quantities of animal remains, including reindeer, mammoth, bison, horse and woolly rhinoceros, suggesting that these presumably Neanderthal hunters followed animal herds northwards into tundra habitats in the warmer season. The industry was mainly of Mousterian flake tools, with a proportion of late hand-axe forms. Apart from the stone implements, there was abundant evidence for the working of bone and horn, including clubs of reindeer antler, points made of mammoth ribs and barbed bone points. The size of the camp and quantity of materials suggest a group of 40 or more individuals and a high degree of specialisation and proficiency in hunting is indicated.

The last appearance of the hand-axe or biface in the British Palaeolithic is among those assemblages which have been compared with the French 'Mousterian of Acheulian Tradition' (Collins, 1970; Mellars, 1974, pp. 64–5), suggested as a particularly Atlantic or west European manifestation of

AGE		CULTURE TRADITION			
		ACHEULIAN	CLACTONIAN	LEVALLOISIAN	MOUSTERIAN
DEVENSIAN	Upton Warren Interstadial				Coygan Hyaena Den Pontnewydd Creswell Crags
	Chelford Interstadial			Ebbsfleet	
					Oldbury Little Paxton Kent's Cavern
IPSWICHIAN	Interglacial	Wolvercote Stoke Newington		Crayford Brundon Acton Selsey Iver West Drayton	
WOLSTONIAN	Interstadial?	Caddington High Lodge Hoxne Swanscombe (Upper Loam)	High Lodge?	Bapchild Baker's Hole Purfleet Chatham	
HOXNIAN	Interglacial	Swanscombe (Mid. Gravels) Hoxne	Little Thurrock Swanscombe (Low. Gravels) Clacton Barnham		
ANGLIAN	Lowestoft Stade				
	Corton Interstadial	Fordwich?			
	Gunton Stade				
CROMERIAN	Interglacial or Temperate Period	Kent's Cavern Westbury			

Figure 3.9: Suggested chronological sequence of some earlier Palaeolithic sites.

Mousterian tradition quite separate from central or eastern European developments. They may have survived as late as the Upton Warren Interstadial in England. Among the richest assemblages are those from Oldbury, Kent (Collins, 1970), where the industry included flake-tools and small hand-axes (Figure 3.8/10–12), and Great Pan Farm, Isle of Wight (Poole, 1924; Shackley, 1973), where the condition of the artifacts suggests little or no transportation by natural processes from the site where they were used or discarded.

At the Hyaena Den, Wookey Hole, Somerset (Tratman *et al.*, 1971), the hand-axes or bifaces are among the smallest known (Figure 3.8/13,14) and the fauna includes hyena, woolly rhinoceros and horse. In the 'far north' of this period, Mousterian artifacts have been recovered from Pinhole Cave, Robin Hood's Cave and Church Hole, Creswell Crags, Derbyshire (Figure 3.8/6,7) (Mellars, 1974), and Pontnewydd Cave, Denbighshire (McBurney, 1965). Collagen from a reindeer antler associated with a 'Mousterian of Acheulian Tradition' industry at Coygan Cave, Carmarthenshire (Grimes and Cowley, 1935) has yielded a radiocarbon date of 38,684 bp (BM-499). The fauna included mammoth, horse and woolly rhinoceros, and the date is similar to that for a full-glacial faunal assemblage from Fladbury, Worcestershire (Coope, 1962), possibly belonging to a cold phase within the Upton Warren Interstadial Complex.

The earlier (Lower and Middle) Palaeolithic in Britain is a phase of slow physical and cultural development which, if the pre-Hoxnian sites mentioned above are correctly dated, extended over a span of time of the order of half a million years. The archaeological evidence from this major evolutionary period is relatively scarce and, allowing for destruction by various processes, suggests only intermittent occupation, with man absent during glacial phases before the last ice age (Figure 3.9). Recent research has revealed a less complex, if still little known, pattern of development. There would now appear to be less need than formerly to seek direct parallels for cultural evolution among French industries and traditions, and more attention is now being given to internal developments, environmental adaptation and functional variation. Two or three main lines of development can be traced. The Clactonian industries appear perhaps as early as the late Anglian, but are less easy to trace after the mid-Hoxnian, apart from their possible ancestry to later flake cultures. By comparison, the Acheulian or hand-axe tradition, which might now be seen as developing earlier than the Clactonian, survives in late and modified forms to the last (Ipswichian) interglacial and merges with Levalloisian and Mousterian industries to appear finally in the early stages of the last glaciation.

Chapter 4

THE UPPER PALAEOLITHIC IN BRITAIN

The date of the first appearance of fossil forms of modern man (*Homo sapiens sapiens*) and his material culture in Europe is now generally accepted to have been between 40,000 and 30,000 years ago, although dates for the earliest Aurignacian in eastern Europe, for example at the Istállóskö Cave, Hungary (Vértes, 1955), are even earlier than this. The earliest manifestations of Upper Palaeolithic material culture in Europe show undeniable links with earlier, Middle Palaeolithic, traditions. The unifacially- and bifacially-worked leaf-shaped points of British Earlier Upper Palaeolithic sites, formerly termed 'proto-Solutrean' in an attempt to correlate with the nearest culture-sequences in France and western Europe, can now be seen to have closer affinities with groups in central and east central Europe of a period much earlier than the classic Solutrean (Davidson, 1974), or even the west European 'Proto-Solutrean'. It has been suggested (McBurney, 1965) that the British leaf-point tradition, with its much earlier origin, might even have developed to the point of influencing the beginnings of the west European Solutrean sequence. In the central and east European cultures, the continuity from Middle Palaeolithic Mousteroid traditions can clearly be seen. The development of specialised points with bifacial working was already traceable in the Mousterian assemblages of, for example, Ehringsdorf, near Weimar, East Germany, and there is evidence for 'hand-axes evolving towards foliates' at many sites (Coles and Higgs, 1969). The size of the 'bifaces' at Wookey Hole, Somerset (Chapter 3 and Figure 3.8) is interesting in this respect. The earliest cultures using these leaf-points may therefore have been regional developments from local Middle Palaeolithic traditions, with perhaps some influences from westward-spreading Aurignacian groups.

The Szeletian of Hungary (from the Szeleta Cave in the Hungarian Bükk Mountains) shows a development from small, thick bifaces resembling hand-axes, and possibly of Eastern Mousterian origin, to longer, bifacially-worked 'laurel leaves' showing advanced working techniques. At Szeleta Cave, a layer just above the earliest occurrence of Szeletian material has been dated to 43,000 radiocarbon years bp, and the main Szeletian layer has a date of 32,620 radiocarbon years bp. A split-based bone point in the earliest layer suggests contemporaneity with Aurignacian I in the region (Vértes, 1955, 1956, 1959; Zotz, 1951; Freund, 1952). A similar industry, the Jerzmanowician, is known from Poland, and the lowermost layer at the type-site of Nietoperzowa has been dated to 38,500 radiocarbon years bp (Chmielewski, 1961, 1972). Further west, a later development, the Altmühlian, is known from the Ilsen Cave in East Germany (Otto, 1951) and Mauern in Bavaria. In the Weinberg caves, near Mauern, the lowermost industry is a form of Eastern Mousterian including plano-convex scrapers and, above this, the Altmühlian assemblage has the 'Blattspitzen' or leaf-points, up to 15 cm in length and with advanced plano-convex or bifacial retouch (Bohmers, 1951; Zotz, 1955, 1960). As already stated, the British Upper Palaeolithic leaf-points would seem to have more links with these groups than with any west European culture-sequence.

It is more difficult, lacking definite evidence, to identify the forms of men associated with these industries. It is known that Neanderthal man survived into the Upper Palaeolithic period in central and western Europe, for example in the somewhat culturally retarded 'Alpine Palaeolithic' (Tschumi, 1949) of Switzerland, south Germany and Austria (a Mousterian industry and cave-bear remains at Salzofenhöhle, Austria, was dated to 34,000 radiocarbon years bp), and that it may be possible to associate the earliest forms of modern man with an early Aurignacian culture, but this transitional period is ill defined.

Whatever the man/culture association, the crucial phase appears to have been a major warmer period or interstadial near the middle of the last 'ice age'. Such a climatic amelioration could have been favourable to groups bearing the initial Upper Palaeolithic culture while at the same time accelerating the decline of Neanderthal/Mousterian traditions.

In Britain, this more temperate period may have been the series of climatic oscillations known as the 'Upton Warren Interstadial Complex' (Figure 4.1). This phase, during which trees had not yet recolonised the British environment, has been recognised at Upton Warren itself (Coope *et al.*, 1961, 1969; Coope and Sands, 1966; Coope *et al.*, 1971) and at Four Ashes, Staffordshire, the stratotype or type-site for the Devensian Stage (Morgan, A., 1973; Morgan, A. V., 1973). Cold conditions towards the end of this 'Interstadial Complex' are indicated by the Lea Valley Arctic Plant Bed from Ponders End, North London (Reid, 1949; Godwin, 1964), dated to 28,000 radiocarbon years bp, where a fauna with mammoth, woolly rhinoceros, horse, reindeer and lemming was associated with remains of arctic mosses, dwarf birch and arctic willow, and a molluscan assemblage comparable with that of present-day Iceland or Lapland. An earlier Devensian interstadial has been demonstrated at Chelford, Cheshire, on the basis of vegetational evidence – a peat bed containing remains of birch, pine and spruce trees (Simpson and West, 1958) – and insect faunas (Coope, 1959), and possibly at Wretton, Norfolk (West *et al.*, 1974), although there is some disagreement between floral and insect evidence at the latter site. Figure 4.1 shows the differences between a climatic curve based mainly on the evidence of insect (beetle) assemblages and one based on glacial deposits and pollen analysis. Some discrepancies may be due to the much quicker response of insect faunas to changes in the thermal environment.

For fifty years, the only comprehensive survey of the Upper Palaeolithic in Britain was that of Garrod (1926). More recently, a new series of excavations and re-excavations of Upper Palaeolithic sites and a re-examination of existing material have produced a modern study of the period (Campbell, 1977). The period has been divided into an Earlier and a Later Upper Palaeolithic on the basis of differing cultural traditions separated by the hiatus of maximum glaciation (Figure 4.1). Campbell (1977, pp. 3–17) lists the raw materials for artifacts associated with British Upper Palaeolithic cultures under the headings of stone, bone, ivory, tooth, antler, shell, snow or ice (as building materials, etc.), sand or silt, clay, gut, skin, fur, moss, herbs, bark or wood. Stone tools

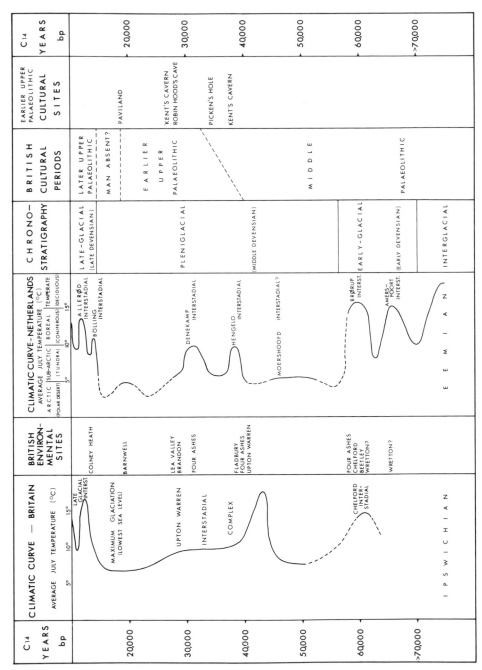

Figure 4.1: Last Glaciation – table of environmental changes and cultural chronology. The British climatic curve is based mainly on evidence of insect faunas and is after Coope, 1975; the Netherlands curve is based on glacial deposits and pollen analysis and is after Zagwijn and Paepe, 1968.

are classified under eight subdivisions:

(1) backed tools – flakes, blades, shouldered and tanged points;
(2) burins;
(3) scrapers;
(4) 'Zinken' – burin type with nosed point, particularly adapted to the 'groove and splinter' technique of working reindeer antler, where parallel grooves were cut into the antler and a long splinter prised loose to be worked into barbed points etc.;
(5) awls and borers;
(6) saws and notches or 'spokeshaves';
(7) combined or composite tools – for example burin/scraper;
(8) retouched blades and flakes, particularly unifacial and bifacial leaf-points ('Blattspitzen').

The remainder of the stone inventory is listed as 'waste' and includes cores, micro-burins, axe-sharpening flakes, hammer-stones, pebble tools and engraved or decorated stones. Artifacts of bone, ivory or antler include awls, needles, points (plain and barbed), spatulae, *'bâtons-de-commandement'*, ornaments and musical instruments (for example whistles).

Most of the stone artifacts, particularly the blunted-back tools, knives, end-scrapers, saws, etc., were produced on blades – approximately parallel-sided, long flakes struck from cylindrical or prismatic cores using a hammer-stone and a wood or bone punch. Blade industries were typical of the Upper Palaeolithic in general, but they can be traced to earlier periods – for example the Levalloisian 'blade-flakes' at Crayford, Kent.

The Earlier Upper Palaeolithic Period

The Earlier Upper Palaeolithic, as already suggested, appears to have originated during the early phases of the Upton Warren Interstadial Complex. The earliest absolute date is one of 38,270 radiocarbon years bp (laboratory number GrN-6324) from bone of horse (*Equus* cf. *przewalskii*) associated with two unifacial leaf-points (Figure 4.2/1,2) and a saw at Kent's Cavern, Torquay, Devon (Campbell, 1977). At Picken's Hole, Somerset, human teeth and animal remains with an undetermined Palaeolithic industry have been dated to 34,265 radiocarbon years bp (BM-654); the animal remains included arctic fox (*Alopex lagopus*), cave hyena, cave lion, horse, woolly rhinoceros, reindeer and mammoth (Tratman, 1964; Oakley *et al.*, 1971). Later radiocarbon dates for Kent's Cavern are 28,720 bp (GrN-6202) for bone collagen of brown bear (*Ursus arctos*) associated with a bifacial leaf-point, 28,160 bp (GrN-6201) for bone of woolly rhinoceros associated with a unifacial leaf-point, two nosed scrapers and a saw, and 27,730 bp (GrN-6325) for bison bone associated with a scraper and a scraper/saw (Campbell and Sampson, 1971). The average radiocarbon age for the Earlier Upper Palaeolithic at Kent's Cavern has been estimated as *c.* 30,720 bp (Campbell, 1977). A 'site-catchment area' of 10 kilometres radius (2 hours walking) centred on Kent's Cavern as a base camp (Campbell and Sampson, 1971) would have allowed

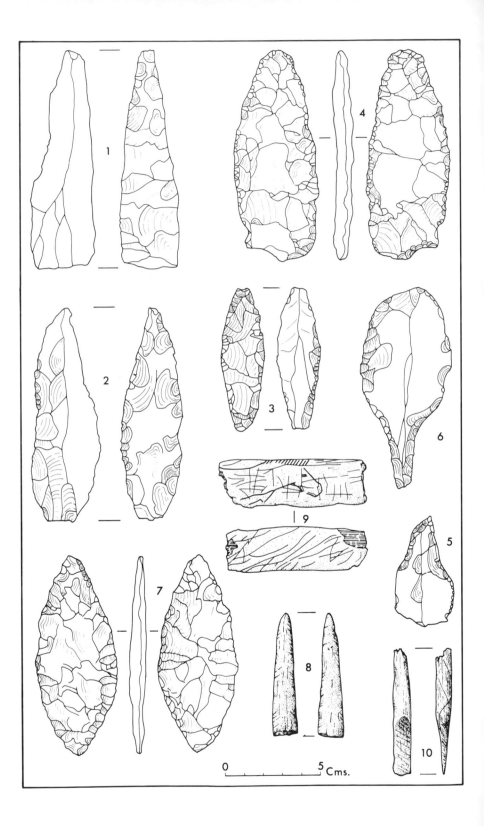

exploitation of the lowlands to the east and south (now covered by the English Channel) as well as the hilly hinterland. Other caves in the vicinity, such as Bench Fissure, Cow Cave and Tornewton Cave, may have been used by the same hunting group. Bench Fissure, Brixham, had a unifacial leaf-point and remains of hyena, wolf, fox and voles (*Microtus* sp.).

There is a major concentration of Upper Palaeolithic sites in the Mendip region of Somerset (Figure 4.3). The main centre of hunting activity appears to have been near Badger Hole, Wookey Hole, where the Earlier Upper Palaeolithic industry consisted of scrapers, awls, saws and leaf-points (Figure 4.2/3), and the fauna included hyena, lion, otter (*Lutra lutra*), fox, brown bear, horse, giant Irish deer (*Megaceros giganteus*) and reindeer. The faunal evidence for cold conditions is supported by pollen analysis, which shows only 22 per cent trees and shrubs but 78 per cent grasses, sedges and ferns (Campbell, 1970, 1977). A radiocarbon determination on charred bone fragments gave a date greater than 18,000 bp (BM-497). At Hyaena Den, Wookey Hole, scrapers, saws and leaf-points are ascribed to a cold period (Tratman *et al.*, 1971), but stratification is not clear. The site at Soldier's Hole is more secure, with an Earlier Upper Palaeolithic industry stratified beneath a Later (Campbell, 1970). The Earlier industry consisted of saws, bifacial leaf-points and an awl or point of ivory (Figure 4.2/4,8); it was associated with a fauna including hyena, lion, wolf, fox, brown bear, mammoth, horse, red deer, giant Irish deer, reindeer and bison, plus birds (teal, grey-lag goose, whooper swan, ptarmigan, grouse, etc.) (Campbell, 1977). Similarities between the Soldier's Hole leaf-points and those from the Altmühl industries of Mauern, Bavaria (Bohmers, 1951), have been noted (Campbell, 1977), further emphasising the affinities of at least one element of the early phase of the British Upper Palaeolithic. Another site in the area, Uphill Cave, near Weston-super-Mare, Somerset, had unifacial leaf-points, saws, scrapers and a burin (Garrod, 1926).

At King Arthur's Cave, Herefordshire, Earlier Upper Palaeolithic material, consisting of at least one unifacial leaf-point and other artifacts subsequently lost or destroyed, was stratified below Later artifacts. Among the animal remains were horse, hyena, giant Irish deer, cave bear, mammoth and woolly rhinoceros (Garrod, 1926; Campbell, 1977). A rare western open site is that at Forty Acres gravel pit, Barnwood, Gloucestershire, where backed tools, scrapers, a possible tanged point and a broken ivory point were recovered (Clifford *et al.*, 1954).

Two further areas of concentration of Upper Palaeolithic material (concentrations mainly due to the higher incidence of survival in these cave-sites and to archaeological interest and activity) are in Glamorgan (particularly the Gower region) and Pembrokeshire. The cave of Long Hole,

Figure 4.2: Earlier Upper Palaeolithic artifacts from England and Wales. Unifacial leaf-points: 1, 2, Kent's Cavern, Torquay; 3, Badger Hole, Wookey Hole, Somerset; 4, bifacial leaf-point, Soldier's Hole, Somerset; 5, '*burin busqué*', Ffynnon Beuno, Flintshire; 6, 'tanged point', Bramford Road, Ipswich; 7, bifacial leaf-point, Charsfield, Suffolk; 8, awl or point of ivory, Soldier's Hole, Somerset; 9, engraved bone, Robin Hood's Cave, Creswell Crags, Derbyshire; 10, bevel-based ivory point, Pin Hole Cave, Creswell Crags. After Garrod, 1926; Campbell, 1970, 1977; Moir, 1922, 1932.

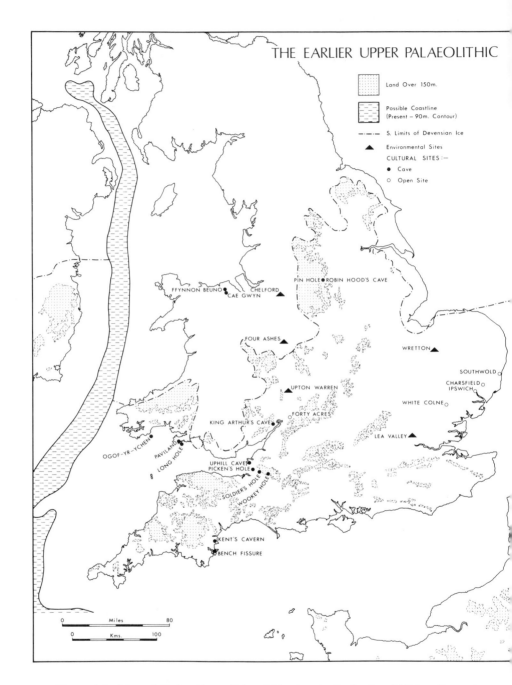

THE EARLIER UPPER PALAEOLITHIC

Land Over 150m.

Possible Coastline
(Present – 90m. Contour)

—·—·— S. Limits of Devensian Ice

▲ Environmental Sites

CULTURAL SITES:—

● Cave

○ Open Site

FFYNNON BEUNO● CHELFORD
CAE GWYN▲

PIN HOLE●ROBIN HOOD'S CAVE

FOUR ASHES▲

WRETTON▲

SOUTHWOLD○
CHARSFIELD○
IPSWICH○

●UPTON WARREN

WHITE COLNE○

KING ARTHUR'S CAVE●●FORTY ACRES

LEA VALLEY▲

OGOF-YR-YCHEN●
PAVILAND●
LONG HOLE●

UPHILL CAVE●
PICKEN'S HOLE●
SOLDIER'S HOLE●
WOOKEY HOLE●

●KENT'S CAVERN
●BENCH FISSURE

Miles 0 — 80

Kms. 0 — 100

Figure 4.3: Map of Earlier Upper Palaeolithic sites in England and Wales, Devensian glaciation limits and possible sea-level.

Glamorganshire, had waste flakes, a burin, a scraper, saws and a leaf-point fragment. There were also remains of fox, horse, reindeer, marten, otter, wolf, woolly rhinoceros and mammoth (Garrod, 1926; Campbell, 1977). Nearby is the site of Goat's Hole Cave, Paviland, which, though lacking any true stratification, is one of the richest caves and a main centre of intense Earlier Upper Palaeolithic activity in Britain. Of the stone tools, scrapers were in the majority (56 per cent), followed by burins (24 per cent), saws/notches (7 per cent), borers/awls (4 per cent), retouched flakes/blades (4 per cent), combined tools (3 per cent) and 11 leaf-points − 10 unifacial, 1 bifacial (2 per cent) (Campbell, 1977). An unstratified fauna included horse, cave bear, aurochs, woolly rhinoceros and reindeer. There was also a wide range of artifacts in bone and ivory, including spatulae, bracelets and pendants (Buckland, 1823; Sollas, 1913; Garrod, 1926). Associated with these was a headless human burial, stained with red ochre, as were some of the bone and ivory artifacts. This was the 'Red Lady of Paviland', wrongly supposed by Buckland (1823) to be female and of the period of Roman occupation, since he could not believe in the contemporaneity of a modern human type and the extinct animals. The skeleton was in fact that of a male, and collagen samples from the long bones have given a radiocarbon dating of 18,460 bp (BM-374) (Oakley, 1968). This is close to the time of maximum glaciation and Bowen (1970, 1972), assuming the correctness of the date, has pointed out that glacier-ice would have been only a few kilometres to the north, although the Gower Peninsula was never completely overrun by ice during the last glaciation. The environment would, however, have been periglacial, with permafrost and only tundra vegetation, and no immediate ameliorating influence from the sea, which was possibly 100 kilometres to the west and as much as 130 metres below present sea level. Approach could only have been from the south, across the lowlands of the present Bristol Channel (Figure 4.3). Campbell (1977) considers the Paviland date to be 'too young', assuming that the burial and stone industry − some of which also had red ochre staining − were contemporary and earlier than maximum glaciation. Another suggestion − and a further argument for the absence of man at the time of most severe climate − is that the date is perhaps too early; that the industry and fauna were contemporary and perhaps pre-date the coldest phase, while the skeleton was buried at a much later period (Molleson, 1976). A further radiocarbon date of 27,600 bp (BM-1367) on humerus of *Bos primigenius* (aurochs) lends support to the idea of Earlier Upper Palaeolithic occupation, with perhaps much later use of the cave purely as a burial site (Molleson and Burleigh, 1978). Despite the uncertainty of dating, Paviland was undoubtedly occupied in Earlier Upper Palaeolithic times and may have been a central base for hunting-groups using other caves in the region. At Ogof-yr-Ychen, Caldey Island, Pembrokeshire, a cold-climate level with a fauna including woolly rhinoceros has been dated to 22,350 radiocarbon years bp (Birm-340) (Nedervelde *et al.*, 1973).

There is a little evidence for Upper Palaeolithic activity in north Wales. At Cae Gwyn Cave, Tremeirchion, Flintshire, Earlier Upper Palaeolithic material has been recovered (Garrod, 1926; Campbell, 1977). The cave was sealed by glacial deposits, probably at the time of maximum glaciation. Mammoth bone from a collection made in the nineteenth century has been dated to 18,000 radiocarbon years bp (Rowlands, 1971). Both faunal remains and artifacts came from beneath glacial till, but there is no direct association and stratigraphy is uncertain, so that the date can only be accepted as a possible upper limit for occupation before the deposition of the glacial till. Nearby, at the cave of Ffynnon Beuno, Flintshire, artifacts were associated with a fauna including hyena, giant Irish deer, reindeer, horse and woolly rhinoceros. Among the artifacts were burins, scrapers and a unifacial leaf-point; one of the burins (Figure 4.2/5) is a type (*burin busqué*) associated with the French Aurignacian culture, and particularly the phase dating to 32,000–29,000 radiocarbon years bp. This should perhaps be seen as an element of western European influence, but insufficient to proclaim a true 'Aurignacian culture' in Britain.

The caves in the Permian limestone of Creswell Crags, Derbyshire, were used earlier by groups with a Middle Palaeolithic culture, but there are only two main sites of Earlier Upper Palaeolithic occupation. Pin Hole has an industry consisting of scrapers, backed implements, awls and a unifacial leaf-point. There are also bone and ivory tools, including a bevel-based ivory point with engraved decoration (Figure 4.2/10) (Garrod, 1926; Armstrong, 1931; Kitching, 1963; Jackson, 1967; Campbell, 1977). At Robin Hood's Cave, there were bone implements and a stone industry with saws/notches, scrapers, combined tools, unifacial and bifacial leaf-points (Garrod, 1926; Campbell, 1969, 1977). One of the bone artifacts is a piece of the rib of a herbivorous animal, on which is engraved a horse's head, possibly *Equus przewalskii* (Figure 4.2/9). Among the animal remains were reindeer, fox, horse and woolly rhinoceros. A radiocarbon date of 28,500 bp (BM-602), from bone of brown bear, was obtained from an upper layer containing later artifacts, but it may have arrived there by nineteenth-century excavation disturbance since it seems more applicable to the Earlier Upper Palaeolithic level (Campbell, 1977, pp. 66–7).

In East Anglia, Upper Palaeolithic evidence has been recovered entirely from open sites with little or no stratification. Among the more certain sites is that of the gravel pit at Bramford Road, Ipswich, Suffolk (Moir, 1932a, 1938), where the assemblage included a 'tanged point' (Figure 4.2/6), scrapers, unifacial and bifacial leaf-points. A fauna with reindeer, mammoth, horse and woolly rhinoceros was recovered from the site, but it cannot be associated directly with the artifacts. Other sites with leaf-points include White Colne, Essex (Layard, 1932), where a point was found above remains of horse, mammoth and ibex (*Capra ibex*), Southwold and Charsfield, Suffolk (Figure 4.2/7) (Moir, 1922), and at Constantine Road, Ipswich (Moir, 1923), where three bifacial leaf-points were found under 5.5 metres of Flood Plain Gravels.

The total quantity of material from this period is very small when compared with a time-range of possibly 20,000 years (Figure 4.1). Campbell (1977, p. 141) gives the total number of existing Earlier Upper Palaeolithic artifacts as 5,860, but as much as 80 per cent of this is waste material from stone-working. The number of known Earlier sites is 37 – only 29 per cent of all Upper Palaeolithic sites. The phases of extreme climatic conditions probably restricted human activity, particularly in the more northerly sites, and winter migration out of Britain may have been necessary over long periods. A fluctuating population of only 100–500 has been suggested (Campbell, 1977), and, during maximum glaciation, for a period of perhaps 4,000 years, there may have been a complete absence of human occupation. The main 'type fossil' of the period is the leaf-point, which seems in general to have been a missile-head but may in some cases have been used as a knife. The most important food animals were horse, reindeer, woolly rhinoceros, mammoth, giant deer, red deer, brown bear and bison, and there is evidence from some sites, particularly Soldier's Hole, Somerset, of bird-hunting. The hunters operated in a tundra or steppe-tundra environment with only dwarf tree-forms and within an effective northern limit of about 53° 30′ latitude. The main finds have been from cave sites, located mostly in lowland/highland transition zones, whereas the open-air sites are mainly in the south-east (Figure 4.3). Much of this distributional evidence is purely the result of chance finds or archaeological activity, but the emphasis on open sites in the south and south-east, apart from the differing landscape, can probably be related to climate and distance from glacial conditions; perhaps the bulk of the evidence for open-site occupation lies beneath the waters of the present Bristol Channel, English Channel and southern North Sea. It has been possible, for a few areas, to indicate probable 'base camps' (for example Kent's Cavern; Paviland) and, within a 10 kilometres/2 hours walking radius, possible subsidiary 'transit camps' (Campbell, 1977), but evidence is insufficient for anything more than the most tentative framework of man/land relationships. Some attention was given to self-ornamentation and decoration of implements (for example Paviland and Robin Hood's Cave), but there is little to compare with the range of artwork from contemporary western European sites. In a study of Upper Palaeolithic human remains from Europe and Asia, Vallois (1961) noted that of more than 70 individuals, fewer than 50 per cent were over 21 years of age and only 12 per cent had attained the age of 40 years, while few females had reached 30. The life expectation could not have been any higher among the hunters in the extreme conditions of Earlier Upper Palaeolithic Britain.

The Later Upper Palaeolithic Period

The Late Last Glacial or Late Devensian (Chronozone ID) has been suggested as beginning about 25,000 years ago and including the maximum ice-advance (Mitchell *et al.*, 1973). Alternatively, a Late Weichselian subdivision commencing about 13,000 radiocarbon years ago, after maximum glaciation, has been proposed (Mangerud *et al.*, 1974), and this may be more in keeping with British evidence (Pennington, 1975) (Figure 4.4).

The Late-glacial sequence (Pollen Zones I-III) is typified at many sites in Britain by two, mainly mineral, layers above and below a level with organic silts, muds or peats representing the more temperate or interstadial Zone II and equating with the continental Allerød oscillation. Lithostratigraphical (for example glacial deposits or sediments) and biostratigraphical (for example flora or fauna) changes do not always coincide, so that this tripartite division may be over-simplified (Moore, 1974). Coope (1975) has shown that discrepancies exist between vegetational evidence and beetle fauna from contemporary sites; as mentioned above, this may be due to a more immediate reaction by Coleoptera to changing climatic conditions.

The vegetational environment of the colder phases, for example park-tundra,

Figure 4.4: Late-glacial and Later Upper Palaeolithic environmental and cultural chronology. The environmental sequence is continued into Post-glacial times in Figure 5.4.

C14 YEARS bp	CHRONO-ZONES	POLLEN ZONES	VEGETATION	CLIMATE	ICE MOVEMENT	ENVIRON-MENTAL SITES	CULTURAL CHRONOLOGY		C14 YEARS bp
	EARLY FLANDRIAN (Fl. 1)	V (BOREAL)	Hazel – birch – pine	Becoming warmer	POST-GLACIAL		GOUGH'S CAVE AVELINE'S HOLE	MESOLITHIC	
10,000	PRE-TEMPERATE	IV (PRE-BOREAL)	Birch–pine rising AP (arboreal pollen)	Sub – arctic improving		ST. BEES	ANSTON STONES SPROUGHTON MESSINGHAM FLIXTON ROBIN HOOD'S CAVE	PALAEOLITHIC	10,000
11,000	LATE DEVENSIAN (l.De.)	III (YOUNGER DRYAS)	Tundra	Sub – arctic	LOCH LOMOND RE-ADVANCE (CORRIE GLACIATION)	NEASHAM GRIMSTON HALL			11,000
		II (ALLERØD)	Birch, poplar, Tundra	Temporarily milder	ICE – FREE?	NEASHAM	SPROUGHTON POULTON-LE-FYLDE		
12,000	LATE GLACIAL	I (OLDER DRYAS)	Tundra with arctic willow and dwarf birch. High N.A.P. (non arboreal pollen)	Sub – arctic	'PERTH' RETREAT STAGE	TADCASTER	KENT'S CAVERN SUN HOLE	UPPER	12,000
13,000									13,000
14,000					FULL GLACIAL	COLNEY HEATH BLELHAM BOG	KENT'S CAVERN	LATER	14,000
15,000					MAXIMUM GLACIATION				15,000
16,000									16,000

consisted of open communities of herbaceous plants, grasses, sedges and only dwarf tree forms such as dwarf birch (*Betula nana*) and arctic willow (*Salix herbacea*). The mountain avens (*Dryas octopetala*), a plant widespread in Britain at this time, has provided the names for Zones I (Older Dryas) and III (Younger Dryas).

After the extreme-cold conditions of the glacial maximum, and with climatic improvement in regions near the centre of the ice masses, there was a decrease in the expansion of the ice fronts. Summer melting surpassed winter accumulation and recession of the ice fronts took place. The resulting ice retreat was neither steady nor continuous. There were long periods when the ice fronts were motionless and, because of fluctuations in climate, times of actual re-advance. The recession of ice in the British Isles is marked by traces of the ridges of end moraines (Chapter 1 above) which show the still-stand positions of the retreating ice fronts (Figure 4.6).

For a period following maximum glaciation, the cold conditions continued, as indicated by the periglacial character of the plant assemblage from Colney Heath, Hertfordshire, dated to 13,560 bp (Q-385) (Pearson, 1962; Godwin, 1964). There is not a great deal of evidence for the short-term milder period during Zone I, the continental Bølling oscillation, at least in western Britain (Pennington and Bonny, 1970; Moore, 1974), although a relative increase in birch pollen noted in Yorkshire (Bartley, 1962) might be suggestive of a comparable mild phase in the north-east.

Whether or not man was completely absent from Britain in full-glacial times, there is evidence for renewed human activity in the fifteenth millennium bp. One of the most important sites is again Kent's Cavern, Torquay, Devon (Campbell and Sampson, 1971), where layers of superimposed hearths indicate intermittent use of the cave in Later Upper Palaeolithic times. The industries typical of this phase have a dominant backed blade element and have been classified, after the Derbyshire and Somerset sites, as Creswellian/Cheddarian (Bohmers, 1956). 'Creswellian points' have a single-angled blunted back, and 'Cheddar points' have a double-angled back producing a trapeze-like shape. They may have functioned as both knives and points (Schwabedissen, 1954; Bohmers, 1956). In the 'Black Band' hearth area of the Vestibule at Kent's Cavern, Creswell and Cheddar points, other backed implements, burins and scrapers, plus a uniserially-barbed point of antler (Figure 4.5/1,2,16), were associated with bone of brown bear, collagen from which has been dated to 14,275 bp (GrN-6203). The dominant artifacts were the backed implements (30 per cent of total tools) followed by retouched flakes and blades (18 per cent), and equal quantities of scrapers (16 per cent), burins (16 per cent), saws and notched tools (16 per cent) (Campbell, 1977). At a later level in the Vestibule, bone collagen from giant Irish deer, associated with a biserial antler point, has been dated to 12,180 bp (GrN-6204).

The Mendip region has several sites with quantities of Later Upper Palaeolithic material. At Aveline's Hole the industry consisted mainly of backed tools plus a double-barbed point (Figure 4.5/15), classified as Magdalenian VIb (McBurney, 1965), and *Neritoides* shells (Campbell, 1970; Oakley *et al.*, 1971; Campbell, 1977). Collagen from human bone from the occupation level gave a date of 9114 bp (BM-471) and Campbell (1977) has suggested, on the evidence of the assemblage plus the late date, that this

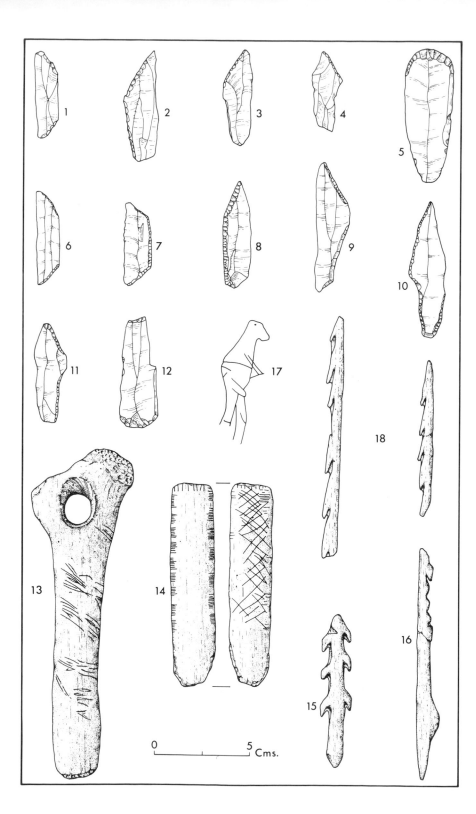

0   5 Cms.

occupation may represent a transitional Later Upper Palaeolithic/Mesolithic phase. Gough's Cave is the most prolific Later Upper Palaeolithic site in Britain (Campbell, 1970; Oakley *et al.*, 1971; Campbell, 1977). Of 799 stone tools, 34 per cent are backed implements (including 87 'Creswell points' and 15 'Cheddar points'), 24 per cent retouched flakes and blades, 14 per cent burins, 10 per cent scrapers, 7 per cent multiple tools, 5 per cent borers or awls, 3.5 per cent saws or notched tools and 2.5 per cent 'Zinken'. Among the backed tools were a number of shouldered points (Figure 4.5/3,4) which have been compared (Campbell, 1977) with those of the Hamburgian culture (Rust, 1962) of north Germany, dating to Zone I. There was a wide range of bone artifacts, including an awl, incised bone segments and '*bâtons-de-commandement*' (Figure 4.5/13). Decoration on Upper Palaeolithic bone and antler artifacts has been analysed (Marshack, 1972a,b,c) and suggested in many cases as notational and perhaps even calendrical. The piece of decorated rib bone from Gough's Cave (Figure 4.5/14) has been studied (Hawkes *et al.*, 1970) and variously suggested as a gauge for spacing barbs on harpoons, etc., a netting guide, a hunter's tally markings, a gaming piece or a system of recording genealogical information; reconsideration of yet another notched piece (Tratman, 1976) has indicated a possible complex numeration system. Human remains ('Cheddar Man') have also been recovered from Gough's Cave, under the same stalagmitic layer which covered the Later Upper Palaeolithic deposits. Collagen from a tibia has yielded a date of 9080 bp (BM-525), but there is no association with the artifacts, which may be much earlier (Tratman, 1975). The assemblage from Sun Hole is small, with mainly backed tools (Figure 4.7), but bone of brown bear from the same level as the artifacts has been radiocarbon dated to 12,378 bp (BM-524) (Tratman, 1955; Campbell, 1970).

King Arthur's Cave, Herefordshire, was also occupied in Later Upper Palaeolithic times; the assemblage had mainly backed tools and a few bone implements (awl, needle and point) (Garrod, 1926; Taylor, 1928). In south Wales, some sites with Earlier Upper Palaeolithic material, such as Paviland, also have evidence of later occupation. At Cat's Hole (Cat Hole, Cathole), Gower, Glamorgan (Garrod, 1926; McBurney, 1959), a possible inland exploitation site, the Later Upper Palaeolithic assemblage had backed tools, burins, scrapers and awls, with a bone awl and needle. A fauna included reindeer, red deer, brown bear, fox, vole and lemming. Occupation is also indicated at various sites on Caldey Island, Pembrokeshire, particularly at

Figure 4.5: Later Upper Palaeolithic artifacts from England and Wales. 1, Cheddar point; 2, Creswellian point, Kent's Cavern, Torquay; 3, 4, shouldered points; 5, end scraper; 6, Cheddar point, Gough's Cave, Somerset; 7, Cheddar point, Sun Hole, Somerset; 8, Creswellian point, Anston Stones, Yorkshire; 9, shouldered point, Oare, Kent; 10, 11, shouldered points; 12, composite burin/end-scraper, Hengistbury Head, Hampshire; 13, antler '*bâton-de-commandement*', which may have served as a shaft-straightener; 14, decorated rib bone, Gough's Cave; 15, biserially-barbed point, Aveline's Hole, Somerset; 16, uniserially-barbed antler point, Kent's Cavern; 17, figure from decorated rib bone, Pin Hole Cave; 18, uniserially-barbed points, Poulton-le-Fylde, Lancashire. After Garrod, 1926; Campbell, 1977; Mellars, 1969; Clark, 1938; Mace, 1959; Armstrong, 1928; Hallam *et al.*, 1973.

Nana's Cave (Lacaille and Grimes, 1955; Ap Simon, 1976). Perhaps the most important site in south Wales, which may also have been a base-camp, is Hoyle's Mouth Cave, Pembrokeshire (Garrod, 1926; Savory, 1973; Campbell, 1977), where the large assemblage of stone tools had 42 per cent backed implements, 15 per cent burins, 15 per cent scrapers, 13 per cent saws and notched tools, 10 per cent retouched flakes and blades, and 5 per cent borers and awls.

As in Earlier Upper Palaeolithic times, there was a concentration of later sites in the Creswell Crags region of Derbyshire. At Robin Hood's Cave, Campbell (1969, 1977) claims to have recognised different phases from Later Upper Palaeolithic to 'transitional Mesolithic', with varying quantities of 'Creswell points', shouldered points and 'penknife points'. Among the animal remains were horse, lemming, reindeer, voles, hare, red deer and hyena. Bones of horse from Later Upper Palaeolithic and Later Upper Palaeolithic/transitional Mesolithic layers have been dated to 10,590 bp (BM-604) and 10,390 bp (BM-603) (Campbell, 1969, 1977). Mother Grundy's Parlour had a large assemblage, with 40 per cent backed tools, 24 per cent awls, 16 per cent scrapers, 7 per cent burins, 7 per cent retouched flakes and blades, and 6 per cent saws and notched implements. Faunal remains included horse, bison and giant Irish deer (Garrod, 1926; Campbell, 1969, 1977). Four radiocarbon dates (Q-551, 552, 553, 554) range between 8,800 and 6,705 bp; this seems too young if the associated artifacts were undoubtedly Creswellian. From Pin Hole Cave (Armstrong, 1928), a decorated rib segment shows the only representation of a (?) human figure known in the British Palaeolithic (Figure 4.5/17), and at Church Hole, Nottinghamshire, a good example of an eyed needle of bone was recovered (Garrod, 1926). A hint of possible ritual practices is provided by the burial of a brown bear skull under a limestone slab at Fox Hole Cave, Derbyshire (Bramwell, 1971); the possibly deliberate burial of the thorax of a young reindeer under limestone slabs at Elder Bush Cave, Staffordshire (Bramwell, 1964) is reminiscent of the reindeer sacrifices of the Hamburgian and Ahrensburgian cultures of north Germany, respectively contemporary with pollen Zones I and III (Rust, 1937, 1943).

At Anston Stones (Dead Man's Cave), south Yorkshire, a small assemblage of mainly 'Creswell points' (Figure 4.5/8) and other backed implements was associated with reindeer bone and a fragment of antler, not directly associated, which have yielded C14 dates of 9940 (BM-440a), 9850 (BM-439) and 9750 bp (BM-440b) (Mellars, 1969). The dates show an unusually late survival for reindeer and Campbell (1977, p. 104) suggests that they may be about 1,000 radiocarbon years too young. At Langwith Cave, Derbyshire, Later Upper Palaeolithic tools were associated with human remains and hearths (Garrod, 1926). A large faunal assemblage included arctic forms, but was not definitely attributable to the cultural layer.

Details of continuity in the last stages of ice-front withdrawal are still imperfectly known. The 'Perth Re-advance', during Zone I, was formerly believed to be a major resurgence of ice after deglaciation (Sissons, 1963, 1964a, 1967a, 1967b), but the evidence of ice-front deposits is now generally interpreted as representing a still-stand position of ice retreat with perhaps minor local re-advances (Jardine, 1968; Francis *et al.*, 1970; Jardine and Peacock, 1973; Paterson, 1974; Sissons, 1974, 1976; Price, 1975; Gray and Lowe, 1977). The Loch Lomond Re-advance, broadly equivalent to pollen

Zone III, is well marked (Sissons *et al.*, 1973) and represents a resurgence of Scottish ice before final deglaciation (Figure 4.6). It is probable that cold-adapted fauna such as mammoth and woolly rhinoceros became extinct in the temporary mild period (Zone II/Allerød) immediately preceding the Loch Lomond Re-advance (Sissons, 1964a).

The process of melting left the north of England free of ice by about 13,000 years ago, apart from local corrie glaciation (for example in the Lake District and north Wales during Zone III). In the cool-temperate Zone II, birch, pine, juniper and poplar woods spread into park-tundra regions. Zone II deposits containing faunal remains (elk) have been dated at Neasham, Co. Durham, where peat and organic silts gave radiocarbon dates of 11,561 (Q-208), 11,011 (Q-207) and 10,851 bp (C-444) (Blackburn, 1952), and plant debris from similar deposits at Grimston Hall, Yorkshire, have been dated to 11,260 bp (Birm-345). At High Furlong, Poulton-le-Fylde, Lancashire, elk (*Alces alces*) remains and barbed points of apparent proto-Maglemosian (or 'proto-Star Carr') type (Figure 4.5/18) have been recovered from Zone II coarse detrital muds dated to 12,200 (St-3832) and 11,665 bp (St-3836) (Barnes *et al.*, 1971; Hallam *et al.*, 1973). The elk had been wounded several times, possibly by flint-tipped missiles or stone axes, and the condition of its antlers suggested that it had been hunted in winter. It was probably drowned while attempting to escape its hunters, in a partially ice-covered lake, one of many in the rather watery environment left by the retreating ice. In terms of winter activities, the same hunting-group may have exploited the open territories made available by a lower relative sea level in the present Morecambe Bay–Liverpool Bay region and, if the 10-kilometre radius/2 hours walking distance 'site catchment area' is applied, their base camp could have been in that area now covered by the Irish Sea (Clark, 1972). There is some further, indirect, evidence of hunting at Flixton, Yorkshire (Moore, 1954), where a 'shouldered point' and an unretouched blade were associated with the remains of at least three horses. Pollen analysis indicated Zone II and organic mud overlying the artifacts and bones has been dated to 10,413 bp (Q-66).*

Zone III saw a return to a mainly treeless landscape with dominant herb, sedge and grass pollen, and solifluction sediments due to alternate freezing and thawing. Wood from a Zone III context at St Bees, Cumberland, has given dates of 10,500 and 10,340 (Q-304) (Walker, 1956; Godwin, 1960), and similar deposits at Scaleby Moss, Cumberland (see Chapter 5, Figure 5.3b) have been dated to 10,828 and 10,316 bp (Q-144, Q-153) (Godwin *et al.*, 1957). An open site at Messingham, Lincolnshire, has evidence of Later Upper Palaeolithic activity in the form of a flint end-scraper associated with bone of possible giant Irish deer in a peat layer under Cover Sand. The peat layer has been dated to 10,250 bp (Birm-349) (Buckland, 1976).

The locations in the south-east and south of England are, as in the Earlier Upper Palaeolithic, open sites, and in some there is a mixing of Upper Palaeolithic and Mesolithic material. This may be the case at Cranwich,

*At Kildale Hall, north Yorkshire, a disarticulated aurochs (*Bos primigenius*) skeleton was found embedded in peaty deposits and associated with a layer of charcoal (birch and shrubs) subsequently dated to 10,350 bp (Gak-2707) (Jones, 1976). This has also been suggested as evidence of early Mesolithic activity (Spratt and Simmons, 1976).

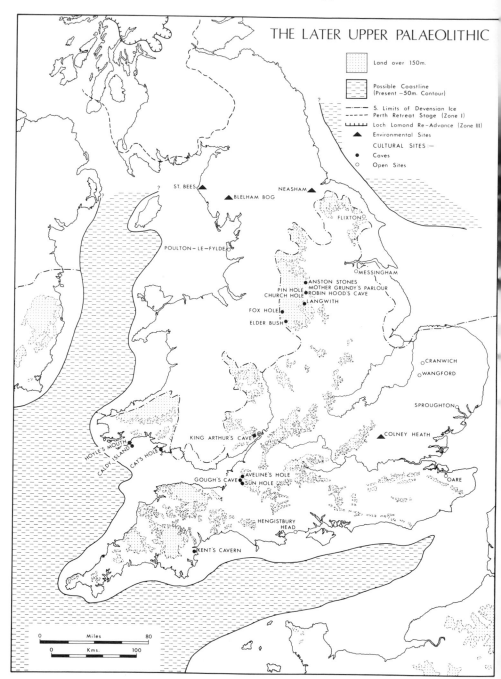

Figure 4.6: Map of Later Upper Palaeolithic sites in England and Wales, retreat stages of Devensian glaciation and possible sea-level.

Norfolk, although Wymer (1971) has identified a few implements as possibly indicating a Zone II/III occupation. At Sproughton, Suffolk (Wymer *et al.*, 1975), two barbed points were recovered from sand and gravel deposits showing the response of fluvial processes to high snow-melt discharge. The older point, which was made of bone, was located above layers from which twigs and leaves gave radiocarbon dates of 11,940 (HAR-260), 11,640 (HAR-261) and 11,370 bp (HAR-262), and under a layer dated to 9880 bp (HAR-259), so that a Zone II–III dating seems likely. The younger point, of antler, was above the latest dated layer and could be of Zone IV–V date, possibly contemporary with the Star Carr points (see Chapter 6 below). The site at Wangford, Suffolk (Garrod, 1926; Clark, 1932) has yielded mainly Mesolithic material, but a few backed implements and 'shouldered points' may date to the Later Upper Palaeolithic.

In searching for British equivalents to the Late-glacial reindeer hunters' summer camps on the Continent, Clark (1938) indicated a few flints of the shouldered point type from the vicinity of Oare, in Kent, as possible evidence for this phase (Figure 4.5/9). A rich site in the south of England is that at Hengistbury Head, near Bournemouth, Hampshire (Mace, 1959; Campbell, 1977), an important location for the exploitation of the English Channel plain. Pollen analysis (Campbell, 1977, Figure 79) might indicate a dating near the Zone I–II transition. The industry comprised 'Creswell points', shouldered points and tanged points, as well as scrapers, awls, burins and multiple tools (Figure 4.5/10–12), and there are similarities to contemporary Continental industries of the Hamburgian and Federmesser (Rissen, Wehlen, Tjonger) groups. Campbell (1977) has noted an oval arrangement of heavier stones (particularly large cores) on the site, surrounding the greatest concentration of flint-working debris, and has suggested possible 'edge-weights' for a skin tent, such as those of Zone I-dated Hamburgian sites in north Germany at Poggenwisch and Borneck (Rust, 1962). The loss of much evidence for Upper Palaeolithic habitations and economy in the regions now covered by the North Seas and English Channel has been noted (for example Schwabedissen, 1962) and the scarcity of open sites in the south and south-east of England may be due to these areas having been peripheral to a much greater concentration in the drowned territories.

The amount of evidence for human activity in Britain during Later Upper Palaeolithic times far outweighs that from the earlier period. The total known sites constitute 71 per cent of all known Upper Palaeolithic locations, and the total possible human remains from Later sites amounts to 105 (a large proportion, though most subsequently lost, deriving from one site – Aveline's Hole (Oakley *et al.*, 1971)) as against 7 from Earlier sites. A tentative population range of 500 to 5,000 (Campbell, 1977, p. 160) has been suggested on the basis of this evidence. Improving climatic conditions allowed expansion northwards, as can be seen in the distribution of sites (Figure 4.6). This distribution shows two main groupings: south-west England/south Wales, and north Wales/Midlands/northern England. Taking into account the possibility of lost sites and hitherto undiscovered sites, plus the emphasis given by relatively intensive archaeological activity in certain areas, if the groupings are realistic then one explanation that might be offered is that the northern sites may have been summer hunting locations while the southerly group could represent winter bases (Campbell, 1977, p. 159).

The main animal food sources appear to have been horse and reindeer, hunted with weapons involving the use of 'Creswell/Cheddar points', shouldered points or tanged points. Environmental conditions in the early phases must have been similar to those of the millennia before maximum glaciation, but with gradual improvement to much milder climate, particularly in the Zone II (Allerød) Interstadial, when an expansion of human activity and population must have been possible. In general, however, the tundra landscape prevailed, particularly in the more northerly areas, until the end of the Late-glacial period.

Little is known of habitations away from the cave sites, apart from hints of a possible tent-like structure at Hengistbury Head, but evidence of open-site dwellings in contemporary Hamburgian, Federmesser and Ahrensburgian groups on the eastern periphery of the North Sea plain may be an indication of what is missing from the British archaeological record. Further comparative evidence may be sought in the late Magdalenian hunters' encampment at Pincevent, Seine-et-Marne, France, where excavation uncovered a tripartite 'hut-tent' with three hearths, sleeping areas (relatively free of flint-working debris) and evidence of cooking. This may have been some form of communal dwelling for 10–15 people on a site probably occupied intermittently over a considerable period of time – six radiocarbon dates ranged from 12,300 to 9840 bp (Leroi-Gourhan and Brézillon, 1972).

Despite the mingling of Upper Palaeolithic and Mesolithic material at some sites, the cultural continuity between the two periods in Britain is not easy to prove, and there are many areas of Mesolithic activity where material culture of the Late-glacial period is completely lacking (Chapter 6 below). However, there seems little doubt as to the degree of chronological overlap between the stages at sites such as Anston Stones, Gough's Cave and Aveline's Hole, and it is perhaps from similar 'epi-Palaeolithic' sites as yet undiscovered that evidence for continuity will be recovered.

Chapter 5

POST-GLACIAL ENVIRONMENTAL CHANGES

The labelling of the Recent or Holocene period as 'Post-glacial' might be taken to suggest that the sequence of glacial/interglacial episodes of the last few hundred thousand years has now ended. This would be wrong, even if we knew more about the mechanisms causing glaciation and deglaciation, since there is nothing 'new' in the evidence for the environmental changes of the past ten thousand years, apart from the far greater role of man in changing the landscape. Interglacials may have varied widely in length, and there may have been many more in the past than present evidence would indicate, but by the criteria mentioned in Chapter 1 (page 22 above) there is no reason to believe that we are not in another interglacial, and perhaps in a quite advanced, 'Late-temperate' stage of that interglacial! To be strictly accurate, if the term 'Post-glacial' is to be used, it should be qualified as 'Post-last-glacial'.

A major agent in shaping the landscape during deglaciation was the water released by the melting ice. Melt-water streams from the retreating ice front carried fluvio-glacial material – stones, gravels, sands, clays – which was left to form ridges, mounds and hummocks, or, in blocking the flow of the melt-water itself, new lakes. Much of this material was deposited in layers in lakes. In any one year the coarser material from the summer melting settled first, forming a relatively thick layer upon which were superimposed the finer deposits carried in suspension and settling only in the winter months, usually when the surface of the lake was frozen over. These annual pairs of laminae – thick plus thin or light plus dark – were named *varves* by de Geer (1912). A chronology of ice retreat in Scandinavia was constructed, based on varve-counts, correlation of similar layer-groupings and cross-checking of exposures. It was possible to show, by the occurrence of a particularly large varve, that the Scandinavian ice-sheet had split into two much smaller ice-caps in the vicinity of Ragunda, central Sweden, about 6800 bc, a date accepted as the end of the ice age in that region (de Geer, 1912, 1940; Zeuner, 1958, pp. 20–45). It has not yet been possible to construct such a chronology for the British Isles, due to the scarcity of sufficiently good exposures of well developed varves.

Land- and Sea-level Changes

The vast quantity of water released by deglaciation caused a major eustatic rise in sea-level. After the maximum of the Devensian glaciation, sea-level rose rapidly in relation to the land until about 9000 bc. Thereafter, isostatic uplift of the land masses, freed from the weight of ice, approximately kept pace with the eustatic rise of the oceans until the later seventh millennium bc, when the some-what faster-rising sea-level, towards the culmination of this main Holocene marine transgression, formed shorelines which in some areas are now up to 10 metres above Ordnance Datum (OD), due to continued isostatic recovery in those regions (Figure 5.1).

The late Devensian and early Post-glacial rise in sea-level was global in scale (Godwin *et al.*, 1958; Fairbridge, 1961), but surviving evidence shows that its effects varied widely according to local conditions of glaciation, isostasy and geomorphological features (Figure 5.1). The 'raised beaches' of this period occur mainly in northern Britain, the area of major isostatic uplift. The highest transgression level of the Late-glacial sea was probably reached before about 12,000 bp (Donner, 1959, 1970; Bishop and Dickson, 1970; Peacock, 1971). The greatest incursions were in central Scotland, particularly in the areas of the present firths and lower valleys of the rivers Clyde, Forth and Tay (Figure 5.1). These regions are near the centre of maximal land-depression during the last glaciation and evidence of sea-level movements is complicated by the degree of subsequent isostatic uplift. The shoreline of this late Devensian sea was named the '100-foot raised beach' in *Memoirs* of the Geological Survey published early in the twentieth century, but this height is not uniform throughout the area where remnants of the shoreline occur. Donner (1959, 1963) suggested an inferential centre of isostatic uplift near Callander, Perthshire, from which the height of the shoreline terrace decreases in all directions. A height of about 155 feet (49 m) above OD was recorded near Doune, in Perthshire (Dinham, 1927), and Sissons (1964a) noted height variations from 73.5 feet (22.4 m) to over 120 feet (36.6 m) in the Glasgow and Stirling areas. The effects of the high sea were counteracted in many areas by the continued presence of Late-glacial ice and perhaps also by glacially produced land forms. The term '100-foot beach' is obviously a misnomer and Sissons (1962, 1964a) has suggested its abandonment, together with the term '50-foot beach' used for a later shoreline. The terms have, however, been used frequently in archaeological literature and the positions of the shorelines are shown in Figure 5.1a.

By early Post-glacial times, isostatic uplift had enlarged coastal territories in the regions most affected. The North Sea was a greatly diminished body of water at this time and might be represented by a uniform drop in modern sea level of about 36.5 metres (see Figure 6.1). At the same time, peat beds were forming which were subsequently submerged during the main Holocene marine transgression. These and other similar organic deposits have been important in demonstrating the land-recovery of certain regions in the Preboreal and early Boreal periods and, where contact-surfaces between the organic deposits and overlying transgression sediments exist, in dating the commencement of that transgression (Figure 5.2). The difficulties in proving that certain 'land bridges' existed in early Holocene times are considerable, but it seems likely that at least the southern region of what is now the North Sea constituted a land connection, probably swampy and with sporadic lakes and pools, between eastern England and northern France, the Low Countries and Denmark. The recovery, by a trawler, of a barbed spear head from peat ('moorlog') deposits, assigned to the Boreal period, at about 36 metres depth off the Norfolk coast (Godwin, 1933), supports this suggestion.

Evidence of rising sea-level in the mid-seventh millennium bc suggests that the main Holocene eustatic rise and the inundation of the southern North Sea Basin had commenced by this time. Sediments accumulated during this transgression occur in many parts of the British Isles: Carse Clays (in Scotland),

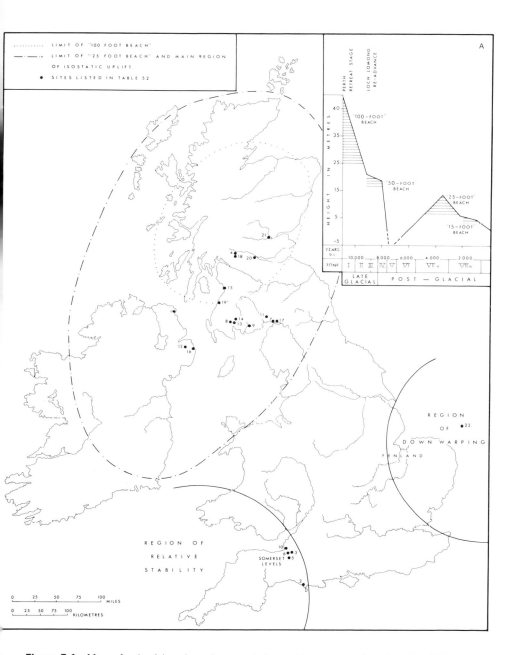

Figure 5.1: Map of raised beach regions and sites with transgression deposits. 5.1a, chronology of transgressions and raised beaches. After Godwin, 1956; Willis, 1961; Donner, 1963, 1970; Sissons, 1976.

C14 YEARS bc		SITE	DATABLE DEPOSIT	LAB NO.	C14 DATE
3000	1	Cushendun, Co. Antrim	Wood from layer on top of grey silts of marine transgression	Q-373	2790 ±110 bc
	2	Chesil Beach, Dorset	Base of peat layer overlying transgression silt	I-3431	3430 ±115 bc
	3	Tealham Moor, Somerset	Phragmites peat at junction with underlying estuarine clay	Q-120	3452 ±130 bc
	4	Flanders Moss, Stirlingshire	Wood peat 10 - 12 cm above upper surface of Carse Clay	Q-533	3542 ±130 bc
	5	Shapwick Heath, Somerset	Phragmites peat just above surface of estuarine clay	Q-423	3550 ±120 bc
	6	Tealham, Somerset	Peat at junction with underlying estuarine clay	Q-126	3610 ±120 bc
	7	Newbie Cottages, Dumfriesshire	Wood from peat layer overlying transgression sediments	Birm-220	3680 ±115 bc
4000	8	Newton Stewart, Wigtownshire	Wood fragments washed into middle strata of marine sediments	Q-339	4209 ±120 bc
	9	Gatehouse of Fleet, Kirkcudbrightshire	Top layer of peat lens overlying marine deposits	Q-818	4294 ±140 bc
	10	Burnham-on-Sea, Somerset	Peat near end of main post-glacial marine transgression	Q-134	4312 ±130 bc
	11	Lochar Moss, Dumfriesshire	Basal peat overlying marine deposits	Q-638	4595 ±120 bc
5000	12	Ringneill Quay, Co. Down	Brackish-water deposit underlying raised beach material	Q-532	5395 ±150 bc 5550 ±150 bc
	13	Palnure Burn, Kirkcudbrightshire	Wood from thin layer within Flandrian estuarine/marine deposits (early stage in marine transgression)	Birm-219	5500 ±200 bc
6000	14	Bargaly, Palnure Burn, Kirkcudbrightshire	Wood at junction of Flandrian marine/esturaine sediments and underlying fluvioglacial gravel	Birm-188	3010 ±350 bc
	15	Troon, Ayrshire	Top 2 cm peat overlain by sands and gravels of Post-glacial emerged beach	IGS-C14/149	3055 ±120 bc
	16	Ballyhalbert, Co. Down	Wood from top of peat bed (Zone VIc) underlying raised beach deposits	Q-214	6170 ±135 bc
	17	Redkirk Point, Dumfriesshire	Wood from peat bed underlying base of Carse Clay deposit	Q-637	6185 ±150 bc
	18	Kippen, Stirlingshire	Top of peat bed underlying Carse Clay	I-1838	6320 ±160 bc
	19	Turnberry, Ayrshire	Wood from upper 5 cm of peat immediately underlying beach sand of Flandrian transgression	Birm-190	6470 ±150 bc
	20	Airth Colliery, Stirlingshire	Peat (early Zone VI) from thin layer between "100 ft raised beach" and overlying Carse Clay	Q-280	6471 ±157 bc
	21	Eastfield of Dunbarney, Perthshire	Peat (Zone VIa) from bed below Carse Clay	Q-421	6471 ±157 bc
	22	Leman and Ower Banks, North Sea	Peat from bed 20 fathoms deep off Norfolk coast	Q-105	6475 ±170 bc

Figure 5.2: Table of sites with radiocarbon-dated transgression deposits as shown in Figure 5.1.

estuarine clay, marine sediments, Buttery Clay (Fenland), 'raised beach deposits', etc., some of which are listed in Table 5.2. No one term can encompass all of these deposits, whether spatially or chronologically. In one region alone, the northern shore of the Solway Firth, Jardine (1967) dist-inguished at least four distinct facies (beach, open-bay, estuarine and lagoonal deposits) associated with the transgression. The rate and extent of the balance between the eustatic rise of sea-level and isostatic land rebound varied greatly, sometimes within quite small areas, due to differences in coastal configuration (for example sand bars, land forms, tidal range, etc.). Using again the Solway Firth as an example, Jardine (1975) inferred, from evidence of deposits at Newton Stewart (no. 8 in Table 5.2), Gatehouse of Fleet (9) and Lochar Moss (11), that the sea had receded from the Lochar Gulf region to the south-east of Dumfries and from part of the estuary of the Water of Fleet, while it was still present in the estuary to the north of Wigtown Bay (Figure 5.2 and Figure 5.1). Radiocarbon dates from Ireland – for example Ballyhalbert (16), Ringneill Quay (12) – also suggest variations in the time of the onset of transgression conditions and perhaps a later transgression maximum, for example at Cushendun (1).

The '25-foot raised beach' associated with the main Holocene transgression is, like the '100-foot' and '50-foot' beaches, inaccurately named, even as an average height of the feature. Provisional isobases for this main Holocene shoreline show heights of more than 13 metres above OD in central Scotland (Sissons and Smith, 1965a; Stephens and Synge, 1966), dropping to less than 6 metres above OD in north-west England and south-east Ireland (Figure 5.1), representing a shoreline formed by the eustatically rising sea and subsequently uplifted differentially to heights ranging between 5.5 and 13.5 metres above OD.

The situation in southern Britain differs considerably from that in the north. In early Holocene times the land seems to have remained relatively stable, so that eustatic sea-level rise was the major factor involved in the formation of shorelines, particularly in the south-west (Churchill, 1965). The East Anglian region, however, apparently was involved in general down-warping of the southern North Sea area, probably encouraging marine transgression in the Fenland (deposition of Fen Clay) soon after 3000 bc (Godwin, 1940b, 1945; Willis, 1961).

This brief coverage of land- and sea-level changes has of necessity been generalised and simplified. The sites and dates discussed above have been selected deliberately to give a broad picture of the major changes in coastal configuration in regions where these changes are outstanding, and it must be emphasised that there is evidence of minor transgressions and regressions included within the major movements mentioned here (for example Stephens, 1968; Binns, 1972; Sissons, 1974; Tooley, 1974).

The effect of changes in coastal configuration on man's activities and on his occupancy of the land is difficult to estimate, particularly for early Holocene times when evidence of, for example, coastal Mesolithic sites may have been destroyed by a transgressing sea. The progressive submergence of the southern North Sea basin, however, undoubtedly had far greater repercussions for Mesolithic cultures than any other Post-glacial environmental change. Between approximately 6500 and 3500 radiocarbon years bc, the configuration and space-relationships of the British mainland altered completely with the loss of the North Sea plain and its enlarged estuaries. There is also a possibility that the submerged region, with its ample wildlife and fishing resources, had previously supported a quite dense seasonal population (by Mesolithic standards) of hunter/fisher communities (Jacobi, 1973). These communities would be displaced subsequently and perhaps forced to re-adapt to new environments and resources, thus greatly affecting cultural continuity and evolution in the later Mesolithic period. The new sea barrier would inhibit continental contact and encourage, to a certain extent, British insular development. Other aspects of Holocene sea-level changes and their effects on cultural development and distribution will be covered regionally (Chapters 6 and 7 below).

Vegetational and Climatic Development

Post-glacial vegetational history is better known than that for any earlier interglacial, but the pattern of development during the last 10,000 years is complex, with many gaps, and certain working assumptions which were necessary in the early days of research are now proving untenable in the light of recent evidence and techniques. A framework for Holocene vegetational succession has been constructed from evidence derived from the study of macroscopic plant remains – seeds, fruits, nut-shells, buds, leaves, bark and wood – preserved and stratified in peats, soils, muds, silts, etc., and from the microscopic study of plant pollen and spores.

Fossil pollen has an extremely high survival rate, due mainly to the toughness of its skin, the exine. The grains have a morphological individuality which makes pollen from different plants relatively easy to recognise under the microscope. Because of this, pollen analysis, pioneered by the Swedish geologist Lennart von Post (1916), has become a basic technique in palaeo-ecological studies. In general terms, a count of the various pollen types included in, for example, a sample from a peat layer should give percentages of the total pollen count which approximate to the proportional quantities and varieties of vegetation occurring in the vicinity when that particular layer of peat was forming. Evidence from samples and counts of pollen from closely spaced layers in a peat-bog, former lake-bed or similar deposit, obtained either by excavation or boring, can be tabulated in the form of a pollen diagram (Figure 5.3a–c) showing the plant succession through time for that locality.

Early work in this field was carried out by Erdtman (1928, 1943) and Jessen (1949), but perhaps the most important programme of research was that of Godwin, beginning in the 1930s, tracing the Post-glacial history of British vegetation (for example Godwin and Clifford, 1938; Godwin, 1940b, 1941, 1948; Godwin and Tallantire, 1951; Godwin, Walker and Willis, 1957), and producing *The History of the British Flora* (Godwin, 1956). Godwin's pollen zonation (1940a, 1956) is shown in the summary chart (Figure 5.4). The scheme is that for England and Wales, given here as a general guide. There are some differences in the zonations for Ireland, Scotland and the Highland Zone in general, with variations in the numbering of the more recent zones in the Irish system (Jessen, 1949; Mitchell, 1951; Smith and Pilcher, 1973).

The Late-glacial vegetation sequence, represented by Pollen Zones I–III, has

HOCKHAM MERE

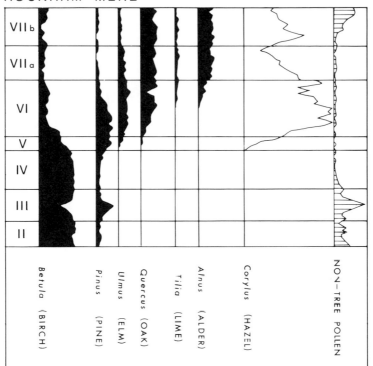

(a)

SCALEBY MOSS A

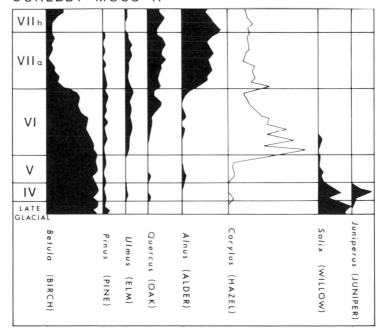

(b)

DRYMEN

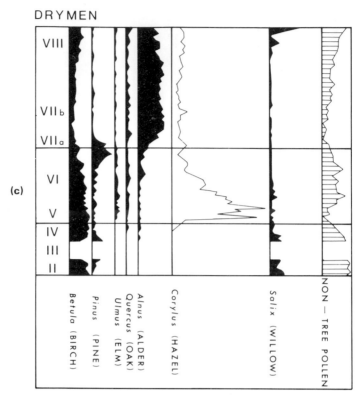

(c)

Betula (BIRCH)
Pinus (PINE)
Ulmus (ELM)
Quercus (OAK)
Alnus (ALDER)
Corylus (HAZEL)
Salix (WILLOW)
NON — TREE POLLEN

Figure 5.3: Examples of pollen diagrams: a, Hockham Mere, Norfolk; b, Scaleby Moss, Cumberland; c, Drymen, Stirlingshire. After Godwin and Tallantire, 1951; Godwin, Walker and Willis, 1957; Donner, 1957.

already been summarised in the discussion of Later Upper Palaeolithic cultures (Chapter 4). Zone IV, the first Post-glacial/Holocene subdivision of the vegetational succession, is remarkable for the sharp decline in non-tree pollen in face of the encroaching closed birch forest. In some areas (for example Scaleby Moss, Figure 5.3b) juniper reaches a maximum at this time, and in southern regions pine infiltrates the birch forest (Hockham Mere, Figure 5.3a). The mainly mineral skeletal soils of the Late-glacial zones begin to mature with increasing humus content and improved drainage. In Zones V–VI the pollen of hazel dominates the diagrams for most of the British Isles, showing a sudden rise to a maximum in Zone VI. Birch is still dominant in Zone V, but in many areas is gradually displaced by pine. An example of man/environment relationships in Zones IV–V was revealed at Star Carr, Yorkshire (C14 dates of 7607 bc and 7538 bc), with an emphasis on the use of the birch tree and its bark and an associated fauna including red and roe deer, elk, aurochs (*Bos primigenius*), boar and varieties of water fowl (Clark, 1954). Oak and elm also appear in Zones V–VI and begin to spread rapidly, offering further competition to the birch forest.

The transition from Zone VI to Zone VIIa (Zone VII in Ireland) is marked

ELEMENTS OF POST-GLACIAL CLIMATE & ENVIRONMENTAL DEVELOPMENT

C14 YEARS bc	STAGE	CHRONOZONES	VEGETATION	POLLEN ZONES	CLIMATIC PERIODS	LAND AND SEA-LEVEL CHANGES	C14 YEARS bc
3000	FLANDRIAN	Late-temperate Fl III	Alder–oak / Elm decline	VIIb	Sub-Boreal — Warm, dry. Continental	ISOSTATIC RECOVERY	3000
4000		Early-temperate Fl II	Mixed oak forest (alder, oak, elm) / 'Climatic Optimum'	VIIa	Atlantic — Warm, wet. Oceanic	TRANSGRESSION MAXIMUM '25-FOOT RAISED BEACH' DEPOSITS	4000
5000							5000
6000		Pre-temperate Fl I (c)	Pine–hazel–elm	VI	Boreal — Becoming warmer and drier	BEGINNING OF MAIN HOLOCENE MARINE TRANSGRESSION	6000
7000		(b)	Hazel–birch–pine	V			7000
8000		(a)	Birch–pine, increasing A.P. (arboreal pollen)	IV	Pre-Boreal — Sub-arctic, improving	ISOSTATIC RECOVERY	8000

Figure 5.4: Summary-table of Post-glacial climatic and environmental changes.

by a vast increase in alder pollen, due probably to the increased oceanicity of the 'climatic optimum'. In the interglacial zonation of Turner and West (1968), this is the Early-temperate or mesocratic period (Zone Fl.II), having a climax vegetation of mixed oak forest consisting of oak, elm, ash, alder, lime and hazel, with alder dominant in regions of high moisture. The highest Post-glacial temperatures and adequate rainfall encouraged maximum density of forest and shade-tolerant vegetation on rich soils. The wetter climate initiated the growth of peat in raised and blanket bogs in the upland areas of the British Isles, principally in the Highland Zone, exterminating large areas of woodland and other vegetation. The arrival of the earliest farming cultures and the beginnings of large-scale forest clearance occurred during this phase, and the period around the Zone VIIa/VIIb transition (Ireland, Zone VII/VIII) is marked by a drastic decline in the percentage of elm pollen in most north-west European diagrams (Figure 5.3a–b).

Climatic zones for the Post-glacial period were proposed by Blytt and Sernander as a result of macroscopic studies of peat stratigraphy and correlation with relative land- and sea-level changes in Scandinavia (Blytt, 1876; Sernander, 1908). The four original Post-glacial zones were eventually expanded to nine: Older (Lower) Dryas, Allerød Interstadial, Younger (Upper) Dryas, Pre-Boreal, Boreal, Atlantic, Sub-Boreal and Sub-Atlantic, taking in the Late-glacial period (Jessen, 1935). The Blytt-Sernander sequence was subsequently applied to the pollen assemblage Zones I–VIII and the two systems have often been accepted as coterminous, despite the differing bases for their construction. For guidance, the climatic sequence is equated with the pollen zonation in Figure 5.4.

Pollen zones are biostratigraphical divisions and are, therefore, liable to be time-transgressive. With a wide range of radiocarbon dates now available for Post-glacial vegetational changes, it has become obvious that the use of zone-boundaries as time-indicators is impossible (West, 1970; Smith and Pilcher, 1973).

It is clear ... that any idea of the *general* synchroneity of pollen zone boundaries in the British Post-glacial must now be abandoned. The radio-carbon dates amply confirm West's contention that pollen zones cannot be treated as units of chronostratigraphy without further evidence (West, 1970). It is perhaps of significance, however, that those horizons which are shown by the radiocarbon dates to have a measure of synchroneity; namely, the *Ulmus* decline and the final decline of *Pinus* (in Ireland), both record the disappearance or reduction of a species rather than its arrival (Smith and Pilcher, 1973, p. 911).

The factors controlling vegetation development and determining habitat in general are numerous and their interaction is complex (see Table 5.1).

Topographic factors include aspect – north, south, east or west, angle of slope, vicinity of hills or mountain ranges, distance from the sea and height above sea-level (OD). *Climatic* factors will have varied from time to time since the Late-glacial period: duration and intensity of sunlight, temperature range,

Table 5.1: Factors Determining Habitat and Vegetation

wind, rainfall and humidity of atmosphere. *Edaphic* factors are soils and the local rocks from which they are derived (limestone, chalks, sandstones, etc.), the air and water content of soils, the presence or absence of lime, mineral salts, humus, etc. The influence of organisms, the *biotic* factor, includes the demands and influences of plants on one another and on their environment; the activities of animals — for example rabbits, moles, mice, birds, earthworms and insects; the activities of bacteria and fungi. The activities of man in felling trees, clearing, draining and cultivating land, introducing grazing animals, etc., represent a major biotic factor expanding with time. Evidence for the influence of man's activities on vegetation and the habitat in general is scarce in the Pleistocene sedimentary record, but becomes more apparent in early Post-glacial times (see below) until the advent of farming and permanent settlement in the fourth millennium bc accelerated the process of the evolving 'cultural landscape'. *Fire* can be regarded as a biotic factor where it is due directly or indirectly to man's activities — the camp-fires of hunting cultures getting out of hand or not completely extinguished, the use of fire in driving animals during the hunt, the deliberate burning of vegetation to improve grazing, for cultivation or settlement — but natural fires due to lightning, volcanic eruption, chemical decomposition, etc., also represent an element influencing the development and composition of plant cover as well as the source of man's first knowledge of fire (Stewart, 1956; Mellars, 1976b).

With such complex factors operating on the habitat, it is unlikely that rapid changes could take place in all of them with sufficient contemporaneity to provide closely datable boundaries for those changes. The delay in the effects of climatic change between one region of the British Isles and another is an obvious example, although individual microclimates or microhabitats might have been affected strongly. Where, also, a regional climax vegetation existed (the dominant plant community most demanding of the edaphic, topographic, climatic and biotic factors of its habitat, and therefore suggestive of a certain equilibrium between those factors), for example, in certain types of closed forest, there may have been inertia to change which prevented rapid colonisation by new species (Smith, 1965). At the other extreme, a 'sensitive' stage may have been reached in the development of a particular vegetation form, where a change of climate in one area of the British Isles or the impact of human activity in another would have been sufficient to upset the balance and produce a decline of certain species (Smith, 1965, p. 340).

Such possibilities do not permit closely dated dividing lines between vegetation sequences. Rather is there a case for biostratigraphic zones of transition, varying regionally and taking into account all the elements influencing habitat change. The interglacial chronozones (Turner and West, 1968; West, 1970a; Sparks and West, 1972) shown in Figure 5.4 have sufficiently widely based characteristics to allow correlation of vegetational development over relatively large areas (see also Figure 1.6).

Human Influence on the Environment

It has been implied above that man's creation of a cultural landscape dates from the beginnings of agricultural activity. It might be argued, however, that even at the hunter/gatherer stage of culture man's selective use of certain types of vegetation for food, fuel or building materials, and his spreading of fire, whether accidental or deliberate, were activities which encouraged the development of some types of plant communities and discouraged others, and therefore represent a transformation of the natural landscape. Evidence of human interference with the natural habitat in early Holocene times is increasing. In France, pollen analyses have shown clearance of forest in some areas during the pre-Neolithic Atlantic period, interpreted as due to 'proto-Neolithic' stock-raising before the appearance of agriculture or pottery (Roux and Leroi-Gourhan, 1956). However, the possibility of hunters burning off vegetation in order to encourage the grazing of wild animals on regenerating plants must also be recognised. At Iping Common, Sussex, pollen analysis of a late Boreal level showed a dominant hazel scrub woodland being replaced by heath and accompanied by increasing acidity of the soil at and above a layer containing Mesolithic flint implements (Keef, Wymer and Dimbleby, 1965). Fire, associated with man's presence, appears to have been the operative factor here, and a large proportion of the flints showed signs of having been subjected to intense heat.

At sites in the Cleveland Hills of north Yorkshire, pollen sampling has shown areas of thick forest cover changing to more open conditions at levels containing charcoal and Mesolithic flints (Dimbleby, 1961, 1962; Simmons, 1969a,b; Simmons and Cundill, 1974; Spratt and Simmons, 1976; Jones, 1976). Simmons has also suggested (1964) that pollen evidence and charcoal from Blacklane, Dartmoor, indicates that, by causing fires, Mesolithic man altered the balance of forest development in favour of alder and at the expense of hazel in Zone VI.

Smith (1970) has noted a number of Mesolithic sites of Zones IV–V where strong evidence for burning coincides with the rapid rise in hazel pollen. Hazelnuts were collected and stored at many Mesolithic sites, and Troels-Smith (1960) records the storage of hundreds of hazel and willow twigs in bundles at Muldbjerg in the Aamosen Bog, Denmark, probably for plaiting into fish traps. It is possible that man's interference by burning did influence habitat development in favour of hazel, and there is no doubt that it was a species used by man, and also eaten by the animals he hunted (Mellars, 1976c). On present evidence for population density in early Holocene times, however, it is unlikely that such a widespread and relatively synchronous change could have been initiated by man alone, and it may be that in certain areas a natural process which was already under way was accelerated by human activity (Smith, 1970, pp. 82–3).

Apart from accidental fires, which may account for much of the evidence already quoted, the major reason for any deliberate burning by Mesolithic man must have been in furtherance of his hunting activities and general food quest. Some initial clearance of camp-sites may have been necessary, but this could have been better tackled with tools, rather than by burning, so that the vegetation cleared could perhaps be used for structures as at Star Carr (Clark, 1954). Fire-clearance of larger areas may have been attempted to improve hunting prospects by removing undergrowth to make sighting of prey easier, or fire may have been used to drive and perhaps trap hunted animals. Burning might also have been used to improve the quality and quantity of growth of plants attractive to grazing animals, particularly deer (Mellars, 1975; Simmons, 1975).

Repeated interference of this type, especially in regions which might be regarded as marginal, for example upland areas of the British Isles such as the North Yorkshire Moors and the Pennines (see Chapter 6 below), could have caused deterioration in vegetation cover due to loss of trees and destruction of regenerating plants by grazing animals, and soil degradation by podzolisation, possibly culminating in blanket peat (Simmons, 1969).

Even closer man/animal relationships and habitat manipulation are suggested by high concentrations of ivy pollen in Mesolithic levels at Oakhanger, Hampshire (Rankine, Rankine and Dimbleby, 1960; Simmons and Dimbleby, 1974), Hockham Mere, Norfolk (Sims, 1973), and Winfrith Heath, Dorset (Simmons and Dimbleby, 1974). The occurrences are in plant communities, for example forest, which might be expected to have prevented the natural growth of ivy in such large quantities as are indicated by the pollen analyses, and it is possible that the ivy was collected elsewhere to be spread out in the forest as a winter fodder to attract deer or other wild animals. This is a form of incipient herding, and demonstrates a developing intimacy between hunting man and a preferred species of animal which in other regions of the world led to eventual domestication.

There can be little doubt that man's activities at the hunter/gatherer stage of cultural development were to a great extent controlled by environment. The vast forests of early Holocene times were barriers to movement, and dwelling-sites were restricted to their fringes, or to lakeside, riverside or coastal locations. Seasonal movement over quite long distances between the summer and winter feeding-grounds of animals determined the form and duration of man's settlements in some areas, although certain environments, for example the coastal habitat, might have allowed longer sedentary periods. But with tools, fire and an intimate knowledge of the flora and fauna within his territorial range, he was already learning to manipulate, if only on a small scale, some elements of the habitat which determined his way of life.

Chapter 6

THE EARLIER MESOLITHIC PERIOD

The Concept of a 'Middle Stone Age'

'What are called mesolithic cultures represent adaptations of various societies to the new [environmental] conditions' (Childe, 1950, p. 25). This very useful working hypothesis has an element of over-simplification and determinism which limits its application in terms of present evidence for Mesolithic cultures. Nevertheless, a general classification of Mesolithic cultures as degrees of adaptation or non-adaptation to the changed and changing Post-glacial climate and landscape can still be a helpful basis from which to proceed in a study of the period. However, cultural origins, diversity and continuity, and the movements of human groups into hitherto unoccupied regions must also be taken into account. Mesolithic culture lasted longest and reached its greatest development and complexity in the region we now know as Temperate Europe, in areas which had been glaciated or subjected to periglacial environmental conditions. Further to the south, there is evidence of a continuity of many elements of late Palaeolithic culture with a degree of deterioration or 'impoverishment' in equipment and even more so in art and decoration. Such epi-Palaeolithic groups perhaps support Childe's idea of environmental adaptation in that they existed in regions remote enough from really drastic Post-glacial changes to allow survival without major cultural alterations. Their place among Mesolithic cultures is justified by dating evidence, the species of animals hunted, and certain type-artifacts (for example the Azilian flat harpoon of red deer antler which succeeded the Magdalenian reindeer antler harpoon of late Palaeolithic times).

The early Post-glacial period can therefore be distinguished from the late Pleistocene on the basis of environmental change (deglaciation, vegetational and faunal changes, land/sea-level fluctuations) and the variety of cultural response (basically a continuation of Upper Palaeolithic hunting/collecting economies but with a change in emphasis due to the disappearance of the large herds of late glacial times, changes in equipment as a result of adaptation to forested environments, and a wider-ranging food quest, and the intensification of particular aspects of subsistence – for example fishing and the collection of shellfish). A number of generalisations characterising the Mesolithic have been listed by Binford (1968). (1) New centres of population growth appeared with the replacement of open steppe/tundra environments by forest and the consequent break-up of the larger, more unified Upper Palaeolithic herd-hunting communities. (2) Major changes in the form of stone tools, with microliths becoming very common and widespread use of the bow and arrow. (3) The likelihood of more specific responses to local environmental conditions as suggested by greater geographical variety in cultural remains. Braidwood and

Willey (1962) support this in the widest sense:

> In general, however, it seems safe to say that this was a time – roughly from 8000 to 2000 B.C. – of multiple and at least semi-independent responses to Post-Pleistocene environmental changes. Man, throughout the world, was becoming adapted to the geological Recent. In most of these adaptations he gradually increased his subsistence efficiency over the millennia.

(4) There was a marked increase in the exploitation of aquatic resources and wild fowl. (5) Smaller-game hunting replacing the big-game hunting of the later Pleistocene. (6) Cultural degeneration of some aspects of Mesolithic society (particularly the graphic arts) when compared with the Upper Palaeolithic.

There have been frequent attempts to abolish the designation 'Mesolithic'. The word has been in existence for more than a hundred years (Wilkins, 1959; Moberg, 1959), but it only came into use when the work of Piette (1889, 1895) at Mas d'Azil began to undermine the theory of a 'hiatus' which was believed to have existed between the disappearance of the big game hunters of the Upper Palaeolithic and the arrival of the first farmers, a cultural gap during which temperate Europe was thought to have been devoid of human occupation. Epi-Palaeolithic, Neothermal, Miolithic, Leptolithic, Proto-Neolithic, Early Neolithic and occasionally simply Neolithic have all been used as labels for this chronologically undeniable but typologically awkward period, which was referred to by MacCurdy (1935, p. 61) as the 'Dark Ages' of the pre-historic era and more recently by Kozlowski (1973, p. 333) as 'a stage of "waiting" or "quarantine" which was realized in an environment where primitive agriculture could not develop'. It is perhaps the lack of cultural advance or achievement implicit in some of these terms, combined with the idea of Mesolithic as 'stop-gap' that has led to the frequent reappraisal of nomenclature. On current evidence, however, the period can be seen as an uninterrupted development of human culture against a background of changing climate and environment, with its own major developments anticipating in some cases those of the later sedentary food-producing communities, perhaps summed up by Friedrich Schlette (1958, p. 57), who sees the Mesolithic as *'eine Zeit, in der vieles sich bereits ankündigt, was dann in der Jungsteinzeit zum endgültigen Durchbruch kommt'.*

The Eighth-Seventh Millennia bc

The locations of earlier Mesolithic finds in England, Wales and Ireland on a distribution map (Figure 6.2) can only show a fraction of the true situation. Where environmental conditions were particularly favourable, ensuring good supplies of game or fish, suitable for habitation, or close to sources of raw materials for tools, then concentrations of such sites on a distribution map would to some extent accurately reflect the importance of these particular regions to Mesolithic communities. But there are many sites of casual finds of Mesolithic artifacts with no evidence of habitation, economy or even cultural affinity. Such sites can give a misleading impression of distribution and population numbers, since these hunting and gathering groups must of necessity have been wide-ranging in their movements. Because of this, sites in different environments could represent the varying seasonal activities of the same general group. Due to the randomness of discoveries of Mesolithic sites or artifacts, it is also likely that particular facets or aspects of these seasonal cycles will receive undue emphasis in the archaeological record at the expense of other, perhaps more important, activities. Such limitations should particularly apply to the British Isles, where Mesolithic population may not have been very large at any given time. The creation of cultures and comparison with Continental industries have been over-emphasised in Mesolithic studies in the past. There is no doubt of the importance of contact with the European mainland, indirectly or directly by movements of people, particularly in the earliest Post-glacial period when the greater areas of dry land facilitated such links. However, the greater importance of variability of equipment and the versatility of individual groups in exploiting a range of subsistence-regions is now becoming clear from modern multidisciplinary studies and a reassessment of the evidence from earlier excavations (Clark, 1972; Evans, Limbrey and Cleere, 1975; Switsur and Jacobi, 1975).

On present evidence, the Earlier Mesolithic period appears to have begun shortly after about 8500 bc. From the Mesolithic onwards, radiocarbon dates will be quoted here as years bc, as mentioned in Chapter 1. For example, one of the Star Carr dates is published as 9557 ± 210 bp (bp = 'before present'). Since the 'present' is internationally accepted as being AD 1950, this figure is deducted from the bp date to give a date of 7607 bc. The standard deviation (± 210) is omitted for convenience, but all Mesolithic dates are shown to one standard deviation in the chronological tables. The beginning of the Mesolithic period must have been towards the end of the last major stadial of the Pleistocene glaciations (Loch Lomond Re-Advance) and of Zone III vegetation forms (see Chapter 5). The evidence does not allow a simplistic environmental change/cultural change correlation, although these processes were often closely linked at early stages of man's technological development.

Some Late-glacial faunal forms had already become extinct or migrated by the time of the Zone II (Windermere) interstadial, and the general climatic improvement then under way may not have been too drastically halted in the final cold phase, particularly in the most southerly regions of the British Isles. It is therefore possible that some adaptations of human material culture to changing environments and animal forms were already taking place during the final stages of the Late Upper Palaeolithic, thus blurring any fine division suggested by the date of 8500 bc mentioned above.

Late Palaeolithic origins for elements of early Mesolithic culture are, however, difficult to prove. The absence of Late Upper Palaeolithic artifacts in areas of England where Mesolithic groups appeared in early Post-glacial times has been noted (Jacobi, 1973), and the shouldered point form does not seem to have developed much after the end of the Palaeolithic period. There is, on the other hand, a strong likelihood that some groups with a form of Creswellian culture survived into the Mesolithic period, if the dates for sites such as Anston Stones, Yorkshire (p. 96 above, and in bc years 7990, 7900 and 7800), and perhaps the earliest determination (6850 bc) from Mother Grundy's Parlour, Creswell Crags (Mellars, 1969; Godwin and Willis, 1962), are correct; and if the scant evidence of battered-back blades accompanying Mesolithic

Figure 6.1: Map of the North Sea area during the eighth millennium bc. The possible coastline is suggested by the present 20-fathom (−37 metre) contour.

microlithic flints at Stony Low, near Sheldon in the Southern Pennines, truly indicates a mixture of two traditions (Radley, 1968). Firmer evidence for continuity and development in bone and antler working is suggested by the barbed points of Zone II date from Poulton-le-Fylde (Barnes *et al.*, 1971; Hallam *et al.*, 1973) which have been compared with the much later Group D points from Star Carr (Figure 6.7/2), and by the finds of barbed bone and antler points from Sproughton, Suffolk (Wymer *et al.*, 1975); the antler mattocks from Star Carr probably also have their prototypes in Late Palaeolithic Northern Europe and there is no doubt about the pre-Mesolithic origins of the 'groove and splinter' technique used to produce the blanks for barbed points (Clark, 1954).

As mentioned in Chapter 5, one of the major influences on the development of the earlier Mesolithic was the configuration, in early Post-glacial times, of what is now the southern North Sea (Figure 6.1). Before flooding and subsidence, a land-link existed between eastern England and Denmark, north-west Germany, the Low Countries and northern France. This large area of low-lying land, although perhaps mainly estuarine and with many swamps and shallow lakes, was probably an extremely rich potential food source, with deer, aurochs, fish, water-fowl and shellfish widely available (Jacobi, 1973, pp. 245–6). The density of occupation by hunter/fisher communities, whose presence is to some extent substantiated by finds of bone and antler implements from the North Sea bed (Clark, 1932; Godwin, 1933; Louwe Kooijmans, 1971), may have been much greater than on the marginal lands of eastern Britain and the north-west European mainland. Eventual dispersal east and west from such an area would undoubtedly have been a major factor in the evolution of Mesolithic culture groups. The similarities in microlithic equipment among north-west European cultures in the earlier Mesolithic are known, and further emphasise the land-link (Jacobi, 1976). More particularly, the relationships between sites such as Star Carr or Flixton I and the north German early Duvensee groups have been referred to by Bokelmann (1972) and explained by the former existence of this 'Northsealand'; Kozlowski (1973) has listed Star Carr as a subculture of the 'Duvensee Complex'.

Most of the earlier Mesolithic artifactual assemblages fall into what Clark (in Warren *et al.*, 1934) described as the 'axe, burin and non-geometric microlith industries', with a microlithic component of limited range, mainly obliquely-blunted points and some large isosceles triangles or trapezes made on broad blades (for example Figure 6.3/1–8), probably used for tipping arrows or spears. These 'Broad Blade' industries are now accepted as typical of the earlier Mesolithic groups in Britain and north-west Europe (Buckley, 1924; Radley and Mellars, 1964; Switsur and Jacobi, 1975; Mellars, 1976a; Jacobi, 1976).

Star Carr

Probably the most important of all British Mesolithic sites is that of Star Carr (Clark, 1954; 1972), where a wide range of organic materials (as opposed to the solely lithic remains recovered from most Mesolithic sites) was preserved in a waterlogged and peaty area, and a great deal of evidence of economy and environment was recovered by an interdisciplinary exploration combining

Figure 6.2: Map of Earlier Mesolithic sites in England, Wales and Ireland. Sites are numbered, Star Carr (3), as in the chronological table at Figure 6.8.

archaeological, botanical and zoological techniques with radiocarbon dating. The site, covering about 240 sq m, may have been occupied by about four nuclear family units. It consisted of a rough platform or flooring (no actual dwelling structures were discovered) of felled birch brushwood, in a reed swamp on the edge of a former early Post-glacial lake in a low-lying area at the eastern end of the Vale of Pickering. Animal remains recovered included red deer, elk, roe deer, aurochs, wild pig, beaver, badger, fox, wolf, birds and domesticated dog (Degerbøl, 1961). Surprisingly, considering the proximity of the lake, no fish bones were recovered. This may have been due to geomorphological features along the course of the River Derwent at this stage of its post-glacial development, preventing the penetration of fish to the upper reaches and to the Star Carr lake (Wheeler, 1978).

Pollen analyses show a late Zone IV/early Zone V vegetation of mainly birch forest with hazel and pine beginning to appear. Samples of wood from the platform gave two radiocarbon dates of 7607 and 7538 bc.* Of the 17,000 flints recovered, 85 per cent were waste material and about half of the remainder consisted of utilised flakes. The main finished forms were burins, scrapers, microliths (mainly obliquely-blunted forms, triangles and elongated trapezes) and awls. There were also seven small core axes and adzes (the marks of this type of implement could be seen on some of the birch brushwood used in the construction of the platform) and five saws (Figure 6.3). Apart from the wood of the platform, part of a wooden paddle had survived (Figure 6.3/19) and also rolls of birch-bark – presumably a source of resin for fixing arrowheads and spearheads; one elongated trapeze microlith had resin adhering to it and resin traces were found on the tangs of two barbed points. A major discovery was the large number of barbed points – 191 altogether, 187 of deer antler (Figure 6.7/1–3), and a series of perforated mattock-heads made of elk antler (Figure 6.3/18). Remains of food animals included red deer (80), roe deer (33), elk (11), ox (aurochs or *Bos primigenius*) (9) and pig (5). Clark (1954, p. 15) has estimated that, due to variations in conditions of preservation on the site, this number could probably be doubled. Evidence from these animal remains, and in particular the red deer, roe deer and elk antler, suggests that the site was occupied from about October until April. Red deer antler frontlets with parts of the antlers remaining and with perforations for tying may have been used as disguises in ritual or actual hunting. The flint industry, with its emphasis on burins and scrapers, and the examples of 'groove and splinter' technique from the site, point to bone- and skin-working as the main activities. Most of the raw materials used at Star Carr could have been obtained within one hour's walk of the site, and Clark (1972, p. 25) has proposed a site-territory or 'catchment area' of 5 km radius within one hour or 10 km within two hours' walk of the site. Star Carr can now be seen as representative of one element of seasonal activity in an annual pattern of Mesolithic hunting and collecting. This realisation was a major advance in Mesolithic studies, and a breakaway from the days when too-great stress was placed upon differences in flint assemblages alone as indicators of 'cultural variation'. The seasonal round of the Star Carr hunters was possibly controlled

*Radiocarbon dates are quoted without laboratory numbers in Chapters 6 and 7, but these numbers are listed in Figures 6.8, 7.4, 7.7 and 7.11.

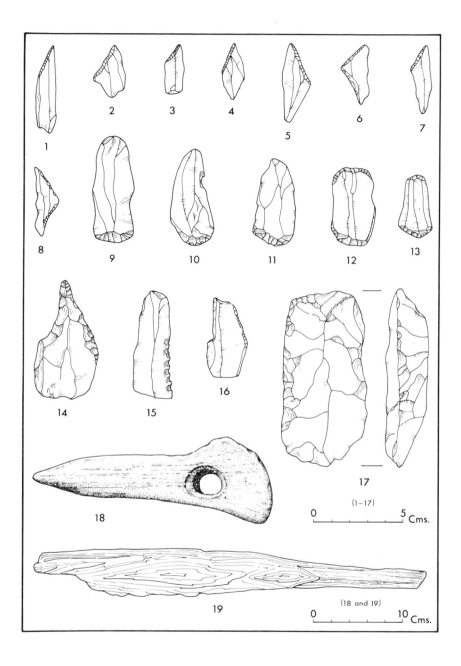

Figure 6.3: Flint, bone and wood artifacts from Star Carr. 1–8, broad blade microliths (obliquely-blunted points, triangles, trapezes); 9–13, scrapers; 14, awl; 15, saw; 16, burin; 17, small core axe; 18, perforated elk antler mattock-head; 19, part of a wooden paddle. After Clark, 1954.

by the movements of the red deer, and the sites of their summer/early autumn activities should coincide with that animal's known preference for upland grazing at that time of year (see below). In a recent study of Mesolithic activity in the Schwabian Alb and in Oberschwaben, on either side of the Upper Danube (Jochim, 1976), it was demonstrated that with exploitation of the resources of different environments at different times of the year, seasonal movement and change in form of the base camp were necessary. The winter and autumn sites were usually sheltered caves, in spring more open rock shelters in river flood plain regions were used, and in summer open lakeside settlements such as the groups of huts on the shores of the Federsee, at Tann-stock. Estimates of population suggest large groups in summer (54 to 108) and much smaller groups (17 to 33) in winter camps.

Near Star Carr and on a gravel ridge, the site of Flixton I (Moore, 1950) had traces of hearths and and a flint assemblage. Finished implements comprised only 4 per cent of the total flints and included 165 scrapers, 78 microliths, 19 burins, 9 awl-like forms and 2 axes or adzes, perhaps indicating similar seasonal activities to those at Star Carr. Surface collections of flints at the Sandbeds, Otley, in the West Riding of Yorkshire (Cowling and Mellars, 1973) may also represent a series of successive occupations of winter camp-sites.

Southern England

Another important early Mesolithic lowland site was that discovered at Broxbourne, Hertfordshire, on the flood-plain of the River Lea (Warren *et al.*, 1934). The industry, which was sealed under Boreal peat, suggesting a date not later than Zone VI, was limited in quantity and scatter, indicating a small site with perhaps only one temporary occupation. The main artifacts (Figure 6.4/9–18) were 28 scrapers, 25 microliths (almost entirely obliquely-blunted points), only 2 burins and 2 core axes. This in itself suggests limited activity and little or no working of bone or antler. A small industry from the Colne Valley, Essex (Layard, 1927; Clark, 1932), associated with hearths and depressions, had a dominance of microliths (80, of which 66 were obliquely-blunted points), with tranchet core axes, a few burins and no scrapers (Figure 6.4/1–8).

It is not possible to make hard and fast interpretations of site-function where perhaps only a surface-scatter of flints has been collected, and statistical analyses are only really useful where excavation has allowed total artifact plus waste recovery. In a recent study of Mesolithic habitation sites (Mellars, 1976c), settlements have been classified tentatively according to dimensions (assumed mainly from the limits of flint-working scatter), location/environment and flint assemblage/site-function. On this basis, Star Carr, Flixton I and Broxbourne are regarded as lowland (below 200 metres) habitat sites, near lake or river, with 'balanced' assemblages (microliths less than 85 per cent and a high percentage – up to 50 per cent – of scrapers), most probably occupied through winter/spring.

At Iping Common, Sussex (Keef *et al.*, 1965), a Mesolithic site defined by a roughly circular stained area on the Lower Greensand was occupied, according to pollen analysis, during a hazel-dominant Boreal phase. Of the flint assemblage, 91 per cent was waste and used cores, and the main implements

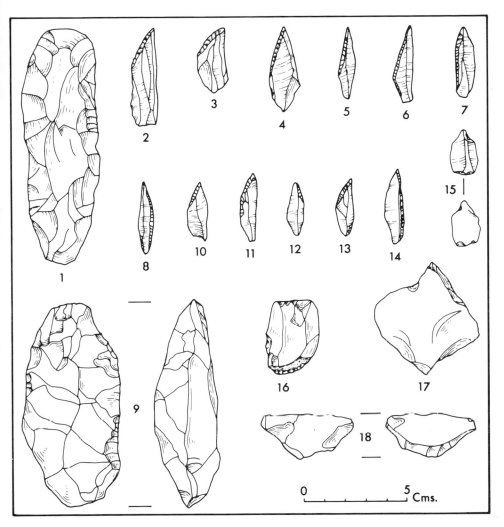

Figure 6.4: Artifacts from the Colne Valley and Broxbourne. 1, core axe; 2–8, microliths, Colne Valley, Essex; 9, core axe; 10–14, microliths; 15, micro-burin; 16, scraper; 17, burin or graver; 18, tranchet axe-sharpening flake, Broxbourne, Hertfordshire. After Layard, 1927; Clark, 1932; Warren *et al.*, 1934.

were 108 microliths (67 classifiable, mainly obliquely-blunted points), 46 'segmented blades', 10 scrapers, 2 certain and 5 doubtful gravers or burins. There were also 7 tranchet axe-sharpening flakes (from core axes, where the cutting edge is formed by the intersection of two flake scars, produced by striking the 'tranchet blow' across the cutting end of the axe, detaching a large flake (for example Figure 6.4/18) which is distinctive enough in itself to suggest the use of tranchet axes even when the axes are absent). A large proportion of the flints had been damaged by fire. This is a 'microlith-dominated assemblage' (Mellars,

1976c) and site-function may have been associated mainly with primary hunting rather than 'domestic' activities. Indeed Wymer (in Keef *et al.*, 1965) suggests a simple bivouac site for itinerant hunters, with flint-working to produce tips for spears and arrows. The pollen analysis shows a change from hazel woodland to heathland at about the time of occupation and this could be interpreted as the result of human activity, involving fire, as suggested by the heat-damaged flints (see Chapter 5 above).

In a group of Mesolithic sites in the Kennet Valley west of Reading, Berkshire, several are of earlier Mesolithic date. A range of six radiocarbon determinations between 8415 and 7530 bc is available for Sites III and V at Thatcham (Churchill, 1962) and single dates of 7350 bc for Marsh Benham (Switsur and Jacobi, 1975) and 6829 bc for Greenham Dairy Farm (Sheridan *et al.*, 1967; Switsur and Jacobi, 1975; Jacobi, 1976) (Table 6.8). The site at Thatcham (Peake and Crawford, 1922; Wymer, 1962) was on a gravel terrace overlooking a reed swamp which may have been a lake in early Post-glacial times, backed by birch and pine forest. The flint assemblage (96.5 per cent waste, 3.5 per cent finished implements) included 285 microliths (187 obliquely-blunted points), 132 scrapers, 61 gravers or burins, 19 saws, 17 axe-adzes and 15 awls (Figure 6.5/1–10). A few artifacts of red deer antler and bone were recovered, including an unbarbed polished bone point or spearhead (Figure 6.5/11). Among the animal remains were red deer, pig, roe deer, aurochs and elk; part of the organic material was recovered by coffer dam excavation in the reed swamp (Site V). No structures were discovered, but concentrations of domestic rubbish and hearth material of roughly 6 m diameter might indicate shelters of branches or skins; quantities of hazel-nuts were found in and around the hearth areas. There are similarities to Star Carr: lakeside location, animal remains, 'balanced' flint assemblage and occupation in the Pre-Boreal and Boreal periods. The Star Carr barbed points are missing, but the overall quantity of bone and antler implements recovered was small. The total evidence suggests a lowland site intermittently occupied by small groups of hunter/fishers for winter and spring seasonal activities with perhaps an emphasis on preparation of skins and bone-working. Visual and computer cluster analysis of the microliths from the earliest-dated locations (8415 and 8080 bc for Site III) at Thatcham and those from Greenham Dairy Farm (Jacobi, 1976) show little typological evolution over the length of time which separates the two sites.

These early sites may represent a penetration by Mesolithic groups from the east via the Kennet Valley towards south-west England, where important collections of flints have been recovered at Dozemare Pool, Cornwall, and at Shapwick and Middlezoy in Somerset (Wainwright, 1960). At Dozemare, the flint assemblage included microliths (mainly obliquely-blunted points) and some scrapers, burins and saws (Figure 6.5/12–18), but no trace of the axe-adze. The assemblages at Middlezoy and Shapwick are very similar,

Figure 6.5: 1–5, microliths; 6,7, scrapers; 8, burin; 9,10, core axes or adzes; 11, bone point, Thatcham, Berkshire; 12–15, microliths; 16,17, scrapers; 18, saw, Dozemare Pool, Cornwall; 19–21, microliths; 22, saw; 23, scraper; 24, tranchet-sharpened flake axe, Middlezoy, Somerset. After Wymer, 1962; Wainwright, 1960.

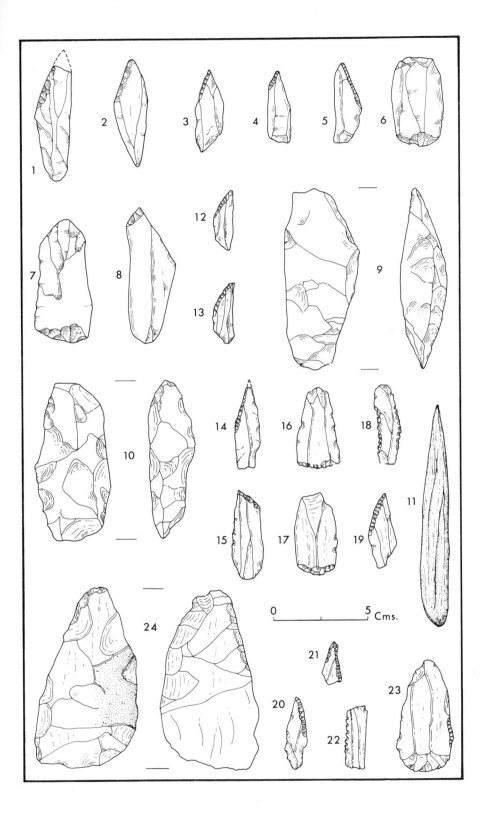

0   5 Cms.

Middlezoy having a few microliths, burins and scrapers with a tranchet-sharpened flake axe (Figure 6.5/19–24). Elsewhere in Somerset (Norman, 1975), an early Mesolithic context is suggested by flint assemblages showing a dominance of obliquely-blunted points among the microliths, the occurrence of burins, saws and truncated blades, plus traces of the core axe element of 'heavy equipment'. Little can be said about the activities of these groups, represented as they are by mainly surface collections of flints, but their affinities would appear to lie with those industries of the Colne Valley, Broxbourne and Thatcham mentioned above (Wainwright, 1960, pp. 200–1).

Wales

In a study of the microlithic industries of Wales (Wainwright, 1963), a pre-dominantly coastal occupation was suggested with sparse representation in the interior. In the intervening years more inland sites have been recognised, but the bulk of evidence for the Welsh Mesolithic has resulted chiefly from investigation of coastal locations. The flints from Burry Holms Island, Gower (Clark, 1932; Grimes, 1951; Wainwright, 1963) include some obliquely-blunted microliths on broad blades, and blunted-back points, scrapers and a burin. These may represent some relationship to the earlier Mesolithic sites of Shapwick and Middlezoy across the Bristol Channel in Somerset (Wainwright, 1963, p. 117), but the evidence is still scant. At Nab Head, Pembrokeshire (Gordon-Williams, 1926; Grimes, 1951; Wainwright, 1963), the occurrence of tranchet axes (Figure 7.3/7) has been attributed to possible contact with the later Mesolithic 'Horsham culture' (see Chapter 7 below) of southern England by way of the Cotswolds and Bristol Channel coasts (Wainwright, 1963). Whether or not these south Welsh littoral sites represent a form of permanent coastal economy is yet to be demonstrated. More excavation of inland and coastal locations is necessary, and seasonality might still be detected when and if site-function can be proved.

More definite evidence of earlier Mesolithic occupation is now available from north Wales. At Trwyn Du, Aberffraw, Anglesey, a flint assemblage from a Mesolithic site located beside, and partly under, a later cairn included 123 blunted points, 87 scrapers and two tranchet axes (White, 1975). Radiocarbon determinations on burnt hazel-nuts gave dates between 6700 and 6000 bc (White, 1975; Jacobi, 1976). At Rhuddlan, Flintshire, in an area where exploitation of both sea coast and Clwyd Estuary resources was possible, a Mesolithic site with a chert non-geometric microlith industry has been excavated (Miles, 1972). Associated with the industry were 4 pebbles with incised patterns reminiscent of the wide range of decoration produced in quantity by the Continental Maglemosian culture (Clark, 1936, pp. 162–89). Carbonised hazel-nut shells gave radiocarbon dates between 6800 and 6500 bc.

The Pennines and Northern England

Some of the lowland sites mentioned above undoubtedly represent the winter and spring locations of seasonally nomadic hunters. The importance of the red deer has already been mentioned in relation to Star Carr, and the movements of many of these groups may have been controlled to a great extent by the animal's feeding requirements and migrations at different times of the year. The carrying capacity of the prehistoric environment for these animals, and their seasonal requirements and movements, have been discussed amply by Mellars (1975) in general and by Clark (1972) in relation to Star Carr. Evidence from studies of present-day red deer populations has demonstrated 'the existence of well-defined patterns of movement between upland areas in the summer months and lowland areas in the winter' and 'a general tendency for the red deer herds to disperse over extensive territories during the summer months and to congregate into much smaller areas during the winter season' (Mellars, 1976, pp. 381–2). It is therefore likely that remains of summer sites of groups which had a hunting economy linked closely to the red deer are to be found in upland regions. The proximity of the North Yorkshire Moors suggests a likely summer hunting territory for the occupants of the Star Carr winter base camp, and a few probably early Mesolithic sites have been identified there, mainly above 200 m (Clark, 1972; Jones, 1975; Spratt and Simmons, 1976).

Much more evidence is available from the Southern Pennines. Excavations at Deepcar, Yorkshire (Radley and Mellars, 1964), at a height of about 150 m, revealed a habitation site, with hearths and roughly circular arrangements of stones which coincided with maximum flint density. From a total of almost 37,000 flints, only 144 (0.4 per cent) were finished implements. This suggests a flint-knapping site for the manufacture of hunting weapons, many of which must have been used and lost in other areas. The industry, in the 'Broad Blade' tradition, included 68 microliths (the majority obliquely-blunted points), 37 scrapers, 21 notched flakes, 8 burins and one very small possible tranchet core axe (Figure 6.6/1–12). The flint was of mainly opaque white colour, suggesting contacts with East Yorkshire where it is found in the Wolds chalk, and there was a small quantity of black chert, probably from Derbyshire. Further to the north-west, in the vicinity of Marden, lie the four sites of Warcock Hill North, Warcock Hill South, Lominot II/III and Windy Hill, all above 305 m, excavated by Buckley in 1922–4 (Radley and Mellars, 1964, pp. 13–22). Over 5,000 flints were recovered from the Warcock North site where they were concentrated in four circular patches. The Lominot II/III sites were probably also two similar concentrations. The flint assemblages from all of these sites are again of 'Broad Blade' type with microliths (Warcock North 60, Warcock South 21, Lominot II/III 44, Windy Hill 33) dominated by obliquely-blunted points, scrapers (Warcock North 32, Warcock South 12, Lominot II/III 31, Windy Hill 24) and burins (Warcock North 5, Warcock South 1, Lominot II/III 2, Windy Hill 8) (Figure 6.6/13–26). At Warcock North, Lominot II/III and Windy Hill, as at Deepcar, opaque white flint comprised, on average, about 95 per cent of the raw material used for tools, again indicative of possible links with south-east Yorkshire or north Lincolnshire. At Warcock Hill South, however, 85 per cent of the flint was of translucent type which, coupled with an absence of opposed retouch on the obliquely-blunted points, has been seen as evidence of links with the lowland sites of Star Carr and Flixton I (Mellars, 1976a). Charcoal samples from the original Buckley excavations have given radiocarbon dates of 7615 bc for Lominot III and 7260 bc for Warcock Hill South (Switsur and Jacobi, 1975). The reliability of dates from charcoal

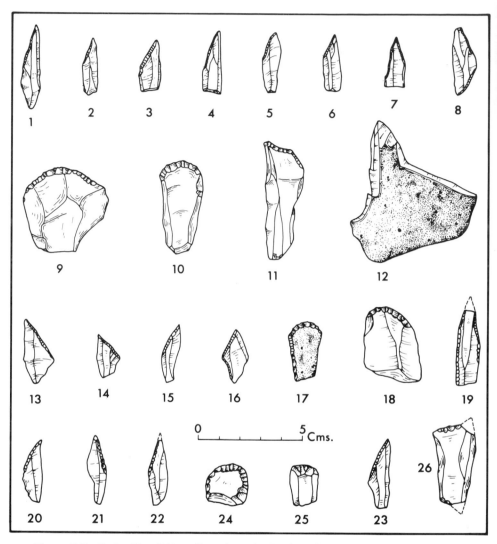

Figure 6.6: Earlier Mesolithic artifacts from the Southern Pennines. 1–8, microliths; 9,10, scrapers; 11, 12, burins, Deepcar, Yorkshire; 13–16, microliths; 17,18, scrapers; 19, steeply-worked awl, Warcock Hill South, Yorkshire; 20–23, microliths; 24,25, scrapers; 26, obliquely-truncated blade, Lominot, Yorkshire. After Radley and Mellars, 1964.

excavated in the 1920s has been questioned (Bonsall, 1975), and it should be noted that some dates have large standard deviations – for example Lominot III (±350) and Warcock Hill South (±340) (Figure 6.8).

At Warcock Hill Site III, charcoal obtained from three 'cooking pits' during Buckley's 1920s excavation has been dated to 6656 bc (Switsur and Jacobi, 1975), and charred wood from Broomhead Moor Site V, in the Deepcar region, which had hearths and stake holes, gave a date of 6623 bc (Radley *et al.*,

1974). Both of these sites have 'Narrow Blade' assemblages (see Chapter 7 below).

These are only a few of the upland Mesolithic sites recorded in northern England alone. In a belt of territory 90 km wide from the west to the east coast across the Southern Pennines, at least 949 Mesolithic sites, both upland and lowland, have been listed (Jacobi *et al.*, 1976). The greatest number (653), constituting 69 per cent of the total, are located at heights above 305 m. Many of these are later Mesolithic sites with differing economies, and not all of the remainder are necessarily the summer encampments of nomadic red deer hunters whose winter base camps were in the lowlands, but a proportion of them must presumably fall into this category. Flint typology and particularly the characteristics of the raw material used suggest that many of these groups may have wintered in the Lincolnshire lowlands or at sites such as Misterton Carr in Nottinghamshire (Buckland and Dolby, 1973). Lest the pattern of winter/summer – lowland/upland be taken as general for all seasonal movements of earlier Mesolithic communities, it should be noted that there are many environments where this would have been unnecessary. Along the Lincoln Edge, there are several sites so situated as to be able to exploit both upland and lowland resources with a minimum of migration (Jacobi, 1973, pp. 243–4).

The limited sizes of upland sites do certainly suggest short occupation by small groups with little in the way of 'domestic' activities. The flint assemblages are limited in range, often of the 'balanced' category, with microliths representing primarily hunting activities, quantities of scrapers suggesting preparation of skins, no 'heavy equipment' of the tranchet axe-adze type and a scarcity of burins at a time of year when antlers were still growing. Assemblages of this type are known from Deepcar, Warcock Hill North and South, Lominot II/III, Windy Hill (all Radley and Mellars, 1964), Pike Low and Mickleden (both Radley and Marshall, 1965).

The removal of tree cover, often by burning, has been shown to improve grazing, increasing the density and influencing the movements and distribution of animal populations such as red deer, while at the same time increasing their average body weight and rate of reproduction (Mellars, 1975, 1976b). Evidence from the Southern Pennines (Jacobi *et al.*, 1976) suggests that regular burning of forest cover may have been practised by Mesolithic hunting groups, leading to permanent modification of vegetation and perhaps contributing to the formation of blanket peat.

The emphasis on red deer and hunting has to some extent detracted from the probability that these groups must have consumed considerable quantities of vegetable foods. Mellars (1976c) refers to modern groups of 'hunters' who derive up to 80 per cent of their food supply from plants and suggests that plant food may have been a major, if not dominant, element of Mesolithic diet, while Clarke (1976) has indicated that greater emphasis should be placed on this element of subsistence when interpreting tool function. The importance of hazel-nuts has already been mentioned (Chapter 5 above), but there is a *caveat* on accepting their appearance on a site as an indication of autumn occupation, since they survive well and could have been stored for winter or later consumption (Mellars, 1976c, p. 376). Some possibly edible plants were listed for Star Carr (Clark, 1954, pp. 13–15) but, in general, the evidence does not survive. Nuts, wild fruits, berries, seeds and rhizomes, mushrooms, bulbs, roots, herbs and certain grasses were all potential food sources and many of them were undoubtedly eaten by Mesolithic communities.

The importance of the coastal environment and resources, particularly in the winter season, must also be stressed (Mellars, 1976c; Morrison and Jardine, 1977), and these will be treated regionally in Chapter 7. Early Mesolithic coastal sites are limited in number, particularly in eastern England, their locations on the greatly enlarged coastal plain of early Post-glacial times having been obliterated by the rising sea-level of the main Holocene transgression. Even in relatively stable regions, such as the south-west, where no major land movements took place (Chapter 5, Figure 5.1), the transgression had a major effect in coastal areas (Churchill, 1965) and traces of submerged forests are known from several sites around the south Welsh coast (Wainwright, 1963).

The apparent absence of evidence for early Mesolithic sites in north-western England is perhaps again due to loss of coastal locations under a transgressing sea-level. Some of the Pennine sites mentioned above may have been the camps of hunters whose winter territories were on the then much more extensive plains of Morecambe and Cheshire, and there is some slight evidence in support of this idea (for example flint at Lominot II may have been brought from Cheshire) (Jacobi, 1973, p. 244).

Ireland

There is no doubt that Mesolithic groups had reached more northerly regions before the mid-seventh millennium bc, though from where and by which routes it is still not possible to say with certainty. The settlement at Mount Sandel, Co. Derry, is an example of this northward expansion before the end of the earlier Mesolithic period. It lies on a sandy area at the edge of fluvio-glacial deposits on a bluff 31 metres above the River Bann, near its estuary. The site covers an area of almost 700 square metres and excavations have revealed traces of the post holes of several near-circular huts up to 6 metres in diameter and with central hearths (Woodman, 1974b, 1974c, 1975, 1976b, 1977a). A series of pits in groups may have been used for storage and some contained fragments of burnt animal bones. The flint assemblage has mainly geometric microliths of Narrow Blade ('microblade') form, with elongated scalene triangles, rods, microburins and 'needle points' with surface retouch (see Figure 7.6 below). The range and number of microliths alone distinguish this industry from the later 'Larnian' (see Chapter 7 below). There are no burins, few scrapers, but a number of core-axes and, surprisingly for this early site, flake-axes. The most common animal remains were wild pig and this animal seems in general to have been more important in the Irish Mesolithic than red deer, which might also partly explain the absence of burins, used so widely elsewhere in the working of red deer bone and antler. Bones of hare, birds and fish were also recovered. Autumn/winter occupation is suggested for Mount Sandel, which was more distant from its contemporary sea-coast than at present, although exploitation of coastal, estuarine and riverine resources may have been possible within the 10 kilometres/2 hours' walking distance 'catchment area' of the site. Hazelnuts were recovered from various locations on the site and a series of radiocarbon determinations on samples of these has given a range of dates between 7000 and 6500 bc (Figure 6.8).

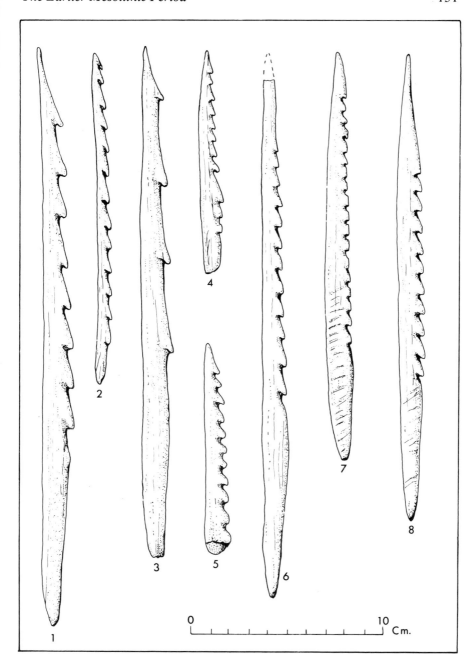

Figure 6.7: Earlier Mesolithic barbed points from Eastern England. 1,3, 'Class A' points, Star Carr, Yorkshire; 2, 'Class D' point, Star Carr, Yorkshire (cf. points from High Furlong, Lancs., Fig. 4.5/18); 4, Skipsea, Yorkshire; 5, Royston, Hertfordshire; 6, Brandesburton, Yorkshire; 7, dredged from the area of the Leman and Ower Banks off the Norfolk coast. After Clark, 1954; Clark and Godwin, 1956; Godwin, 1933.

Barbed Points

Apart from the sites and flint collections mentioned, evidence of earlier Mesolithic activities is represented by a number of finds of barbed bone and antler points from eastern and south-eastern England (Map, Figure 6.2), with a particular concentration in the Holderness region. The distribution suggests an outlook towards the lost territories of the southern North Sea as a major centre of activity, at least until the early seventh millennium bc, with most of the west representing a peripheral region. The points from Star Carr (Figure 6.7/1–3) are dated, with the site, to the mid-eighth millennium bc. An antler point, dredged from the Leman and Ower Banks of the North Sea (Figure 6.7/7), was enclosed in a chunk of peat or 'moorlog'; similar peat from a depth of 37 metres has been dated to 6475 bc (Figure 5.2) (Godwin and Willis, 1959); it must be emphasised that this is not a date for the peat which actually enclosed the point, and Jacobi (in Wymer *et al.*, 1975) would prefer an earlier, Zone V, dating for the point. The Skipsea bone point (Figure 6.7/4) may be dated by its association with Boreal deposits (Armstrong, 1922, 1923; Godwin and Godwin, 1933) and most of these points can be referred to the Pre-Boreal and Boreal periods by typology and comparison with continental forms (Clark and Godwin, 1956; Louwe-Kooijmans, 1971; Mellars, 1976c).

Conclusions

In summary, our picture of the earlier Mesolithic period is a very incomplete one. The quantity of evidence is small and interpretation is difficult due to the limitations of what is, after all, in many cases only the lithic component of material culture, and perhaps only an incomplete or single aspect of that component. Despite these restrictions, major advances have been made in recent years as a result, particularly, of the multidisciplinary approach, where the work of the botanist, zoologist, geologist, chemist and physicist has complemented and often surpassed that of the archaeologist in extracting all possible information from the available evidence. Particularly important has been the recognition of seasonality in the movements of hunting groups, and this in turn has influenced the functional analysis of stone tool assemblages and the classification of sites in terms of function, environment, economy and season. All of this can be set against a well established sequence of environmental change and fluctuations in relative sea-level, from Late-glacial to full Boreal. The major event of this period must have been the drowning of the North Sea lands, with the consequent loss of hunting territories and restriction on cultural contacts with the Continent, and the loss of large coastal areas elsewhere after the start of the main Holocene marine transgression. It is these landscape changes, rather than the Broad Blade/Narrow Blade succession in flint-working traditions, that have been used here as a divide between earlier and later Mesolithic developments.

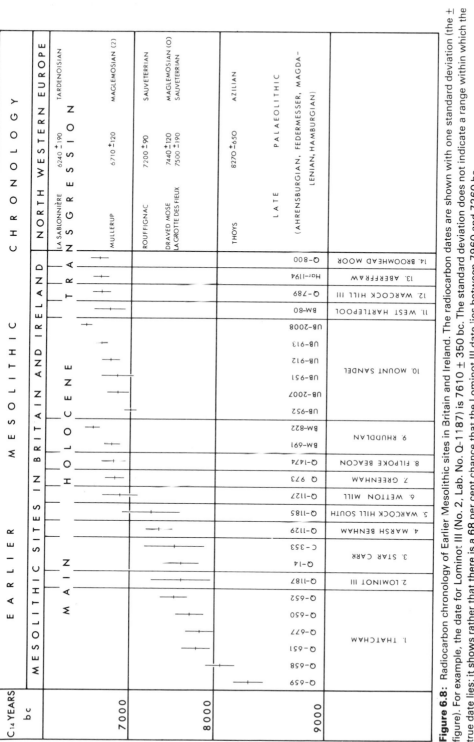

Figure 6.8: Radiocarbon chronology of Earlier Mesolithic sites in Britain and Ireland. The radiocarbon dates are shown with one standard deviation (the ± figure). For example, the date for Lominot III (No. 2, Lab. No. Q-1187) is 7610 ± 350 bc. The standard deviation does not indicate a range within which the true date lies; it shows rather that there is a 68 per cent chance that the Lominot III date lies between 7960 and 7260 bc.

Chapter 7

THE LATER MESOLITHIC PERIOD

On typological grounds, as mentioned in the previous chapter, the Mesolithic has been subdivided into an earlier and a later phase according to the major forms of microlith in use, the earlier Broad Blade 'non-geometric' types being succeeded during the seventh millennium by the Narrow Blade 'geometric' industries (Jacobi, 1973, 1976; Mellars, 1976a, 1976c). There is no sharp division, however, and combinations of both forms are known from quite late Mesolithic sites, while Scottish industries cannot easily be accommodated within this classification. The earliest Narrow Blade site so far discovered is Mount Sandel, Co. Londonderry (Chapter 6), with dates between 7000 and 6500 radiocarbon years bc. Another early Narrow Blade site is that at Filpoke Beacon, Durham, where an industry including narrow rods and narrow scalene triangles ('micro-triangles') has been dated (on nut shells) to 6810 bc (Coupland, 1948; Jacobi, 1976).

These later Mesolithic Narrow Blade industries consist in general of microliths which are smaller and narrower than the Broad Blade forms, with widespread occurrence of small scalene triangles and, particularly among the earliest-dated assemblages, rod-like forms. Assemblages with purely Narrow Blade forms have been further subdivided according to whether they (1) are dominated by scalene triangles, (2) comprise mainly rod-like forms, or (3) comprise a high proportion of small rhomboidal and trapezoidal forms (Radley and Mellars, 1964; Radley *et al.*, 1974). The Narrow Blade assemblages have forms showing close affinities with west European industries, and some of the British sites with these forms have dates early enough to indicate the possibility of some direct movement or diffusion of cultural elements from the Continent before the flooding of the southern North Sea basin. Such contacts appear to have ceased by the last quarter of the seventh millennium bc (Jacobi, 1976; Mellars, 1976a).

Further evidence for an Earlier/Later Mesolithic transition can perhaps be traced in change of functional emphasis among artifact assemblages. As mentioned in Chapter 6, a recent study of 'industrial variability' (Mellars, 1976c) has shown certain functional patterns in groups of flint tools from different sites, albeit from a still limited amount of evidence. Among the various classifications, the Type A ('microlith dominated') assemblage has been assigned mainly to the Later Mesolithic. At Broomhead Moor Site 5, Yorkshire, a Type A assemblage has a microlithic element forming 90 per cent of all retouched tools (Radley *et al.*, 1974; Switsur and Jacobi, 1975). These are mainly scalene triangles with some rod and crescent shapes (Figure 7.2/1–11) and there were also a few scrapers, notched blades and awls. Mellars (1976c, p. 389) has also noted the general scarcity of scrapers in these assemblages,

Figure 7.1: Map of Later Mesolithic sites in England and Wales. Sites are numbered, for example Freshwater West (14), as in the chronological table at Figure 7.4.

suggesting less need for the treatment of skins and hides, and thus possibly indicating mainly summer activities at most sites with Type A assemblages.

Microliths were, in general, manufactured from blades, bladelets or flakes; some geometric forms were produced by a technique involving gradual notching until the blade could be snapped across, or by direct snapping to produce a rectangular or rhomboidal blade segment. The notching process usually left the 'micro-burin' as a by-product (Figure 7.2/41a–f, 42).

Although microliths occur in large quantities and have been used as major indicators of change and variation in the classification of Mesolithic cultural assemblages, their real function cannot be demonstrated with any certainty. Some Broad Blade forms undoubtedly served as missile points, but the smaller

Narrow Blade industries seem too flimsy to have been used individually. The appearance of the Narrow Blade microliths has been suggested as indicating a change from earlier Mesolithic use of barbed bone and antler points for inland hunting, to later use of spears and missiles barbed with microliths (Mellars, 1976a,c), and some writers refer to geometric microliths in general as 'armatures' (for example Rozoy, 1978). Breuil and Lantier (1965, p. 211) note that 'at White Hill (Yorkshire) was found a linear group of thirty-five triangles, spaced 1½–2 cm apart, constituting the barbs on a wooden shaft that had rotted away', referring to Francis Buckley's discovery in the Pennines (Petch, 1924). Further examples of groups of microliths found *in situ*, sometimes in linear arrangements, have been quoted in support of this theory (Mellars, 1976c, pp. 396–7), and Leakey (1951, p. 34) has noted discoveries, in East Africa, of sets of five microliths suggesting barbs for wooden-shafted missiles (Figure 7.2/43), although Rozoy (1978) doubts the efficacy of this particular reconstruction. The use of self-barbed bone and antler points continued in the Later Mesolithic, but by this period they appear to be restricted to coastal sites, and particularly in western Scotland (see Figure 7.10). In a recent essay on forms of Mesolithic subsistence alternative to the meat quest and on the need to avoid 'stereotyped assumptions' in the identification of function in the tools of hunting/collecting societies, Clarke (1976) has made a plea for recognition of the possibility that microliths might have been used as parts of composite tools employed in the gathering or harvesting of plant foods.

Further differences between the Earlier and Later Mesolithic phases can be seen in the increased number of sites and greater variety of environments exploited in the later stage. A growing body of evidence shows no obvious cultural unity within the British Isles, but rather local developments and environmental adaptations in which some groups show apparently similar responses in their artifactual assemblages whereas others, depending on location, types of raw material available and range of animals hunted, have left quite different forms of evidence. Far less importance is now attached to possible links with Continental cultural groupings and to the use of labels such as 'Sauveterrian' or 'Tardenoisian'. For these reasons it is perhaps useful to examine the Later Mesolithic cultural groupings on a regional basis.

England and Wales

As already mentioned, the possibility of diffusion of Continental Mesolithic cultural elements into Britain after the late seventh millennium bc is, on present evidence, unlikely. Clark (1955) indicated sites where part of the microlithic component could be defined as 'of Sauveterrian affinities', and this element may have appeared between 7000 and 6500 bc (Jacobi, 1976). Later sites show combinations of these forms with others, indicating continuity from earlier phases plus internal development.

A site which combines microliths of earlier Broad Blade type with later forms is Peacock's Farm, Shippea Hill, in the Cambridgeshire Fenland (Clark *et al.*, 1935; Clark and Godwin, 1962). The industry had Broad Blade obliquely-blunted points along with smaller geometric forms such as scalene triangles and trapezoids (Figure 7.2/32–40), also burins, scrapers and awls.

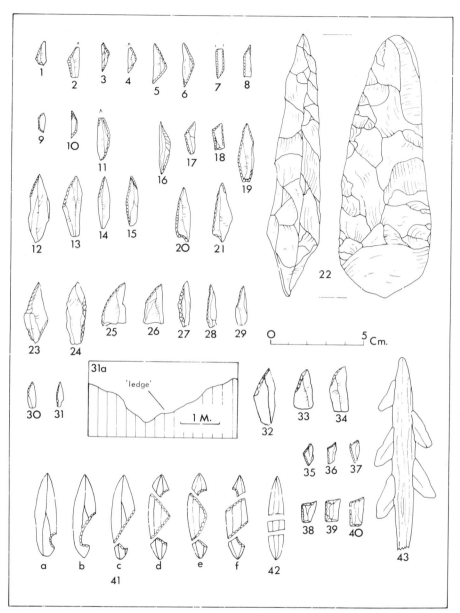

Figure 7.2: Later Mesolithic artifacts from the Pennines and south-east England. 1–11, 'Narrow Blade' geometric microliths (scalene triangles, rods, crescents), Broomhead Moor Site 5, Yorkshire; 12–22, 'Broad Blade' and 'Narrow Blade' microliths, 'Horsham points' (19–21) and tranchet core-axe (22), Selmeston, Sussex; 23–31, microliths (23–31) and cross-section of 'pit-dwelling' (31a), Abinger, Surrey; 32–40, microliths from Peacock's Farm, Shippea Hill, Cambridgeshire; 41, 42, suggested methods of microlith production – notching and snapping technique leaving 'microburin' as by-product (41a–f) and direct snapping to produce rectangular or rhomboidal blade segment (42); 43, suggested technique for hafting microliths as 'barbs' (43). After Radley *et al.*, 1974; Clark, 1934; Leakey, 1951; Clark, 1955; Rankine, 1956.

Pollen analysis shows occupation in the latest Boreal period (Vegetation Zone VIc), and there is a radiocarbon date of 5650 bc.

Mixed sites are in general to be found south of the Bristol Channel–Wash line and particularly in the south-east. A group distributed over the sandy heath areas of Kent, Sussex, Surrey and Hampshire combines both forms of microlith with a 'heavy element' of tranchet axes or adzes. The first major analysis of these sites was based on a concentration in the vicinity of Horsham, in Sussex (Clark, 1934a), and the association of forms of hollow-based microlithic points ('Horsham point') was noted. Further excavations gave rise to the idea of a separate Horsham culture (Clark and Rankine, 1939), but since the 'Horsham point', which was considered to be a type-implement, is known to occur outside the main area, and as far north as Port St Mary and Glen Wyllan, on the Isle of Man (Clark, 1935, 1955), the group is no longer regarded as a distinct culture (Woodcock, 1973).

Among the more important sites in this south-eastern grouping are those at Farnham and Abinger, in Surrey (Figure 7.2/23–31) and at Selmeston, in Sussex (Figure 7.2/12–22) (Clark and Rankine, 1939; Leakey, 1951; Clark, 1934b). At these excavated sites a number of scooped hollows were discovered which were interpreted as 'pit-dwellings'. The depression at Abinger is a distorted oval with a maximum depth of 1.07 m, greatest length 4.27 m and a maximum width of 3.20 m (Figure 7.2/31a). At Selmeston (3 pits), pit no. 1 had a maximum depth of 1.12 m and was 4.57 m in greatest length. By comparison, the 4 pits at Farnham varied from 6 to 8 m in length, but were at most only 0.75 m deep; Leakey (1951, p. 38) attributes the greater depths at Selmeston and Abingdon to the ease of digging in the softer Greensand by contrast with the gravels at Farnham. The Abinger pit had a sloping 'ledge' running along its eastern side, suggested as a possible sleeping-place (Leakey, 1951, p. 36). Two post holes were discovered, at right angles to the long axis of the pit and just beyond its edge on either side of the north-western end.

> It would seem possible that these two post holes carried short forked poles with a horizontal cross piece between the forks, and that the structure forming the roof of the pit consisted of a framework of branches and saplings leaning against the cross piece and with their ends resting on the land surface surrounding the edge of the pit. Some such structure, covered with grass and bracken, and then perhaps the skins of deer, would provide a reasonably waterproof roofing to the pit and convert it into comfortable and warm sleeping quarters (Leakey, 1951, p. 37).

The flint industries at these three sites have been classified by Mellars as Type B1, that is closely related to his Type B ('balanced') assemblages, but with a high percentage (70–85 per cent) of microliths and an important element of end-scrapers (Mellars, 1976c). The pits are seen as an indication of cold-season occupation. At Deerleap Wood, near Wotton, Surrey, about 2 km to the north of Abinger, a Mesolithic flint-knapping site was overlain by a Bronze Age bell-barrow (Corcoran, 1963). The flint industry was of the type common to the West Surrey Greensand, the 'heavy element' represented by a small tranchet axe (Plates VII–VIII). At Belle Tout, Sussex, on a headland just west

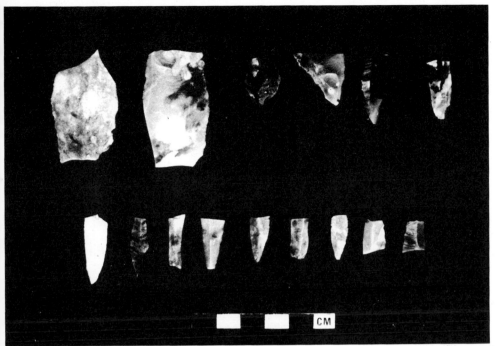

Plate VII: An awl or borer, a 'saw' (top row, first and second from left), and a selection of smaller flints and microliths. Deerleap Wood, Surrey. Dept. of Archaeology, University of Glasgow.

Plate VIII: Small tranchet axe, Deerleap Wood, Surrey. Dept. of Archaeology, University of Glasgow.

of Beachy Head, a small Mesolithic flint industry was recovered during the excavation of a Beaker Settlement site (Bradley, 1970).

The difficulties involved in basing any meaningful interpretation of site-function on flint assemblages alone can be demonstrated by the evidence from Kettlebury, West Surrey (Rankine, 1949b). Kettlebury II had an industry which has been classified (Mellars, 1976c) as Type A ('microlith-dominated'), whereas the 180 m distant site of Kettlebury I had an assemblage with only 4 microliths but with 18 scrapers (82 per cent of the 'essential tool inventory'). This could indicate either two contemporary sites with differing functions (II perhaps involved mainly with hunting and I with more 'domestic' activities), or sites in use at completely different times or seasons, although the excavator has assumed contemporaneity on the basis of both groups of flints being unpatinated.

A large site at Oakhanger Warren, Hampshire, has an assemblage in which Broad Blade types of microlith, mainly obliquely-blunted points, are dominant, with only a few geometric forms (Rankine and Dimbleby, 1960). Radiocarbon dates (on hazel-nut shells and pine charcoal) of 4350 and 4430 bc have been obtained, but the possibility of contamination by recent humus has been suggested, and the samples were not pretreated (Jacobi, 1973, pp. 238–9). A type of stone implement found at Oakhanger and in Mesolithic contexts elsewhere in south-eastern England is the hour-glass perforated pebble or 'mace-head' and the partially hollowed or 'cupped' pebble (Rankine, 1949a, 1956). Similar artifacts are known in the Sandinavian Mesolithic, for example at Svaerdborg and Ertebølle (Clark, 1936). The perforated forms may have been intended for hafting, although some have no traces of wear of any kind, and the cupped stones may have been held between thumb and forefinger as general-purpose hammer stones (Figure 7.3/1).

Further traces of shelters might be represented by the pits at Wakefords Copse, near Havant, Hampshire (Bradley and Lewis, 1974), where charcoal from a pit containing Mesolithic flints has been dated to 3730 bc. Stronger evidence for actual dwelling structures has been excavated at Broom Hill, Braishfield, Hampshire (O'Malley, 1976, 1978). Several pits were discovered on the site, the largest (Pit 3) located within a rough oval of 14 post holes. The post holes were on average 17 cm in diameter, with a depth of up to 11 cm, and scattered around them were smaller stake holes. The tent or structure thus delimited would have measured about $4\frac{1}{2}$ by 5 m across. So far, almost 90,000 pieces of worked flint have been recovered from the site, including gravers or burins, scrapers, over 100 core adzes and about 2,600 microliths. The microliths were mainly of later, geometric forms – rods, scalene triangles, trapezoids and rhomboids. The sealed deposits in Pit 3 within the 'dwelling structure' area contained enough charcoal for several radiocarbon dates. The bottom of the pit gave dates of 6590 ± 150 bc (Q-1192), 6565 ± 150 bc (Q-1528) and 6365 ± 150 bc (Q-1383); the top of the pit infill yielded a date of 5880 ± 120 bc (Q-1460) and some charred hazel-nuts from a level some 5 cm above the top of the filling of the pit were dated to 5270 ± 120 bc (Q-1191). A nearby pit (2) with a hearth was dated to 4584 ± 125 bc (Q-1128). These dates are not shown in Figure 7.4. The scatter of stake holes associated with a late Mesolithic industry at Downton, in Wiltshire (Higgs, 1959), might indicate a light form of shelter.

Evidence for coastal activity, as mentioned above, is greater in the later Mesolithic, earlier sites having been lost to marine transgression and deposition, and in the sinking of the southern North Sea region. Ample evidence for the exploitation of this habitat has been recovered at Culver Well, on the Isle of Portland, Dorset (Palmer, 1970, 1976). A large shell midden consisting of limpet (*Patella*) and winkle (*Littorina littorea*) remains, flint artifacts and charcoal was partly covered by a 'floor' of limestone slabs 3–4 m wide and over 31 m long. The most common form of microlith was the scalene triangle and there were many heavier, pointed implements ('picks'). The most important raw material appears to have been Portland chert; Mesolithic artifacts of this material have been traced to locations as distant as Land's End and the Bristol Channel. Charcoal from hearths within the midden and under the limestone slab 'floor' gave dates of 5200 and 5151 bc. At Westward Ho!, Devon, a midden containing oyster (*Ostrea edulis*), mussel (*Mytilus edulis*) and limpet shells, remains of deer, pig and hedgehog, and flint artifacts, was overlain by a layer of peat dated to 4635 bc (Churchill and Wymer, 1965).

In Wales, the best-known sites at present are coastal and the evidence for these has been reviewed (Wainwright, 1963). At Freshwater West, south-west Pembrokeshire (Wainwright, 1959), the flint industry consisted mainly of scrapers (72 per cent), blades, awls and burins, with only one doubtful microlith despite the presence of 4 microburins. This would be classified as a 'scraper dominated' (Type C) assemblage (Mellars, 1976c), perhaps indicating the working of skins or hides as a major activity. There were quantities of mussels, limpets and whelks (*Buccinum undatum*), and among the stone tools, 11 'limpet scoops' – used elongated beach pebbles (Figure 7.3/9), an implement common to many British west coastal sites, but on present evidence restricted in Wales to sites in the south (Livens, 1972). Peat associated with the Freshwater West artifacts has been dated to 4010 bc. On Caldy Island, excavations at Daylight Rock (Lacaille and Grimes, 1955) have revealed an industry with microliths consisting of larger obliquely-blunted points associated with smaller trapezes, crescents, scalene and isosceles triangles.

A rare example in the west of the association of geometric microliths with tranchet axes is at Nab Head, Pembrokeshire (Gordon-Williams, 1926; Wainwright, 1963) mentioned in Chapter 6 above. Microlithic rods, triangles and needle points, as well as a number of obliquely-blunted points, were recovered along with 3 tranchet axes and about 20 'limpet scoops' (Figure 7.3/2–9). At Aberystwyth, Cardiganshire (Wainwright, 1963), obliquely-blunted points and geometric microliths (Figure 7.3/10–15) were associated with about 30 'limpet scoops'. These sites are not definitely datable, but the tranchet axes at Nab Head might represent a late intrusion.

Another site with geometric and non-geometric microliths is Prestatyn, Flintshire (Clarke, 1938, 1939; Wainwright, 1963). Obliquely-blunted points formed 28 per cent of the microliths and scalene triangles accounted for 50 per cent. The total 'essential tools' comprised 81 per cent microliths and 19 per cent scrapers, classified as a Type B1 assemblage – 'balanced', but with a large percentage of microliths and a significant scraper element (Mellars, 1976c). Despite the coastal emphasis, information for inland sites is increasing, although surface collections are still the main form of evidence. Mesolithic material discovered under a Bronze Age cairn during rescue excavations in the

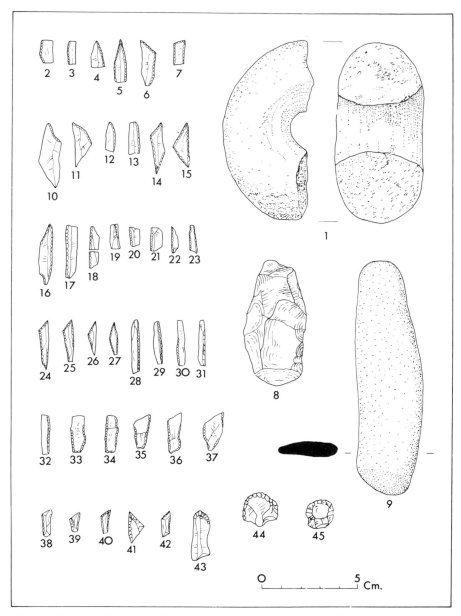

Figure 7.3: 1, perforated pebble 'mace-head', Oakhanger, Hampshire; 2–7, microliths; 8, small tranchet axe; 9, 'limpet scoop', Nab Head, Pembrokeshire; 10–15, microliths, Aberystwyth, Cardiganshire; 16–23, microliths, Dunford Bridge Site B, Yorkshire; 24–37, microliths, White Gill, Yorkshire; 38–42, microliths; 43–45, scrapers, Lyne Hill, Northumberland. After Wainwright, 1963; Rankine and Dimbleby, 1960; Radley *et al.*, 1974; Radley, 1969; Raistrick, 1933.

Brenig Valley, Denbighshire, has been dated to 5700 ± 80 bc (HAR-656) (Lynch and Allen, 1975).

Reference has already been made to sites of earlier Mesolithic date in the Pennines and the likelihood that some of them may have been the summer season equivalents of lowland settlements such as Star Carr. Others are of later Mesolithic date and the assemblages are small enough to indicate short-term occupation. From the site of March Hill, West Yorkshire, excavated by Francis Buckley in the 1920s, a quantity of charcoal from what might have been a cooking pit, associated with geometric microliths and under about 60 cm of peat, has been dated to 4070 and 3900 bc (Radley *et al.*, 1974; Switsur and Jacobi, 1975). At Rocher Moss, West Yorkshire, a small recently excavated site with a 'microlith-dominated' assemblage consisting mainly of rod-like forms has been dated to 3880 bc (Switsur and Jacobi, 1975; Mellars, 1976c). A further site with a microlithic assemblage dominated by rod-like forms is that at Dunford Bridge (Site B), West Yorkshire (Figure 7.3/16–23). Charcoal from a hearth gave a date of 3430 bc. Twenty metres distant, the site of Dunford Bridge A had an assemblage in which the dominant microlith form was the scalene triangle; a roughly oval patch of flat stones may have provided a crude paving around the hearth area and suggests a temporary shelter possibly 2.6 m in diameter. The number of artifacts and generally small size of most of these Pennine Narrow Blade sites, together with the mainly hunting function implied by microlith-dominated assemblages, suggest mobile groups perhaps no larger than the single nuclear family, or possibly without women (absence of evidence for 'domestic' activites such as the preparation of skins), engaged in summer hunting and halting briefly at camp-sites where only the minimum quantities of artifacts necessary for the hunt were manufactured (Radley *et al.*, 1974; Mellars, 1976c).

In a lower-lying and less exposed location is the rock shelter at Thorpe Common, near Thorpe Salvin, south Yorkshire (Mellars, 1976c). Again the industry appears to be dominated by microliths, indicating hunting as a major activity, but the suggestion of summer occupation, implied at the higher Pennine sites, is not so obvious here. The dwelling is a more substantial structure, with a row of limestone blocks perhaps serving as a support or foundation for a tent or hut habitation. This, plus the somewhat more tenuous evidence of a fragmentary hazel-nut shell, has been taken to suggest winter occupation. Burnt wood and bone fragments (including red deer) have given three radiocarbon dates between 4500 and 3700 bc (*Radiocarbon*, 17 (1975), p. 45).

Radley (1969) has described sites with mainly microlithic assemblages at White Gill, Mauley Cross and Farndale Moor, and others at Danby Low Moor, Glaisdale Moor and Commondale Moor, all on the North Yorkshire Moors. The evidence is mainly from surface collections, and the richest site is that at White Gill, about 380 m above present sea level, where microliths formed 97 per cent of the assemblage studied. Rods (317) and triangles (278) were dominant and there were a few tranchet forms (Figure 7.3/24–37). At Farndale Moor, the microliths were mainly rods and at Mauley Cross roughly equal quantities of rods, triangles and points. On the basis of the tranchet forms and the occurrence of the flints *in* the peat layer rather than under it, Radley (1969, p. 323) has suggested a late date, perhaps 4000–3000 bc, for these assemblages. The sites are seen as small hunting camps, probably used by summer-season groups pursuing red deer, pig and birds and perhaps clearing vegetation by burning. In a study of the effects of early human activity on the vegetation of the North Yorkshire Moors in initiating a change from forested to moorland and heath conditions (Simmons 1969a,b, 1975b; Sprat and Simmons, 1976), a 5 cm thick layer of charcoal was discovered within the blanket peat at North Gill. This has been dated to 4416 bc (BM-425) and may be related to these later Mesolithic hunting activities.

Intermediate between the Moors upland region and the lower coastal environment is a group of sites on the Upleatham Hills, north Yorkshire. These are located at about 165–170 m above present sea-level and overlooking the Tees estuary (Spratt *et al.*, 1976). Site1 had 51 per cent microliths, 42 per cent scrapers and a few burins. The microliths consisted of rods and triangles. The favourable location of the sites has been noted:

> eustatic rise in sea level created inter-tidal habitats quite far inland in the case of long estuaries such as those of the southern Lake District and the Tees. The littoral and off-shore fauna would have had a higher species diversity and biomass than that of today and thus spatially and biologically have presented a rich opportunity for subsistence gatherers and fishermen (Simmons, 1975b, p. 4).

The location of the sites, the 'balanced' aspect of the tool assemblages plus the presence of large numbers of hearth stones has led to their interpretation as base camps or intensive exploitation camps. They may have had a catchment area from the sea coast and Tees estuary to the inland hills, and been concerned more with activities such as food preparation than with hunting, occupied for lengthier periods, and perhaps representing the winter sites of the hunters on the Moors, possibly an example of the Later Mesolithic functional equivalent of the Star Carr base camp (Simmons, 1975b). Sites at Lyne Hill, near Newbiggin, Northumberland (Raistrick, 1933) have flint industries with almost equal proportions of microliths and scrapers (Figure 7.3/38–45), a further example of the 'balanced' assemblage at coastal sites (Mellars, 1976c).

The scarcity of evidence for earlier Mesolithic sites in north-west England has been mentioned, but there is a growing body of material indicating human occupation in later phases. Sites have been identified at Tarnflat, St Bees, Drigg and Eskmeals, in Cumberland (Cherry, 1963, 1969, 1973; Cherry and Pennington, 1965; Nickson and MacDonald, 1955). The flints are mainly surface collections with raw material including volcanic tuff (particularly at St Bees) as well as beach-pebble flint. A particular concentration of sites in the Eskmeals area lies along an old shoreline, now averaging 7–8 m above modern sea level, and running from Newbiggin in the north to Skelda Hill in the south. Excavations at Monk Moors, Eskmeals (Bonsall, 1976 and in press), have revealed a flint industry associated with hearths and stake holes. The raw material here is again beach pebble flint and the assemblages are microlith-dominated with an emphasis on micro-triangles, but including a few obliquely-blunted points of Broad Blade type. The catchment area would have included exploitation of the sea coast and combined estuaries of the Esk, Mite and Irt (with the advantages already quoted for the Tees estuary), plus inland hunting to the foothills of the Fells to the east. Dates so far obtained (not shown in Figure 7.4) are

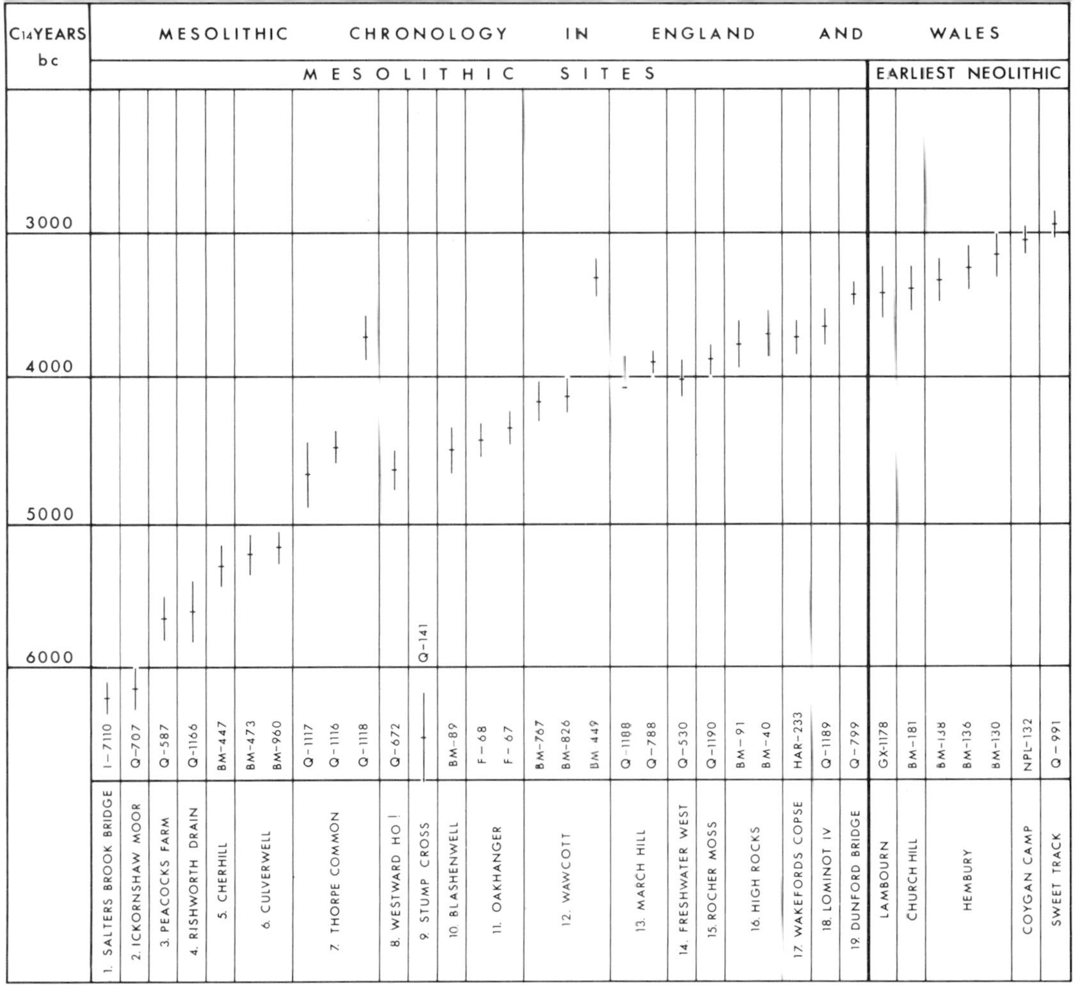

Figure 7.4: Radiocarbon chronology of later Mesolithic sites in England and Wales. The radiocarbon dates are shown with one standard deviation (the ± figure). For example, the date for Westward Ho! (No. 8, Lab. No. Q-672) is 4635 ± 130 bc. The standard deviation does not indicate a range within which the true date lies; it shows rather that there is a 68 per cent chance that the Westward Ho! date lies between 4765 and 4505 bc.

MESOLITHIC CHRONOLOGY IN ENGLAND AND WALES

MESOLITHIC SITES

C14 YEARS bc	Site	Lab. No.
3000 / 4000 / 5000 / 6000	1. SALTERS BROOK BRIDGE	I-7110
	2. ICKORNSHAW MOOR	Q-707
	3. PEACOCKS FARM	Q-587
	4. RISHWORTH DRAIN	Q-1166
	5. CHERHILL	BM-447
	6. CULVERWELL	BM-473
		BM-960
	7. THORPE COMMON	Q-117
		Q-1116
		Q-1118
	8. WESTWARD HO !	Q-672
	9. STUMP CROSS	Q-141
	10. BLASHENWELL	BM-89
	11. OAKHANGER	F-68
		F-67
	12. WAWCOTT	BM-767
		BM-826
		BM 449
	13. MARCH HILL	Q-1188
		Q-788
	14. FRESHWATER WEST	Q-530
	15. ROCHER MOSS	Q-1190
	16. HIGH ROCKS	BM-91
		BM-40
	17. WAREFORDS COPSE	HAR-233
	18. LOMINOT IV	Q-1189
	19. DUNFORD BRIDGE	Q-799

EARLIEST NEOLITHIC

Site	Lab. No.
LAMBOURN	GX-1178
CHURCH HILL	BM-181
HEMBURY	BM-138
	BM-136
	BM-130
COYGAN CAMP	NPL-132
SWEET TRACK	Q-991

5430 ± 370 bc (Q-1356) and 4802 ± 156 bc (BM-1216), from charcoal from Site 1.

Evidence for Mesolithic occupation on the Isle of Man now seems well established (Clark, 1935). The presence of forms of hollow-based point and other microliths at Glen Wyllan and Port St Mary has been mentioned. A recent summary of the evidence suggests two major Mesolithic phases: a microlithic tradition which may represent the initial occupation of the island, and a later 'heavy-bladed' industry which has been compared with the later Mesolithic of Ireland (Woodman, 1978).

Ireland

The earliest inhabitants of Ireland, on present evidence, had arrived by the end of the eighth millennium bc. The main excavated site is that at Mount Sandel, Co. Derry (Woodman, 1977a), described in Chapter 6 above, but there are others at Castleroe, Co. Derry, Glynn, Co. Antrim, and as far south as Lough Boora, Co. Offaly (Woodman, 1978b; Ryan, 1978). Radiocarbon dates have recently been obtained for two of these sites: at Castleroe the dates are 6805 ± 135 bc (UB-2171) and 6610 ± 75 bc (UB-2172), and at Lough Boora the dates are 6525 ± 75 bc (UB-2199) and 6400 ± 70 bc (UB-2200) (Woodman, 1978b). These dates are not shown in Figure 7.7. The industries show a controlled flaking technique, producing microliths (including scalene triangles, needle points and rods), micro-awls, face-trimmed core axes and flake axes (Figure 7.6/1–11). On the basis of the microliths, these assemblages have been classified with the British Later Mesolithic 'Narrow Blade' industries, although in terms of radiocarbon chronology the earliest known English site at Filpoke Beacon, Co. Durham (6810 bc) is still somewhat younger than the earliest dates for Mount Sandel. The core axes may be a survival of British Earlier Mesolithic forms, although these do not appear in the Later Mesolithic of England and Wales.

As a result of early work in the Larne Lough area (Larne, Curran Point, Island Magee), the term 'Larnian' was introduced to indicate a cultural grouping, later extended to embrace the whole of the Irish Mesolithic (Movius, 1940a, 1942, 1953a; Mitchell, 1949a, 1970, 1971; Herity, 1970; etc.), and eventually imposed on the Mesolithic of south-west Scotland (Lacaille, 1954). More recent research, particularly at Mount Sandel and Newferry 3, and reassessment of the available evidence, have suggested a division of the Irish Mesolithic into an earlier and a later phase, with the later phase showing a very insular development of implement styles and techniques. It has been proposed to retain the label 'Larnian' only in the restricted sense of a later Mesolithic technique of uncontrolled direct percussion (i.e. by using a hammer stone instead of a wood or bone punch) in the production of a heavy blade industry from large single-platformed cores (Figure 7.6/21). A common form of implement in these later assemblages is the 'Bann Flake' (for example Figure 7.6/17), used either as a knife or projectile-point (Woodman, 1974a,b, 1978b). 'The Larnian industry has all the appearance of being an industry which has been developed with the knowledge of the local flint and its limitations. It is an

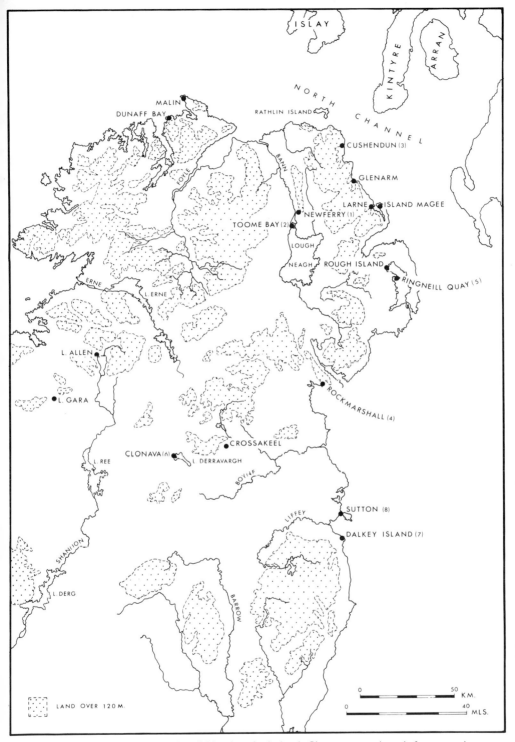

Figure 7.5: Map of later Mesolithic sites in Ireland. Sites are numbered, for example Rockmarshall (4), as in the chronological table at Figure 7.7.

industry at the end rather than the beginning of its development' (Woodman, 1974a, p. 248).

At the moment there is no evidence for an overlap between the earlier sites represented by Mount Sandel, Castleroe, etc., and the later Mesolithic of Ireland, so it is difficult to assess the degree of continuity or development. Recent excavations at Newferry (Site 3), Co. Antrim (Woodman, 1977b), have revealed a sequence of intermittent occupation over a long period of the later Mesolithic and a range of artifacts which change little in form but which show signs of changing techniques of manufacture and differences in the raw material used.

The site of Newferry (Site 3) lies on the eastern (Antrim) bank of the River Bann just north of the point where that river issues from the northern end of Lough Beg. On both banks in this vicinity there are several archaeological sites which have been excavated in the past (Movius, 1936; Whelan, 1938; Smith and Collins, 1971). The excavation at Site 3 shows a sequence of eight zones, the stratigraphical divisions being sedimentary rather than cultural, in which a sand bank site becomes gradually inundated with diatomite deposits. Apart from one level (Zone 7), there was little evidence of flint-working on site, so that most of the implements must have been made elsewhere, emphasising the scarcity of good flint in the Bann valley and supporting the idea of the site as a purely 'extraction' location. The raw materials for axes and other stone implements also had to be obtained at some distance from the site. The main forms in the flint assemblages were butt-trimmed and distally-trimmed flakes and blades, points and bar forms, backed knives and 'spokeshaves' (Figure 7.6/12–18). Only 5 burins and 13 scrapers were recovered from the whole sequence. The blades show a development from longish forms to shorter, broader types. There were also more than 40 polished stone axes and fragments (Figure 7.6/19–20), a tool hitherto accepted as diagnostic of Neolithic culture. The axes were found throughout the sequence, with concentrations in Zone 8 (several radiocarbon dates in the second half of the sixth millennium bc), Zone 5 (two dates in the mid-fifth millennium bc) and Zone 4 (one date of 4265 bc). In the earlier levels, the raw material for the stone axes was predominantly schist, but from Zone 5 onwards mudstone became more important. Fragments of three bone points were recovered from Zone 5; these points differ from the polished unbarbed point from Thatcham, Berkshire (Figure 6.5/11) in that they are rounded rather than flattish. They are typical of the bone points used in the Bann River area (Whelan, 1952; Woodman, 1978b, Figure 43) and on some coastal sites (Woodman, 1978b, Plate 4). Bones of eel (*Anguilla anguilla*) and a species of Salmonid were also recovered from the site. Seventeen radiocarbon dates were obtained from the site (not all shown in Figure 7.7), the main sequence being that between about 5500 and 3500 bc.

Woodman (1977b, pp. 192–4), in considering the function and possible seasonality of the Newferry site, has noted the scarcity of organic material – due mainly to the acidity of the deposits, which has affected even the cutting edges and surfaces of some of the polished axes. The location of the site right out in the middle of the river valley, with the possible hazard of flooding at certain times of the year, plus the presence of fish remains, has suggested a seasonal fishing encampment, occupied intermittently and briefly over a period of at least two thousand years, being gradually abandoned in the late fourth millennium bc as diatomite deposits developed across the site. The main activity may have been the catching of eels during their runs from Lough Neagh to the sea, probably between June and December, and before the severe winter floods. The range of tools, with its prominent heavy element of polished stone axes and scarcity of burins and scrapers, could be interpreted as the equipment necessary for the construction and maintenance of a system of weirs and fish-traps in a favourable area close to the exit-point of the Bann from Lough Beg. It has been suggested (Woodman, 1978b) that the Newferry sites, briefly occupied and seasonal, were within a 10 km 'site-catchment' radius of a possible base camp at Culbane, further north on the west (Derry) bank of the Bann, where Mesolithic material has also been recovered.

South of Newferry and Lough Beg, at Toome Bay, Co. Derry, on the northern shores of Lough Neagh just west of the Bann River exit, a small quantity of undiagnostic Mesolithic material was recovered by Mitchell (1955) in association with a hearth. Charcoal from the hearth gave a radiocarbon date of 5730 bc. The large number of sites now known along the course of the River Bann indicate its value as food-source and the degree of exploitation by Mesolithic hunter/fishers. This concentration is typical of the known evidence for Mesolithic sites in north-eastern Ireland, being confined mainly to lakeside, riverside and coastal locations. So far, there is little evidence of occupation much higher than about 35 m above present sea level. When this is compared with the distribution of Mesolithic sites in, for example, the Pennines of England (see above and Chapter 6) and when, moreover, the scarcity of red deer remains is taken into account, there appears to be a different pattern of seasonal movement and exploitation from that of the possibly over-simplified lowland/upland routine postulated above for England.

Many groups made use of the good flint obtainable from the chalk outcrops of the Antrim Plateau, and this material is particularly plentiful as derived flint nodules in the deposits of the north-eastern coasts. Sites here consist of temporary occupations, with flint-knapping debris, often inundated and disturbed by stages of the Holocene marine transgression (Chapter 5). In some areas shell heaps contain remains of limpets, oysters and periwinkles, and although there is less evidence, fish were undoubtedly a major part of the diet. At Cushendun, on the Antrim coast, in lower gravel and lower lagoon silt deposits, archaeological material was recovered in both fresh and heavily rolled condition (Movius, 1940a). Earlier and Later Mesolithic forms appear to be present and there was undoubted mixing. Charcoal and wood samples from the lower lagoon silts gave radiocarbon dates of 5720 bc and 5445 ± 65 bc, the latter date (UB-689) not shown in Figure 7.7. At Glenarm, Co. Antrim (Movius, 1937), flints were recovered from beach shingle and overlying topsoil. The assemblage consisted mainly of cores, broad flakes and end scrapers. The lower material, from the shingle, had many double- and multi-platformed (polyhedral) cores, suggesting a greater need for flakes rather than the heavy blades produced from the large single-platformed cores which seem to be typical of the later Mesolithic. Woodman (1967, 1974a) has suggested that this might be an early Neolithic industry associated directly with the raised beach. This is one example of the reassessment of a coastal flint assemblage, so many of which have automatically been classified as 'Mesolithic' in the past, yielding information which can shed some light on the early and perhaps 'pioneering' phase of the Neolithic in Britain and Ireland.

At Larne, the Curran Point peninsula has been investigated and excavated

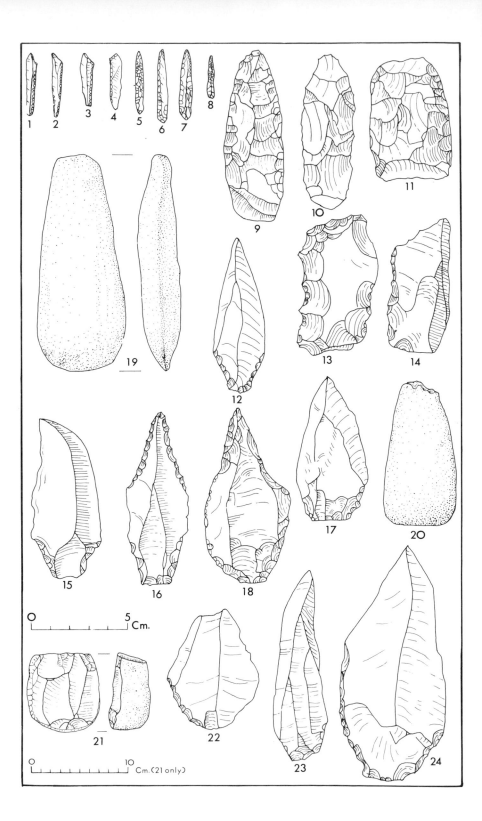

O ⊢——┼——┼——┼——┼——┤ 5 Cm.

O ⊢—┼—┼—┼—┼—┤ 10 Cm.(21 only)

many times in the past, most recently by the Harvard Excavation (Movius, 1953a), when it was described as 'the type site of the Irish Mesolithic'. Many thousands of flints, mostly derived and resorted flint-knapping debris, were recovered. However, in one gravel layer (Movius's Level C), large single-platformed cores (Figure 7.6/21) and flakes appear to be mainly fresh and unrolled. These have been classified by Woodman (1974a) as Later Mesolithic (Late or 'Ultimate' Larnian) and possibly just predating the maximum marine transgression. At Rough Island, Strangford Lough, Co. Down (Movius, 1940b), both rolled and fresh Earlier (microliths and small core and flake axes) and Later (single-platformed cores and short, wide blades) Mesolithic material has been either collected or excavated. A radiocarbon date of 3430 bc has been obtained for an occupation level at Ringneill Quay, also on Strangford Lough. This is shown in the table of radiocarbon dates at Figure 7.7, but its Mesolithic attribution must be in doubt, since the industry is undiagnostic and there appear to be bones of domesticated animals in association (Collins and Stephens, 1960).

On a coastal site at Rockmarshall, Co. Louth, three middens have been excavated (Mitchell, 1947, 1949b, 1971). Blades, flakes, single-platformed cores and bevel-ended beach pebbles (the 'limpet punches' or 'limpet hammers' of many British west coastal sites) were recovered, as well as shells of oyster, periwinkle and carpet-shell (*Paphia decussata*). Charcoal from Midden III, which was above the highest level of the maximum marine transgression, gave a radiocarbon date of 3520 bc.

A large midden, covering about 2000 square metres but fairly shallow, at Sutton, Co. Dublin, was excavated in 1949 and 1970 (Mitchell, 1956, 1972a). The industry had blades and flakes (including 'Bann Flakes'), single-platformed cores, two elongated bevel-ended beach pebbles and two broken polished axes of quartz-chlorite schist. In the report on the Sutton site and elsewhere, Mitchell (1972a, 1971) notes that flint knappers using a core to produce blades would often be faced with ridges or 'spurs' developing between the flake scars on the core. In trimming away these spurs, small scars would be left around the edge of the striking platform and these may often have been mistaken for wear scars, giving rise to the idea of a 'core-scraper'. Blade-flakes struck after this 'spur-trimming' would also have the scars, resembling secondary working (Hodges, 1964, p. 102).

Two shell middens (Sites II and V) at Dalkey Island, Co. Dublin (Liversage, 1968), contained quantities of Later Mesolithic material – single-platformed cores, Bann Flakes, blades, 'spokeshaves', polished stone axes and a large quantity of bevel-ended and elongated beach pebbles (Figure 7.6/22–24). A cache of 13 blades and flakes was discovered under the Site II midden. Charcoal from the Site V midden gave a radiocarbon date of 3350 bc.

Figure 7.6: Mesolithic artifacts from Ireland. 1–8, microliths, Mount Sandel; 9, 10, core axes; 11, flake axe, Mount Sandel; 12, butt-trimmed implement (Zone 8); 13, 'spokeshave' (Zone 7 main); 14, backed knife (Zone 6); 15, butt-trimmed (tanged) flake (Zone 5); 16, butt-trimmed borer (Zone 5); 17, butt-trimmed flake ('Bann Flake') (Zone 4); 18, heavy point (Zone 4); 19, ground stone axe (Zone 7); 20, ground stone axe (Zone 3), Newferry, Site 3; 21, large single-platformed core, Curran Point, Larne; 22–24, Dalkey Island. After Woodman, 1974a, 1977a,b, 1978b; Liversage, 1968.

The greatest concentration of sites away from the coast is, on present evidence, in the valley of the Bann and its tributaries, but a few sites are known from central Ireland. At the north-western end of Lough Derravaragh, Co. Westmeath, between the points where the River Inny enters and exits from the lough, a low knoll in Clonava Townland has a number of sites with Mesolithic material (Mitchell, 1970, 1972b). The only excavated area (Site 1) had a collection of blades and flakes of grey chert, mostly undiagnostic. Some charcoal in association gave a date of 3410 bc. Charred hazel-nuts were scattered around and it has been suggested that seeds of yellow water lily (*Nuphar luteum*), also found on the site, may have augmented the food supply. Mitchell (1970) mentions surface collections of flint and chert flakes from the vicinity of Crossakeel, near Kells, Co. Meath. Further west, on the shores of Lough Gara (Cross, 1953; Mitchell, 1970; Woodman, 1978b), collections of flint and chert were made when the water level was artificially lowered. The assemblages appear to be mixed, but there are quantities of the Later Mesolithic large, leaf-shaped Bann Flakes. Chert flakes and blades, including at least one large, leaf-shaped Bann Flake, have also been collected from the northern shore of Lough Allen, Co. Leitrim (Mitchell, 1970; Woodman, 1978b).

In the far north, at Dunaff Bay and Malin Head, Co. Donegal, collections of implements manufactured from beach-pebble flint have been recovered (Addyman and Vernon, 1966; Mitchell, 1970; Woodman, 1978b). Woodman notes the high percentage of single-platformed cores and the dominance of rough scraper or 'spokeshave' tools in the collection from Dunaff Bay.

As a result of recent excavations and discoveries plus a reassessment of existing collections, the Mesolithic period in Ireland has begun to develop a basic form which can perhaps be used as a framework for future research. As in England, there would appear to be a division into Earlier and Later stages with, however, the major differences that Ireland's Earlier Mesolithic has the 'Narrow Blade' geometric microliths of England's Later stage combined with core axes resembling English Earlier Mesolithic forms. The Irish Later Mesolithic would seem to be a mainly insular development with little or no exterior influences, consisting on the whole of a heavy blade industry combined with quantities of pre-Neolithic polished stone axes. The seasonal movements suggested for England, and based to some extent on the migrations of red deer herds, seem less important in Ireland. There are no truly upland sites in the Pennine sense, and red deer may well have played a lesser role in the hunting activities. Coastal regions and river valleys, with the emphasis at the moment on the Bann Valley, were the main areas exploited. Pig bones were recovered at Mount Sandel, Lough Boora, Cushendun, Sutton and Dalkey Island, and this animal could have been of greater economic importance than the red deer. Much work has still to be done, particularly in the south and west. More faunal remains are needed and much more information on seasonal activities, since the evidence at the moment appears to be from briefly-occupied 'extraction' sites rather than base-camps. The period of transition from earlier to later industries is largely unknown, as is the reason for the change. It is perhaps significant that Woodman ends his recent study (1978b, p. 211) of the Irish Mesolithic with a list of problems and questions.

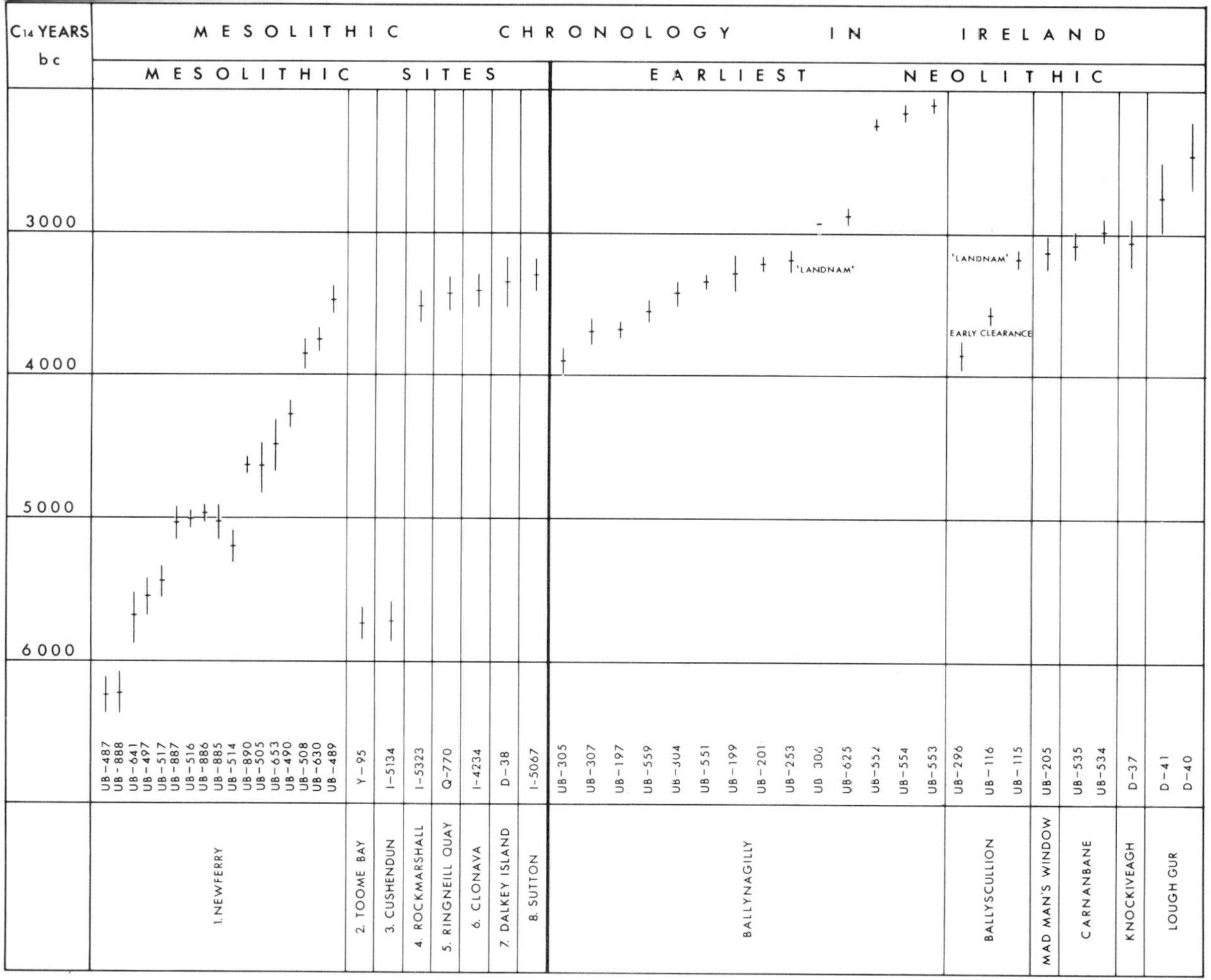

Figure 7.7: Radiocarbon chronology of Later Mesolithic sites in Ireland. The radiocarbon dates are shown with one standard deviation (the ± figure). For example, the date for Toome Bay (No. 2, Lab. No. Y-95) is 5730 ± 110 bc. The standard deviation does not indicate a range within which the true date lies; it shows rather that there is a 68 per cent chance that the Toome Bay date lies between 5840 and 5620 bc.

MESOLITHIC CHRONOLOGY IN IRELAND

MESOLITHIC — MESOLITHIC SITES — EARLIEST NEOLITHIC

C14 YEARS bc: 3000, 4000, 5000, 6000

LOUGH GUR: D-40, D-41
KNOCKIVEAGH: D-37
CARNANBANE: UB-534, UB-535
MAD MAN'S WINDOW: UB-205
BALLYSCULLION: UB-115, UB-116, UB-296 ('LANDNAM', EARLY CLEARANCE)
BALLYNAGILLY: UB-553, UB-554, UB-552, UB-625, UB-306, UB-253, UB-201, UB-199, UB-551, UB-304, UB-559, UB-197, UB-307, UB-305 ('LANDNAM')

8. SUTTON: I-5067
7. DALKEY ISLAND: D-38
6. CLONAVA: I-4234
5. RINGNEILL QUAY: Q-770
4. ROCKMARSHALL: I-5323
3. CUSHENDUN: I-5134
2. TOOME BAY: Y-95
1. NEWFERRY: UB-489, UB-630, UB-508, UB-490, UB-653, UB-505, UB-890, UB-514, UB-885, UB-986, UB-516, UB-887, UB-517, UB-497, UB-641, UB-888, UB-487

Scotland

The Mesolithic period in Scotland has in recent times been less studied than in other areas of Britain. There have been few detailed investigations or excavations, and the majority of sites are known from surface collections of flints. The nature of the sites themselves, the forms of raw material available and the small number of modern excavations on the whole preclude any direct comparisons with established culture-groups elsewhere; therefore the groupings used here are mainly geographical.

A body of evidence is now available for the effects of the main Holocene marine transgression on parts of the coastlands bordering the Firths of Clyde and Solway (Jardine, 1975b; Jardine and Morrison, 1976; Chapter 5 above), and some idea of the distribution of Mesolithic sites has been built up from casual finds and surface collections, careful field-work and one or two recent excavations (Figure 7.8). Along the Solway Firth some sites are located near the top of an old marine cliff rising above the landward edge of the main Holocene raised coastline. Their positions suggest activity when the present beach was covered by the sea. Typical of these locations and perhaps, therefore, typical of the coastal Mesolithic of the western Solway Firth are the sites of excavations at Low Clone and Barsalloch in Wigtownshire, where a radiocarbon date from the latter site of 4050 bc could indicate occupation at a period when the transgressing sea-level was at near-maximum stand (Cormack and Coles, 1968; Cormack, 1970). A number of sites lie between 9 and 15 metres above present sea level, and excavation evidence shows use of natural or scooped hollows as camp sites, usually at or near a point where freshwater streams flow into the sea, and with a very few stake holes indicating perhaps some form of light shelter or windbreak. Animal bone has not survived well on these sites, but fragments of burnt bone, possibly of red deer, from Low Clone show some exploitation of landward resources. Among the flint tools, microliths (Low Clone 46 per cent, Barsalloch 42 per cent), scrapers (Low Clone 32 per cent, Barsalloch 47 per cent) and burins (Low Clone 22 per cent, Barsalloch 11 per cent) suggest a 'balanced' assemblage (Mellars, 1976c), but perhaps emphasising only the littoral element in the subsistence economy of groups whose seasonal activities might have involved a cycle of both inland and coastal habitat exploitation (Cormack and Coles, 1968). In the western Solway Firth (Luce Bay and Wigtown Bay) raw material for artifacts was of mainly local origin, flint from beach pebbles and nearby glacial drift. At sites with surface collections from the Nith estuary eastwards, however, use of non-local and non-flint (chert, amethyst, etc.) materials and a somewhat more numerous microlithic element has suggested closer links with some inland sites located at Loch Doon, in Annandale and in Eskdale, and perhaps as far east as the Tweed Valley (Cormack, 1970; Mulholland, 1970). The 'heavy element' of equipment is non-existent, although Coles (1964) thought he might have identified a flint axe or adze tip from Stairhaven, on Luce Bay. At Barsalloch the burin is scarce, but a number of awls, 'reamers' and notched and utilised flakes have suggested to Cormack (1970, p. 80) possible activities connected with the manufacture of basketry or fish traps.

A barbed point of red deer antler found in 1895 in the bed of the River Dee at Cumstoun, Kirkcudbrightshire (Figure 7.10/13 and Plate IX) is further

Plate IX: Barbed points from north-east England and south-west Scotland. Top, red deer antler, bed of River Irvine, Shewalton, Ayrshire. Centre, red deer antler, River Dee, Cumstoun, Kircudbright. Bottom, antler, shore at Whitburn, Co. Durham. Casts in Hunterian Museum.

suggestive of estuarine/coastal activity in the area, but there is no secure evidence for its Mesolithic affinity or dating (Munro, 1908; Lacaille, 1939), nor for the shell 'middens' reported at Stranraer and on Heston Island in the Urr estuary (Truckell, 1963).

In Lacaille's study of the Scottish Mesolithic, the Ayrshire coast of the Firth of Clyde has only two main site-groupings, at Ballantrae and at Ardeer and Shewalton on either side of the mouth of the River Irvine (1954, Map, Figure 58). More recent surface collection and field-work have shown a greater density of sites between Ballantrae in the south and West Kilbride in the north of Ayrshire (Morrison, 1978, in press). At Ballantrae, the flints were collected from a stretch of beach lying between about 6 and 15 metres above present sea-level, and many were revealed by ploughing. Accurate stratigraphy is lacking, but the locations appear to have been on top of beach material or within an overlying sandy soil which also contained shells of *Littorina* sp. (Edgar, 1939; Lacaille, 1945, 1954). The location on the beach suggests occupation after maximum sea-level, and there is a mingling of possible Mesolithic material with what Lacaille (1945) has termed 'Neolithic facies' and 'Bronze Age facies'. Raw materials, apart from beach-pebble flint, included Arran pitchstone, quartz, chert and chalcedony. The combined environment of the Stinchar estuary and coastal area would have been ideal for exploitation by Mesolithic hunter/fisher groups, but little can be inferred as yet from the mixed assemblages.

Surface collections have also revealed Mesolithic activity in the Girvan area

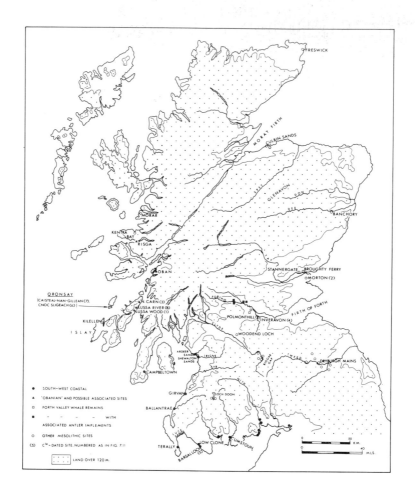

Figure 7.8: Map of Later Mesolithic sites in Scotland. Sites are numbered, for example Barsalloch (5), as in the chronological table at Figure 7.11.

(Morrison, 1978, in press), where lagoonal, estuarine and coastal habitats may have been available contemporaneously during the period of maximum marine transgression. The assemblages from this area consist of large quantities of flakes, many trimmed and retouched, cores, worked blades and a few microliths (backed blades, bladelets and points) with little evidence of geometric forms. The dominant raw material is beach-pebble flint with some chert and quartz.

At several sites in Ayrshire it has been possible to show, from radiocarbon dates for organic material immediately underlying coastal sediments, that the main Holocene marine transgression was under way between 6500 and 6000 radiocarbon years bc (Jardine, 1975b; Jardine and Morrison, 1976; Morrison, 1978, in press; Chapter 5 and Figure 5.3). Many sites are clustered along the landward margin of the raised coastal sediments deposited by the transgression and this is suggestive of occupation during the period of highest sea-level, although this cannot be proved definitely for sites lacking additional dating evidence, and many may be of a period post-dating the beginning of land recovery. Maximum sea-level may have been reached by about 4000 radiocarbon years bc, but in some areas recovery did not commence until about 3500 bc or later (Jardine, 1975b).

At Shewalton Sands and Moor, just south of the estuary of the River Irvine, many collections of flints have been made in dunes and areas which would have been covered by the maximum stand of Holocene sea-level and others from just beyond the landward margin of the transgression. It is not now possible to locate the exact provenance of some of the assemblages described (Lacaille, 1930), but some of the microliths might now be defined as Later Mesolithic (Figure 7.5/1–12) – rods, trapezes, lunates, scalene and equilateral triangles. As at Ballantrae and Girvan, the combined estuaries of the Garnock and Irvine, plus the enlarged coastal territory, would have offered wide hunting and food-collecting possibilities. A barbed antler point, undated but possibly of this general period, was recovered from the bed of the River Irvine at Shewalton in 1938 (Figure 7.10/12 and Plate IX) (Lacaille, 1939). The use of the phrase 'coastal Mesolithic' to describe these south-west Scottish sites should be taken to indicate coastal location rather than to imply a perennial coastal culture, which is as yet unproven.

At Campbeltown, in Kintyre, flint artifacts were discovered at Dalaruan, Millknowe and Albyn Distillery (Gray, 1894; McCallien and Lacaille, 1941). The location of the Dalaruan and Millknowe artifacts apparently within the upper level of raised beach deposits could indicate occupation before maximum sea-level was reached, but might also be attributable to a period when land recovery had already commenced, with minor marine re-advances. Some of the implements appear to have been rolled, but most are quite sharp. The flints from Albyn Distillery were either on top of beach deposits or within overlying material, suggesting post-maximum sea-level occupation.

None of these discoveries shows any trace of the wide range of artifacts made of organic materials which have survived in the caves near Oban and on open, shell-heap sites on some offshore islands. These sites have been labelled 'Obanian', taking the cultural name, proposed by Movius (1940a), from the type-site at MacArthur Cave, Oban, but the unifying element may be no more than similar responses to coastal economic environments, or one specialised facet of the more general western Scottish coastal groups. The cultural status is, in any case, overdue for reassessment, particularly in view of recent work on Jura and Oronsay. The important elements are: the large number of implements made of bone and antler (barbed points, 'limpet scoops', mattocks, awls, pins, etc.); the wide use of flat, elongated beach pebbles as 'limpet scoops/punches' or hammers; the presence of large shell heaps or middens.

The major mainland sites are all in and around Oban – MacArthur Cave, Mackay Cave, Distillery Cave, Gasworks Cave, Dunollie Cave and Druimvargie rock shelter (Anderson, 1895, 1898; Macdougall, 1907; Turner,

1895). At MacArthur Cave, 10 metres above present sea-level, many bone 'tools' were recovered – lengths of bone with rounded ends showing traces of rubbing, polishing and abrasion. These have often been classified as 'limpet scoops', but many were possibly used in the preparation of skins; there were also some pins and awls of bone. Of seven barbed points of antler, only two were complete (Figure 7.10/2,3) and one of the these has a perforated base like a harpoon, resembling a smaller version from Whitburn, Co. Durham (Mellars, 1970) (Figure 7.10/1 and Plate IX). A broken point (Figure 7.10/4) has been re-used with the fracture smoothed into a rounded butt. Stone and flint were poorly represented at MacArthur Cave, and shells included limpet, periwinkle, whelk, mussel, oyster, scallop (*Pecten* sp.) and cockle (*Cardium* sp.).

The rock shelter of Druimvargie, south of the town of Oban, stood at about 15 metres above present sea-level in an area which would have been a shallow arm of the sea at maximum transgression. Occupation material, 1.2 m thick, contained shells, remains of crab, mammal bones and charcoal from hearths. The main form of artifact was again the round-ended bone 'limpet scoop' or smoother, one made of a boar's tusk. Highly unusual were the two broken barbed points of bone (Figure 7.10/5,6), uniserially barbed, and unlike any other Scottish barbed points apart, perhaps, from the small point from Glenavon, Banffshire (see below). Lacaille (1954) has compared the Druimvargie points to those of Maglemosian Gohra-Wohrle type (Clarke, 1936, p. 116), but there are also resemblances to the deeply slashed notches on the group of points from Brandenburg, Germany (Clark, 1936, p. 119; Gramsch, 1973, p. 35), if such distant links need to be mentioned.

The main island sites of the 'Obanian' group are Oronsay and Risga. Oronsay lies off the southern end of the larger island of Colonsay, about 15 km west of Jura and about 10 km north of Islay. The sites are shell heaps or middens – Cnoc Sligeach, Cnoc Riach, Cnoc Coig (Cnoc = Gaelic 'mound, knoll'), Caisteal-nan-Gillean I and II, Priory Midden, etc. Some of the sites have been known since the nineteenth century (Grieve, 1885; Anderson, 1898) and early twentieth century (Bishop, 1914), while modern investigations are continuing to add to the evidence of chronology, economy and environment (Mellars and Payne, 1971; Jardine, 1977a, 1978). The early excavations led to the idea that shellfish were the major item of diet, but modern sieving techniques have yielded large quantities of very small fish bones, showing that sea fish, and in particular the saithe (*Pollachius virens*) were probably more important, either fresh or smoked, than shellfish.

There is a somewhat larger flint industry than that represented by the mainland caves, but distinctive microlithic forms are scarce. The beach-pebble hammer stones or 'limpet punches' occur in large quantities (Plate X) and there are much larger hammer or anvil stones. Grooved or furrowed pebbles and pieces of pumice stone may have served as hones or grinding-stones for the many bone and antler points and pins recovered from the shell heaps; antler had also been used for mattock-like tools (Plate XI). Barbed points of antler or bone vary widely in form or cutting technique, from the comparatively free-standing barbs on the point from Cnoc Sligeach (Figure 7.10/10 and Plate XII) to the slightly notched forms (now lost) from Caisteal-nan-Gillean I (Figure 7.10/7–9). Shells include limpet, periwinkle, whelk, oyster, cockle, scallop and razor (*Ensis* sp.). Some of the scallop shells (*Pecten maximus*) show edge wear,

Plate X: Three beach-pebble hammer-stones ('limpet hammers', 'limpet punches') and two bone points or awls, Cnoc Sligeach, Oronsay. Hunterian Museum.

Plate XI: Three antler 'mattocks', one perforated for hafting, Cnoc Sligeach, Oronsay. Hunterian Museum.

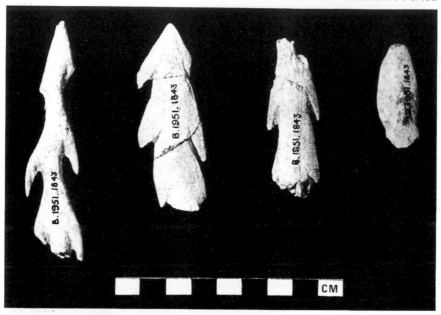

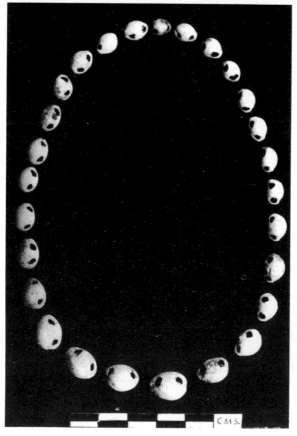

Plate XII: Parts of barbed points, one of antler (second from left), three of bone, Cnoc Sligeach, Oronsay. Hunterian Museum.

Plate XIII: A selection of double-perforated cowrie shells (*Trivia* sp.). Cnoc Sligeach, Oronsay. Hunterian Museum.

suggesting use as scoops or ladles. Large numbers of cowrie shells (*Trivia* sp.) from Cnoc Sligeach have twin perforations, probably for stringing as necklaces (Plate XIII).

Most of these sites are located between 10 and 15 metres above present sea-level and none is more than 400 metres from the present shore, probably quite close to the shoreline of the maximum transgression and perhaps contemporary with it. Recent dates on charcoal from Cnoc Coig (not shown on Figure 7.11) are: base of midden, 3695 ± 80 bc (Q-1353) and 3585 ± 140 bc (Q-1354); upper part of midden, 3545 ± 75 bc (Q-1351) and 3480 ± 130 bc (Q-1352) (Jardine, 1977a). Radiocarbon dates from all sites range between 3800 and 3200 bc, suggesting a relatively short duration for this somewhat specialised form of hunting and gathering. Compared with fish and shellfish, land mammal remains and bird bones are scarce, a point which could be taken to indicate seasonal occupation. Post or stake holes suggest only the flimsiest of shelters, or perhaps the supports for drying or smoking racks. Apart from Colonsay, the nearest land of any size is represented by the islands of Jura and Islay, whereas the supposedly 'culturally linked' mainland caves at Oban are about 65 km to the north-east. Further analysis of food remains from recent excavations on Oronsay may throw more light on the possibility of permanent occupation as against seasonal visits.

The small island of Risga lies at the mouth of Loch Sunart, in North Argyllshire, between Ardnamurchan to the north and Morvern to the south. The island is roughly oval, measuring approximatley 460 m east-west by 365 m north-south. Near its eastern end is a shell midden, about 18 m from the shoreline and about 9 m above present high-water mark, excavated in 1920 (Mann, 1920; Lacaille, 1951, 1954), but not yet fully published. There is quite a large flint and quartz industry, Morvern being one of the few recognised sources of flint in Scotland, and a number of the end-worn beach-pebble hammer stones, as well as quantities of larger, unworked stones perhaps used as clubs or anvils. The bone and antler industry has the usual range of artifacts, barbed points, round-ended 'limpet scoops', pins and awls, mattocks and a bone fish hook, suggesting line fishing (Plate XIV). Shellfish include mussel, oyster, scallop, cockle, razor-shell, limpet, whelk and periwinkle. There were also remains of common crab (*Cancer pagurus*) and fiddler crab (*Portunus puber*). Among the fish remains were tope (*Galeus canis*), spiny dog fish (*Acanthias vulgaris*), angel fish (*Squatina squatina*), skate (*Raia batis*), thornback ray (*Raia clavata*), conger eel (*Conger conger*), grey mullet (*Mugil capito*), haddock (*Gadus aeglefinus*) and black sea-bream (*Cantharus lineatus*). Among the bird bones were those of the great auk or garefowl (*Alca impennis*), which was last seen on St Kilda about 1820 and finally exterminated on Iceland in 1844 (Grieve, 1885). It has been suggested that some of the club-like stones may have been used to kill this flightless bird. Other birds represented were gannet (*Sula bassana*), goose (*Anser* sp.), cormorant (*Phalacrocorax carbo*), shag (*Phalacrocorax aristotelis*), red-breasted merganser (*Mergus serrator*), water rail (*Rallus aquaticus*), gull (*Larus* sp.), common tern (*Sterna hirundo*), razorbill (*Alca torda*) and guillemot (*Uria aalge*). A number of mammal bones included red deer, wild boar (*Sus scrofa*), otter (*Lutra vulgaris*), marten (*Martes foina*), common seal (*Phoca vitulina*), grey seal (*Halichoerus grypus*) and rorqual (*Balaenoptera* sp.). It is likely that

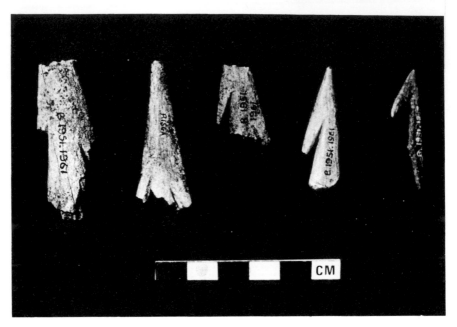

Plate XIV: Fragments of barbed points and a 'fish hook'. The fish hook could be a re-used fragment of a broken barbed point, such as the second from the right. Risga Island, Loch Sunart, Argyllshire. Hunterian Museum.

some of the land mammal remains were brought to the island by the hunter/gatherer groups.

Sites with stone industries which might reflect the activities of the Risga or similar groups on the mainland are known around the coasts of Ardnamurchan, Moidart, Arisaig and Morar in northern Argyllshire and southern Inverness-shire (Lacaille, 1951). On Islay, a number of sites are known from surface collections and some have been reported in various issues of *Discovery and Excavation, Scotland*, particularly in the 1960s and 1970s. Excavations at Kilellan Farm, on the western shore of Loch Gruinart, North Islay, have revealed an assemblage of microliths, scrapers, cores and knapping debris 'of Mesolithic aspect' beneath a Late Neolithic/Early Bronze Age occupation (Burgess, 1976).

Excavations on the island of Jura have recovered evidence of Mesolithic occupation for various periods from possibly pre-transgression to late third millennium bc (Mercer, 1968, 1970a,b, 1971, 1972, 1974a,b,c). Three periods are recognised, the earliest represented at Lussa Bay and Lussa Wood I. The Lussa Bay microliths include backed bladelets, triangles and trapeze forms (Figure 7.9/13–16); there are also awl-like points (Figure 7.9/15) and flake and blade end-scrapers (Figure 7.9/16). At Lussa Wood I, a stone feature consisting of three rings (Figure 7.9/17), interpreted as cooking places, enclosed a scatter of minute bone fragments, limpet shell, red ochre and charred hazel-nut shells and wood. The latter material has given dates of 6244 bc, for a sample from one ring, and 6013 bc for combined samples from the two other rings (Mercer, 1974a).

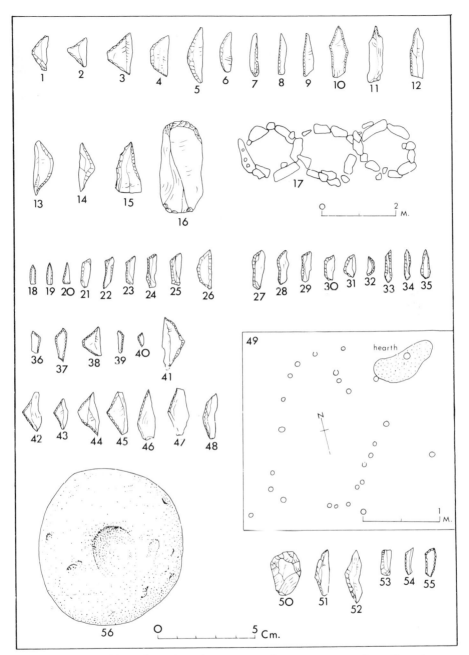

Figure 7.9: Mesolithic artifacts from Scotland. 1–12, geometric microliths, Shewalton, Ayrshire; 13, 14, microliths; 15, awl-point; 16, end-scraper, Lussa Bay, Jura; 17, hearths or cooking places, Lussa Wood I, Jura; 18–26, microliths, Lealt Bay, Jura; 27–35, microliths, Lussa River, Jura; 36–41, microliths, Deeside, Aberdeenshire; 42–48, microliths, Morton, Tentsmuir Sands, Fife; 49, stake-hole setting and hearth, Morton, Tentsmuir Sands, Fife; 50–55, scraper and microliths, Woodend Loch, Lanarkshire; 56, cupped pebble hammerstone, Tweed Valley. After Lacaille, 1930, 1954; Mercer, 1968, 1970a, 1971, 1974b; Coles, 1971; Davidson et al., 1949.

A later stage of occupation is recorded at Lealt Bay and North Carn. The Lealt Bay assemblage includes 1,283 microliths, with points, isosceles and scalene triangles, crescents and trapezoids (Figure 7.9/18–26). At North Carn, charcoal from an L-shaped stone setting and adjoining boulder (fireplace and seat?) gave a radiocarbon date of 5464 bc, taken as dating the beginning of this phase, which possibly lasted through maximum sea-level.

The latest period of occupation is represented at Lussa River. The flint assemblage included 254 microliths, with rod, triangle, crescent and trapezoid forms (Figure 7.9/27–35), 334 'chisels', 149 scrapers and 30 gravers. Among plant remains were seeds of chickweed (*Stellaria media*), bramble (*Rubus* sp.), barren strawberry (*Potentilla sterilis*), charred acorn husks (*Quercus* sp.) and a large quantity of carbonised hazel-nut shells. Red ochre, a piece of pumice of possible Icelandic origin and a black human hair fixed to a flint implement by an iron concretion were also discovered. Radiocarbon dates of 2670 and 2250 bc were obtained for this phase, which bring it well into the west Scottish Neolithic period.

What makes Jura unique in the Mesolithic of Scotland is the large quantity of microliths in the flint assemblages, particularly at Lussa River and Lealt Bay, by comparison with 'Obanian' sites and indeed with sites in the west and south-west in general. The Lussa Wood I dates are also the earliest for the Scottish Mesolithic, suggesting that similar early sites are yet to be found further south. A missing element is the assemblage of bone and antler implements so well represented on the mainland and Oronsay sites. This could be explained by the poor survival of such materials in the acid soils of Jura, in contrast with the shelly sands environment of some 'Obanian' sites. On the other hand, if 'uniqueness' can perhaps be equated with functional variation, it could be that the Jura sites, with their emphasis on the microlith, represent the camps of groups of hunters of mainly land animals, such as wild boar and red deer, whereas the Oronsay people were involved in fishing, seal-hunting and the gathering of shellfish, seasonally or permanently (Mercer, 1970b, 1974b).

In the north-east of Scotland, a number of sites exist which at various times have been included in discussions of 'Mesolithic' occupation. At Freswick Sands, Caithness, and between Golspie and Dornoch, in Sutherland, middens and shell heaps have been discovered, containing flints, but also pottery and other remains suggesting later dating (Lacaille, 1954; Tait, 1868, 1870). On present evidence none of the material can be seen as unequivocally Mesolithic. At the Culbin Sands, Moray, as at Luce Sands, Shewalton, Freswick and other sand-dune sites, flint forms have been collected which would not be out of place in established Mesolithic assemblages, but there is mixing with material which could be from later periods, and often the exact location is not known (Lacaille, 1944, 1954). An unusual object is the uniserial barbed bone point from Glenavon, Banffshire (Figure 7.10/11, Plate XV), now in the Hunterian Museum of the University of Glasgow (Lacaille, 1954, pp. 184–5). It is said to have been found in a peat moss, but nothing more is known about it. The only other Scottish uniserial barbed points are those from Druimvargie rock shelter, Oban (Figure 7.10/5,6), and these would seem to be of a different type – the Glenavon point looks flimsy by comparison. Lacaille (*loc. cit.*) has compared it with Danish forms and would like to see this as indicating a 'spread of the Baltic tradition'. The point alone is not enough to suggest this; the Glenavon

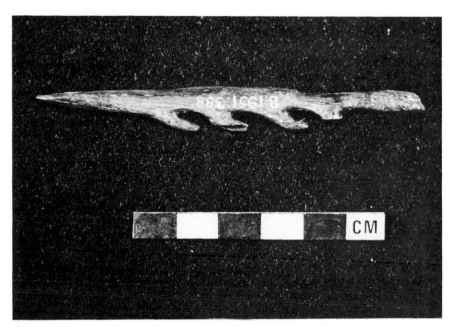

Plate XV: Uniserially barbed bone point from a peat moss. Glenavon, Banffshire. Hunterian Museum.

provenance is all that is known about it and, if this is an exact location, the shortest distance to the coast, by the Avon and Spey valleys to the mouth of the Spey, is more than 70 kilometres. We know little enough about inland Mesolithic groups in general and the evidence is not enough to postulate a diffusion of cultural influence into what must have been an extremely inaccessible area.

A small excavation and many surface collections have produced quantities of flints, some of them undoubtedly Mesolithic, from the lower terraces of the River Dee, near Banchory, Aberdeenshire (Paterson and Lacaille, 1936; Lacaille, 1944, 1954). Stratigraphy is uncertain, and modern excavation is required, but some of the microliths could come under the heading of Narrow Blade forms or later Mesolithic (Figure 7.9/36–41). Some of the Deeside material was listed by Clark (1955) as of 'Sauveterrian affinities'.

Excavations in the nineteenth century uncovered middens at Broughty Ferry and at Stannergate, on the coast of the Firth of Tay to the east of Dundee (Mathewson, 1879; Hutcheson, 1886). A number of flint artifacts were recovered from the Broughty Ferry midden, but these were subsequently lost; the midden at Stannergate was stratified below Beaker cist burials and the refuse consisted of charcoal, the shells of cockle, mussel, periwinkle, whelk and limpet, and a number of artificially split animal bones, one perhaps cut with a sharp implement, plus red deer antler tines. The worked flints are undistinguished and difficult to assign to any particular period.

One of the few Scottish Mesolithic sites excavated in recent times and to modern standards is that at Morton, Tentsmuir Sands, Fife (Coles, 1971). Located about 9.7 m above present mean sea-level and 4 km west of the

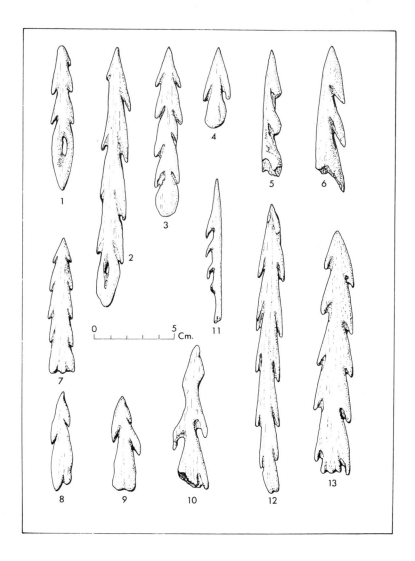

Figure 7.10: Later Mesolithic barbed points. 1, Whitburn, Co. Durham; 2–4, MacArthur Cave, Oban; 5,6, Druimvargie rock shelter, Oban; 7–9, Caisteal-nan-Gillean I, Oronsay, Argyllshire; 10, Cnoc Sligeach, Oronsay, Argyllshire; 11, Glenavon, Banffshire; 12, Shewalton, Ayrshire; 13, Cumstoun, Kirkcudbrightshire. After Mellars, 1970; Anderson, 1895, 1898; Bishop, 1914; Lacaille, 1939, 1954; Munro, 1908.

present North Sea coast, the location was, at the time of maximum Holocene sea-level, on the coast and connected to the mainland by a sandspit or tombolo at low water, but was probably a small island at high tide. Retouched or utilised stone artifacts numbered 2,637 and included utilised pieces (1,556), small edge tools (427), miscellaneous forms (229), microliths (226), burins (101), end-scrapers (54), microburins (49), large edge tools (37) and awls (7). Microliths included triangles, trapezes, obliquely retouched and curved forms (Figure 7.9/42–48). Raw materials for the lithic industry consisted of flint from beach, river or glacial gravels; chalcedony, carnelian, agate, opal and other minerals from Lower Old Red Sandstone lavas, particularly along the south shore of the Firth of Tay, from which region they might have been collected; other rocks and minerals, which must have been brought to the site, included vein quartz, quartzite, green mudstone, schistose grit and jasper/quartz. Heavier equipment included stones which had probably been used for hammering, polishing or grinding. There were also a number of bone tools, made from the long bones of red deer and probably also aurochs, with rounded and abraded ends resembling the 'limpet scoops' of west coast 'Obanian' assemblages. The excavator does not consider that the evidence from the stone industry is clear enough to allow any definite statement as to cultural affinity, particularly over a long period of intermittent occupation, but emphasises that differences in assemblages could be more functional or seasonal than cultural. The differences in assemblages between the Morton occupation site (A) and the midden site (B), which were separated by a distance of only 40 m, are suggested as being perhaps due to butchering and some preparation of food at the midden, compared with activities such as the making of weapons, working of skins and cooking on the occupation site. Mellars (1976c) has classified the Morton assemblage as 'balanced', again stressing the recurrence of this class at coastal sites.

The Morton structures show a remarkable variety. An arc of stake holes was uncovered at the south-eastern end of the occupation site, where the volcanic material of the promontory rises in a bank. This bank may have formed the southern wall of a shelter or at least a permanent wind-break, and might even have been cut back for this purpose. Another roughly rectangular setting of stake holes, 2 m long by about 1.2 m wide (Figure 7.9/49), may have formed a 'lean-to' type of shelter at one phase in the occupation of the site. Two arcs of stake holes (4 each) on either side of a scooped area were very small, almost armchair size, and may have been 'one-man' wind-breaks, easily changed to suit wind direction.

Pits and stake holes were numerous on the site, and not all necessarily connected with shelters or wind-breaks. On coastal sites, post holes could also indicate possible racks for nets, or for the drying or smoking of fish, particularly where they are associated with hearths.

Land mammal remains included red deer, aurochs, roe deer (*Capreolus caprea*) and pig. The most important bird remains were guillemot, gannet, razorbill and cormorant. Fish included cod (*Gadus morhua*), haddock, turbot (*Scophthalmus maximus*), sturgeon (*Acipenser sturio*) and salmon or sea trout (*Salmo* sp.). More than 20 species of marine molluscs were represented, among the most abundant being periwinkle, cockle, Baltic tellin (*Macoma balthica*) and striped venus (*Venus striatula*); remains of common crab were also present in quantity. Among the plant remains were weeds known to have been used as food in prehistoric times, such as corn spurrey (*Spergula arvensis*), orache (*Atriplex patula*), fat hen (*Chenopodium album*) and chickweed (*Stellaria media*). The presence of cod, and particularly the bones of large specimens, suggests that offshore fishing, from some type of boat, was an important activity of the Morton hunter/gatherers. That suitable boats were available is suggested by the find of a dug-out canoe, now lost, some time before 1880 on the River Tay at Friarton, Perth (Geikie, 1880). The canoe was recovered from a river terrace, resting on a peat bed and overlain by 3.4 m of clays and silts. The clays and silts are probably related to the Carse Clays, deposited during the main Holocene marine transgression. The boat was made of 'Scots fir' (*Pinus sylvestris*) and measured not less than 4.5 m in length and about 1.0 m in width. The dug-out cavity was about 1.8 m long by about 0.6 m deep and traces of charring indicated that the canoe had been hollowed out by a combination of burning and gouging or scraping.

The Morton evidence suggests discontinuous occupation by small groups ranging over a territory that may have extended from the Firth of Tay in the north to the Firth of Forth in the south, and inland to the Ochil Hills, seasonally exploiting a variety of habitats – coastal, estuarine, lowland and upland. If the Stannergate and Broughty Ferry sites could be interpreted as Mesolithic they might represent an alternative occupation site for the groups who camped at Morton. Some of the radiocarbon dates were obtained by combining quite small quantities of charcoal from different occupations or from separate trenches, but there seems to be a concentration around 4500 to 4300 bc (Figure 7.11).

The estuary and lower valley of the River Forth were inundated by the main Holocene marine transgression, creating a body of water far greater than that of today. Whale remains have been recovered from several sites in the Forth valley, mainly from transgression deposits (Blackadder, 1824; Turner, 1889; Morris, 1898, 1925; Clark, 1947; Lacaille, 1954), the furthest west being the find at Cardross, on Flanders Moss, now almost 40 km from the main estuary. Jamieson (1865) figures a cross-section of the Forth valley deposits showing the Carse Clays of the transgression period with whale remains in their lower levels overlying a peat bed with remains of trees. Shallow water, large tidal range and shifting mud- and sand-banks must have caused the stranding of many whales and some of these providential food supplies may have been exploited by hunter/fisher groups, as suggested by finds of implements of red deer antler – possibly used in stripping the carcases of blubber and meat – in association with whale remains at Airthrey, Causewayhead, Meiklewood and Blair Drummond. A very white antler implement from Causewayhead has the brow tine artificially smoothed to a point, and the adze/mattock from Meiklewood (Plate XVI) was reported to have had part of a wooden handle in the socket when found. These implements have also been suggested as showing Baltic influence, and there is certainly plenty of evidence for their use in Maglemosian and later groups. A shaft-hole antler tool of the Dyrholm II stage of Ertebølle culture from Dyrholmen in Denmark is similar to the Meiklewood find (Mathiassen *et al.*, 1942), but there are much earlier occurrences of implements, such as the shaft-hole antler 'axe' from a Late Palaeolithic site in Orlagau, Thuringia (Richter, 1955), almost a twin of the Meiklewood mattock,

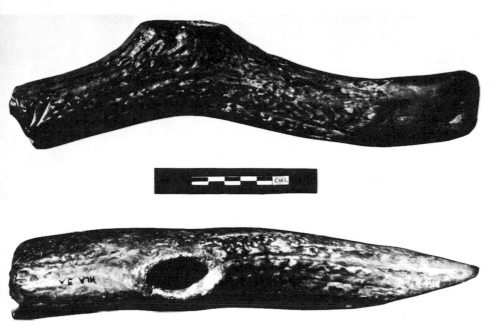

Plate XVI: Red deer antler 'axe/mattock', found in the Carse Clays resting on the skull of a whale at Meiklewood Estate, Gargunnock, Stirlingshire. Cast in Hunterian Museum.

suggesting similar responses to the exploitation of resources of a particular kind by differing culture groups.

Mounds or banks of shells containing patches of charcoal and stones have been reported from the region near the mouth of the River Avon on the lower Forth Estuary and in particular at Polmonthill, Inveravon and Kinneil (Grieve, 1872; Peach, 1879; Callander, 1929; Stevenson, 1946; MacKie, 1972). Some appear to date from a period of maximum or post-maximum transgression sea-level. Oyster is common and there are also whelk, horse mussel (*Modiolus modiolus*), periwinkle and crab remains. Four radiocarbon dates have been obtained for the mound at Inveravon (MacKie, 1972), one from charcoal and three from shell. The shell dates have not been corrected for isotopic fractionation or any of the other effects mentioned in Chapter 1 which can produce 'too old' or 'too young' dates from marine shells, but two (including the charcoal date) are around 4000 bc and two around 2200 bc (Figure 7.11). Activities at these locations, where it can be shown that the mounds were artificially accumulated, may have been part of the general food-collecting cycle of the groups who made use of the stranded whales farther up the Forth Valley.

A number of inland sites, identified mainly by surface collections or minor excavation, have yielded flints which could be classified as Mesolithic. A site on the north shore of Woodend Loch, near Coatbridge, Lanarkshire, had utilised and retouched blades and flakes, scrapers and microliths (Figure 7.9/50–55). The raw material consisted of flint, radiolarian chert and mudstone, not all of which could be obtained in the vicinity (Davidson *et al.*, 1949). In southern Lanarkshire, on either side of the River Clyde between

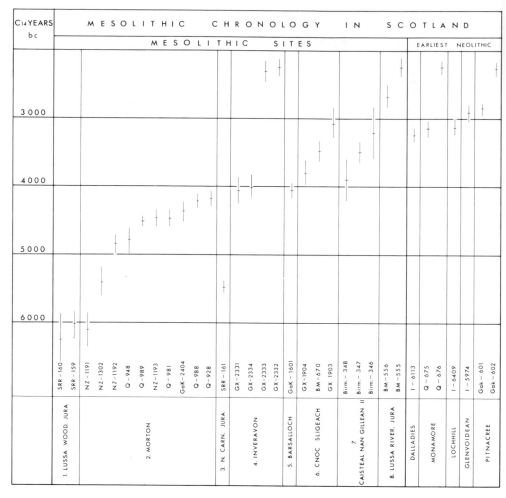

Figure 7.11: Radiocarbon chronology of Mesolithic sites in Scotland. The radiocarbon dates are shown with one standard deviation (the ± figure). For example, the date for Barsalloch (No. 5, Lab. No. GaK-1601) is 4050 ± 110 bc. The standard deviation does not indicate a range within which the true date lies; it shows rather that there is a 68 per cent chance that the Barsalloch date lies between 4160 and 3940 bc.

Carstairs and Biggar, surface collections of worked flints have been obtained from fields, suggesting possible routeways from the Tweed valley via the Biggar Gap to north and west.

Thousands of flints have been collected, mostly on the surface, in the Tweed valley (Corrie, 1916; Callander, 1927, 1928; Mason, 1931; Lacaille, 1954; Mulholland, 1970). Pebble flint and chert were used for tool production, and the occurrence of a few artifacts made in Arran pitchstone supports to some extent the idea of contact with the west coast. Mesolithic artifacts exist in quantity, and many microlithic forms can be classified as Narrow Blade, but there is undoubted mixing with later material – as much as 50 per cent of the finds from Airhouse Farm, Berwickshire, have been classed as Neolithic (Mulholland, 1970) – and there is a lack of precise stratigraphy. A feature of the assemblages from the region is the number of hour-glass perforated pebble 'mace-heads' and cupped pebble hammerstones (Figure 7.9/56), similar to those already described from the south-east of England.

In summary, it would be difficult to say much at present on the origins and affinities of the Scottish Mesolithic groups listed here. The distribution over-emphasises the coastal regions, a concentration which, in terms of 'seasonal' interpretation, might be taken to reflect only one aspect of a year's activities and therefore be functionally biased. However, the general inhospitableness of much of Scotland's inland regions and the difficulty of movement due to bodies of water, swamps and dense forests might have forced the use of coastal sites for a greater part of the year than would have been necessary further south, and future excavation and research might yet reveal the existence of perennial coastal groups. Bias could also be caused by the greater facility for discovery and collection of flints in beach and sand-dune areas. Estimation of population is always difficult for nomadic hunter/fisher peoples. Based on a minimum population density of five per square mile for Tasmania at the time of discovery, Clark (1957, p. 242) suggested a possible total of 4,500 for Great Britain in Mesolithic times. Assuming that the Star Carr inhabitants numbered about 25 and that they required a hunting territory of about 200 square miles, Piggott (1965, p. 32) proposed a total population of about 10,000 for Britain around 7500 bc. Atkinson (1962, pp. 6–7) noted the meagreness of the Scottish evidence, proposing that 'the wanderings of a single family could account, in the space of no more than a few years, for all the finds of microlithic flints in the whole of southern Scotland'. His estimate of 60–70 for the total Mesolithic population at any one time, based on perhaps one hundred known sites, must be the minimum for Scotland. Although the number of sites could now be at least trebled, when we take into account more recent evidence and theories of seasonality of subsistence patterns and functional variability in flint assemblages, it is obvious that several sites could represent the presence of the same group in different years or involved in different activities in different seasons of the same year. Therefore, although Atkinson's estimate should be increased, the calculation has been made more complex by the qualifications on the new evidence and the longer time scale produced by radiocarbon dating.

Mesolithic to Neolithic

The Mesolithic/Neolithic 'transition' is often referred to and discussed in archaeological literature, but its existence is far from being clear cut. There are a few probably Late Mesolithic radiocarbon dates, enough to show an undoubted overlap with early Neolithic activities in Britain and Ireland (Figures 7.4, 7.7 and 7.11), but it is the nature of this overlap that is as yet undefined. There are a few sites with interesting evidence of Neolithic occupation overlying something earlier. At Port St Mary, Isle of Man, a 'mound with megalithic cists' overlay a layer containing Mesolithic 'Tardenoisian' flints (Clark, 1935), and at Glecknabae, Isle of Bute, a Neolithic chambered tomb partly covered a shell midden (Bryce, 1904). Elsewhere, Early Bronze Age burial and habitation sites have been found overlying or close to evidence for apparent Mesolithic occupation. Unfortunately, no undoubted links can be demonstrated between the occupations and the juxtaposition remains tantalising.

Lacaille (1954) saw the simple hunting and food-collecting way of life continuing into much later periods, with sand-dune environments being especially favoured. Archaeological material from such areas ranges from simple flint and bone artifacts to pottery, metal objects and coins, as well as traces of habitations and burial ritual. The idea that this might indicate 'small unenterprising societies' pursuing a basic food-collecting economy and coming into contact from time to time with more advanced cultures without themselves undergoing any drastic change has been suggested (Lacaille, 1954, p. 276) as an indication of 'epimesolithic' survival. Clark (1932, p. 51) referred to the material from Shewalton, Ayrshire, as representing 'one of the final developments of our Tardenoisian, extending in time into the Bronze Age'. Certainly sites at Luce Sands, Ballantrae and Shewalton, in south-west Scotland, and in coastal sand-dune sites elsewhere, have assemblages with Mesolithic, Neolithic and Bronze Age flint types, but the preponderance of evidence from surface collection, the undoubted mixing of material, and the general lack of controlled excavation in these regions prohibit unqualified acceptance of 'survival' theories.

Evidence from the site of Châteauneuf-les-Martigues, Bouches du Rhône, in the south of France, showed that domesticated sheep were kept by the Mesolithic Castelnovian culture well before the arrival of the 'true Neolithic' in this area (Ducos, 1958; Escalon de Fonton, 1967). We cannot expect to find evidence of such 'proto-Neolithic' activity in Britain and Ireland, since sheep and other domesticates had to be brought in by the first farmers. The sites in Ireland which have been traditionally regarded as 'transitional' offer no more secure evidence when closely examined. At Dalkey Island, Co. Dublin, there were middens with later Mesolithic material and some pottery sherds, but the sherds could be intrusive from an overlying Neolithic occupation (Liversage, 1968; Woodman, 1978). At Sutton, Co. Dublin, the Mesolithic midden had a fragment of bone of domesticated ox (*Bos longifrons*) as a possible indicator of contact or overlap between the periods (Mitchell, 1972a; Woodman, 1976a), but generally the evidence is scarce or has more than one possible interpretation.

Evidence for clearance of vegetation well before the 'Elm Decline' is now available from several sites and the earliest dates indicate a pioneering phase of Neolithic activity preceding the period of stability and population expansion expressed in the construction of chambered tombs and ritual sites. At Ballynagilly, Co. Tyrone, early Neolithic occupation has four radiocarbon dates between about 3800 and 3500 bc, several centuries before the *landnam* horizon (Figure 7.7). The excavator (Ap Simon, 1976) noted the complete absence of Mesolithic forms or influence in the flint assemblages at Ballynagilly over a period long enough to have produced some degree of acculturation, but suggested also that the site is not typical of the normal later Mesolithic coastal, riverside and lakeside locations.

On the basis of comparison with recent and modern food-collectors and primitive agriculturists, and the greater labour involved in even elementary crop-raising as against hunting and gathering in some regions of the world (Woodman, 1976a), there is a strong possibility that many Mesolithic groups which had developed efficient means for maximum exploitation of the resources of their environment would have had little need or perhaps desire to change a way of life that had lasted for millennia. Clark (1962, pp. 108–9) has emphasised that

> however important the role of immigrant peasant societies, the mesolithic peoples were far from being passive recipients of a higher form of culture; and this was especially true in relatively marginal territories like the Alpine and West Baltic areas or even the British Isles. Mesolithic peoples were not only responsible in certain parts of Western Asia for the basic discoveries that underlay the so-called Neolithic Revolution; they provided the medium through which the new way of life was propagated and influenced more or less profoundly the pattern of culture that emerged in different regions as these became Neolithic. The Mesolithic peoples realised their essential meaning in maintaining continuity between the old Palaeolithic world and that which, securely based on the domestication of animals and plants, emerged in the course of a few thousand years into the light of recorded history.

BIBLIOGRAPHY

Although it is not possible in a book of this size to cover the various aspects of the Palaeolithic and Mesolithic periods in any great detail, it will be appreciated that a knowledge of the basic elements of Quaternary environments and of climatic change is absolutely essential to the understanding of these early stages of human cultural development, perhaps more so than in any other prehistoric period. To this end a full, but not exhaustive, classified bibliography has been provided which, it is hoped, will serve to emphasise the importance of interdisciplinary studies in archaeology. All references in the text have been listed and these have been augmented by extra and, where possible, alternative sources. A few of the titles have been duplicated under different headings for convenience, but it may be necessary to seek a reference under a different heading from that of the chapter in which it is listed.

Pleistocene – General and European

There are several good general studies of the Pleistocene period which make useful reference works – Flint, 1971, West, 1968, and Zeuner, 1959, are examples of this – and one pioneering attempt to show human biological and cultural development against the changing environment background (Butzer, 1972).

Alimen, M.-H. 'The Quaternary of France' in K. Rankama (ed.), *The Quaternary*, Vol. 2, pp. 89–238 (New York, 1967).
Butzer, K. W. *Environment and Archaeology: an Ecological Approach to Prehistory* (London, 1972).
—— and Isaac, G.Ll. (eds.) *After the Australopithecines: Stratigraphy, Ecology and Culture Change in the Middle Pleistocene* (The Hague, 1975).
Chaline, J. *Le Quaternaire* (Paris, 1972).
Charlesworth, J. K. *The Quaternary Era* (2 vols., London, 1957).
Cornwall, I. *The World of Ancient Man* (London, 1964).
——, *Ice Ages: their Nature and Effects* (London, 1970).
Flint, R. F. *Glacial and Quaternary Geology* (New York, 1971).
Holmes, A. *Principles of Physical Geology* (London, 1965).
Ives, J. D., and Barry, R. G. (eds.) *Arctic and Alpine Environments* (London, 1974).
Jong, J. D. de 'The Quaternary of the Netherlands' in K. Rankama (ed.), *The Quaternary*, Vol. 2, pp. 301–426 (New York, 1967).
Kurtén, B. *The Ice Age* (Stockholm, 1972).
Mangerud, J., Andersen, S. T., Berglund, B. E., and Donner, J. J. 'Quarternary stratigraphy of Norden, a proposal for terminology and classification', *Boreas*, 3 (1974), pp. 109–28.
Ters, M. 'Études sur le Quaternaire dans le Monde', *Proceedings of the VIIIth Congress of INQUA, Paris, 1969* (Paris, 1971).
Turner, C. 'Pre-Elsterian interglacial deposits from the Middle Pleistocene of North-West Europe' in V. Šibrava (ed.), *Quaternary Glaciations in the Northern Hemisphere*, pp. 79–95 (IUGS/UNESCO International Geological Correlation Programme, Prague, 1974)
Vita-Finzi, C. *Recent Earth History* (London, 1973)

West, R. G. *Pleistocene Geology and Biology* (London, 1968)

Woldstedt, P. *Das Eiszeitalter,* 'Band I – Die allgemeinen Erscheinungen des Eiszeitalters' (Stuttgart, 1954)

——, *Das Eiszeitalter,* 'Band II – Europa, Vorderasien und Nord-Afrika im Eiszeitalter' (Stuttgart, 1958)

——, 'The Quaternary of Germany' in K. Rankama (ed.), *The Quaternary,* Vol. 2, pp. 239–300 (New York, 1967)

Wright, H. E. Jr. 'Late Pleistocene climates of Europe: a review', *Bull. Geol. Soc. America,* 72 (1961), pp. 933–84

Wymer, J. J. 'Clactonian and Acheulian industries in Britain – their chronology and significance', *Proc. Geol. Ass.,* 85 (1974), pp. 391–421

Zeuner, F. E. *Dating the Past,* 4th edn (London, 1958)

——, *The Pleistocene Period,* 2nd edn (London, 1959)

Pleistocene Climate, Flora and Fauna

Arambourg, C. 'Les plages soulevées du Quaternaire', *Quaternaria,* 1 (1954), pp. 55–60

Cornwall, I. *Prehistoric Animals and their Hunters* (London, 1968)

Emiliani, C. 'Pleistocene temperatures', *Journ. Geol.,* 63 (1955), pp. 538–78

Fairbridge, R. W. 'Eustatic changes in sea level', *Physics and Chemistry of the Earth,* 4 (1961), pp. 99–185

——, 'World sea level and climatic changes', *Quaternaria,* 6 (1962), pp. 111–34

Frenzel, B. *Die Klimaschwankungen des Eiszeitalters* (Brunswick, 1967)

Kaiser, K. 'The climate of Europe during the Quaternary Ice Age', *VIIIth International Congress on the Quaternary (INQUA), Paris, 1969,* Vol. 16 (1969), pp. 10–37

Klute, F. 'Das Klima Europas während des Maximums der Weichsel-Würm- Eiszeit und die Änderungen bis zur Jetztzeit', *Die Erdkunde,* 5 (1951), pp. 273–83

Koenigswald, W. von 'Veränderungen in der Kleinsäugerfauna von Mitteleuropa zwischen Cromer und Eem (Pleistozän)', *Eiszeitalter und Gegenwart,* 23/24 (1973), pp. 159–67

Kurtén, B. *Pleistocene Mammals of Europe* (London, 1968)

——, 'Pleistocene mammals and the origin of species' in D. Brothwell and E. Higgs (eds.), *Science in Archaeology,* pp. 251–6 (London, 1969)

Laporte, L. F. *Ancient Environments* (New York, 1968)

Manley, G. 'The range of variation of the British climate', *Geogr. Journ.,* 117 (1951), pp. 43–68

Martin, P. S., and Wright, H. E. (eds.) *Pleistocene Extinctions: the Search for a Cause* (Yale, 1967)

Simpson, G. C. 'World temperatures during the Pleistocene', *Quart. Journ. Roy. Meteorol. Soc.,* 85 (1959), pp. 332–49

Woldstedt, P. 'Der Ablauf des Eiszeitalters', *Eiszeitalter und Gegenwart,* 17 (1966), pp. 153–8

Wright, H. E. Jr. 'Quaternary Geology and Climate', *VIIth Congress of INQUA, Colorado, 1965,* vol. 16 (Washington, 1969)

Pleistocene Dating and Chronology

Barker, H. 'Radiocarbon dating: its scope and limitations', *Antiquity,* 32 (1958), pp. 253–63

Bilal, U. H. *et al.* 'Corrected age of the Pliocene/Pleistocene boundary', *Nature,* 269 (1977), pp. 483–8

Bishop, W. W., and Miller, J. A. (eds.) *Calibration of Hominoid Evolution* (Edinburgh, 1972)

Broecker, W. S. 'Isotope geochemistry and the Pleistocene climatic records' in H. E. Wright and D. G. Frey (eds.), *The Quaternary of the United States,* pp. 737–54 (Princeton, 1965)

—— and van Donk, J. 'Insolation changes, ice volumes and the O^{18} records in deep-sea cores', *Review of Geophysics,* 8 (1970), pp. 169–98

Burleigh, R. 'Radiocarbon dating: some practical considerations for the archaeologist', *Journ. Archaeol. Sc.,* 1 (1974), pp. 69–87

Cooke, H. B. S. 'Pleistocene chronology: long or short?' *Quaternary Research,* 3 (1973), pp. 206–20

Cox, A. 'Geomagnetic reversals – their frequency, their origin and some problems of correlation' in W. W. Bishop and J. A. Miller (eds.), *Calibration of Hominoid Evolution*, pp. 95–105 (Edinburgh, 1972)

Curtis, G. 'Potassium-argon date for early Villafranchian of France', *Trans. Amer. Geophys. Un.*, 46 (1965), p. 178

Dalrymple, G. B. 'K/Ar dating in Pleistocene correlation' in R. B. Morrison and H. E. Wright, Jr. (eds.), 'Means of Correlation of Quaternary Successions', *VIIth Congress of INQUA, Colorado, 1965*, Vol. 8 (University of Utah, 1968), pp. 175–94

——, 'Potassium-argon dating of geomagnetic reversals and North American glaciations' in W. W. Bishop and J. A. Miller (eds.), *Calibration of Hominoid Evolution* pp. 107–34 (Edinburgh, 1972)

Damon, P. E. 'Radiocarbon and climate', *Meteorological Monographs*, 8 (1968), pp. 151–4

Einarsson, T., Hopkins, D. M., and Doell, R. R. 'The stratigraphy of Tjörnes, northern Iceland, and the history of the Bering Land Bridge' in D. M. Hopkins (ed.), *The Bering Land Bridge*, pp. 312–25 (Stanford, 1967)

Emiliani, C. 'Cenozoic climatic changes as indicated by the stratigraphy and chronology of deep-sea cores of Globigerina-ooze facies', *Ann. New York Acad. Sci.*, 95 (1961), pp. 521–36

——, 'Palaeotemperature analysis of Caribbean cores A 254-BR-C and CP-28', *Bull. Geol. Soc. Amer.*, 75 (1964), pp. 129–44

——, 'Palaeotemperature analysis of Caribbean cores P 6304–8 and P 6304–9 and a generalized temperature curve for the past 425,000 years', *Journ. Geol.*, 74 (1966), pp. 109–26

——, Mayeda, T., and Selli, R. 'Palaeotemperature analysis of the Plio-Pleistocene section at Le Castella, Calabria, Southern Italy', *Bull. Geol. Soc. Amer.*, 72 (1961), pp. 679–88

Ericson, D. B., and Wollin, G. 'Pleistocene climates and chronology in deep-sea sediments', *Science*, 162 (1968), pp. 1237–44

——, Ewing M., Wollin, G., and Heezen, B. C. 'Atlantic deep-sea sediment cores', *Bull. Geol. Soc. Amer.*, 72 (1961), pp. 193–286

——, Ewing, M., and Wollin, G. 'Pliocene-Pleistocene boundary in deep-sea sediments', *Science*, 139 (1963), pp. 727–37

——, Ewing, M., and Wollin, G. 'The Pleistocene epoch in deep-sea sediments', *Science*, 146 (1964), pp. 723–32

Evans, P. 'Towards a Pleistocene time-scale', Part II of *The Phanerozoic Time-scale – a supplement*, Special Publication of the Geological Society, No. 5, pp. 123–356 (London, 1971)

——, 'The present status of age determination in the Quaternary (with special reference to the period between 70,000 and 1,000,000 years ago)', *24th International Geological Congress, Canada, 1972*, Section 12 (Quaternary Geology), pp. 16–21 (1972)

Evernden, J. F., Savage, D. E., Curtis, G. H., and James, G. T. 'Potassium-argon dates and the Cenozoic mammalian chronology of North America', *Amer. Journ. Sci.*, 262 (1964), pp. 145–98

Evernden, J. F., and Curtis, G. H. 'The potassium-argon dating of late Cenozoic rocks in East Africa and Italy', *Current Anthropology*, 6 (1965), pp. 343–85

Flint, R. F. 'The Pliocene-Pleistocene boundary', *Special Paper, Geol. Soc. Amer.*, 84 (1965), pp. 497–533

Glass, B. *et al.* 'Geomagnetic reversals and Pleistocene chronology', *Nature*, 216 (1967), pp. 437–42

Godwin, H. 'Half-life of radiocarbon', *Nature*, 195 (1962), p. 984

Grommé, C. S., and Hay, R. L. 'Geomagnetic polarity epochs: age and duration of the Olduvai normal polarity event', *Earth and Planetary Science Letters*, 10 (1971), pp. 179–85

Isaac, G.Ll. 'Chronology and the tempo of cultural change during the Pleistocene' in W. W. Bishop and J. A. Miller (eds.), *Calibration of Hominoid Evolution* (Edinburgh, 1972)

Koenigswald, G. H. R. von 'Das absolut Alter des *Pithecanthropus erectus* Dubois' in G. Kurth (ed.), *Evolution und Hominisation*, pp. 112–19 (Stuttgart, 1962)

Laporte, L. F. *Ancient Environments* (New York, 1968)

Michael, H. N., and Ralph, E. K. *Dating Techniques for the Archaeologist* (Cambridge, Mass., 1971)

Morrison, R. B., and Wright, H. E. Jr. 'Means of Correlation of Quaternary Successions', *VIIth Congress of INQUA, Colorado, 1965*, Vol. 8 (University of Utah Press, 1968)

Oakley, K. P. 'Fluorine, uranium and nitrogen dating of bone' in E. Pyddoke (ed.), *The Scientist and Archaeology*, pp. 111–19 (London, 1963)
——, 'The date of the "Red Lady" of Paviland', *Antiquity*, 42 (1968), pp. 306–7
——, *Frameworks for Dating Fossil Man*, 3rd edn (London, 1969)
——, 'Pliocene men', *Antiquity*, 44 (1970), pp. 307–8
Olsson, I. U. (ed.) *Radiocarbon Variations and Absolute Chronology*, Proceedings of the 12th Nobel Symposium, Uppsala, 1969 (New York, 1970)
Penck, A. 'Das Alter des Menschengeschlechtes', *Zeitschrift für Ethnologie*, 40 (1908), pp. 390–407
—— and Brückner, E. *Die Alpen im Eiszeitalter* (1909) (3 vols., Leipzig, 1901–9)
Ralph, E. K., Michael, H. N., and Han, M. C. 'Radiocarbon dates and reality', *MASCA Newsletter*, 9, no. 1 (University of Pennsylvania Museum, 1973)
Rosholt, J. N. *et al.* 'Absolute dating of deep-sea sediments by the Pa^{231}/Th^{230} method', *Journ. Geol.*, 62 (1961), pp. 162–85
Savage, D. E., and Curtis, G. H. 'The Villafranchian stage-age and its radiometric dating', *Special Paper, Geol. Soc. Amer.*, 124 (1970), pp. 207–31
Selli, R. 'The Pliocene-Pleistocene boundary in Italian marine sections and its relationship to continental stratigraphies' in M. Sears (ed.), *Progress In Oceanography*, pp. 67–86 (New York, 1967)
Shackleton, N. 'Oxygen isotope analyses and Pleistocene temperatures reassessed', *Nature*, 215 (1967), pp. 15–17
Shackleton, N., and Turner, C. 'Correlation between marine and terrestrial Pleistocene successions', *Nature*, 216 (1967), pp. 1079–82
Shotton, F. W. 'The problems and contributions of methods of absolute dating within the Pleistocene period', *Quart. Journ. Geol. Soc. London*, 122 (1967), pp. 357–83
Suess, H. E. 'Bristlecone pine calibration of the radiocarbon time-scale, 5200 B.C. to the present' in I. U. Olsson (ed.), *Radiocarbon Variations and Absolute Chronology*, Proceedings of the 12th Nobel Symposium, Uppsala, 1969 (New York, 1970)
Suggate, R. P. 'Pliocene/Quaternary boundary in Australia and New Zealand', *Abstracts, IXth Congress of INQUA, New Zealand, 1973*, pp. 350–1
Szabo, B. J., and Collins, D. 'Ages of fossil bones from British interglacial sites', *Nature*, 254 (1975), pp. 680–2
Waterbolk, H. T. 'Working with radiocarbon dates', *Proc. Prehist. Soc.*, 37 (1971), Part 2, pp. 15–33
Zagwijn, W. H. 'A model-theory for the Plio-Pleistocene boundary determination based on past climatic changes', *Quaternary Newsletter* (Quaternary Research Association), 10 (June 1973), pp. 1–4
——, 'The Pliocene-Pleistocene boundary in western and southern Europe', *Boreas*, 3 (1974), pp. 75–98

Pleistocene – British Isles

Bartley, D. D. 'The stratigraphy and pollen analysis of lake deposits near Tadcaster, Yorkshire', *New Phytologist*, 61 (1962), pp. 277–87
Blackburn, K. B. 'The dating of a deposit containing an elk skeleton found at Neasham, near Darlington, County Durham', *New Phytologist*, 51 (1952), pp. 364–77
Bowen, D. Q. 'The Quaternary of Wales' in T. R. Owen (ed.), *The Upper Palaeozoic and Post-Palaeozoic Rocks of Wales*, pp. 373–426 (University of Wales Press, 1974)
Bristow, C. R., and Cox, F. C. 'The Gipping Till: a reappraisal of East Anglian glacial stratigraphy', *Journ. Geol. Soc. London*, 129 (1973), pp. 1–37
Coope, G. R. 'A late Pleistocene insect fauna from Chelford, Cheshire', *Proc. Roy. Soc.*, B 151 (1959), pp. 70–86
——, 'A Pleistocene coleopterous fauna with arctic affinities from Fladbury, Worcestershire', *Quart. Journ. Geol. Soc. London*, 118 (1962), pp. 103–23
——, 'The response of Coleoptera to gross thermal changes during the Mid-Weichselian interstadial', *Mitteilungen Intern. Verein Theor. Angew. Limnol.*, 17 (1969), pp. 173–83
——, 'Climatic interpretations of late Weichselian Coleoptera from the British Isles', *Rev. Géogr. Phys. Géol. Dyn.*, 12 (1970), pp. 149–55

——, 'Climatic fluctuations in north-west Europe since the last interglacial, indicated by fossil assemblages of Coleoptera' in A. E. Wright and F. Mosely (eds.), *Ice Ages: Ancient and Modern, Geol, Journ., Special Issue No. 6* (1975), pp. 153–68

——, 'Quaternary Coleoptera as aids in the interpretation of environmental history' in F. W. Shotton (ed.), *British Quaternary Studies*, pp. 55–68 (Oxford, 1977)

——, Shotton, F. W., and Strachan, I. 'A late Pleistocene flora and fauna from Upton Warren, Worcestershire', *Phil. Trans. Roy. Soc.*, B 244 (1961), pp. 379–421

—— and Sands, C. H. S. 'Insect faunas of the last glaciation from the Tame Valley, Warwickshire', *Proc. Roy. Soc.*, B 165 (1966), pp. 389–412

——, Morgan, A., and Osborne, P. J. 'Fossil Coleoptera as indicators of climatic fluctuations during the last glaciation in Britain', *Palaeogeography, Palaeoclimatology, Palaeoecology*, 10 (1971), pp. 87–101

Evans, J. G. *Land Snails in Archaeology* (London, 1972)

——, *The Environment of Early Man in the British Isles* (London, 1975)

Francis, E. H., Forsyth, I. H., Read, W. A., and Armstrong, M. 'The Geology of the Stirling District', *Mem. Geol. Survey Scotland* (1970)

Godwin, H. 'Radiocarbon dating and Quaternary history in Britain', *Proc. Roy. Soc.*, B 153 (1960), pp. 287–320

——, 'Late-Weichselian conditions in south-eastern Britain: organic deposits at Colney Heath, Herts.', *Proc. Roy. Soc.*, B 160 (1964), pp. 258–75

——, Walker, D., and Willis, E. H. 'Radiocarbon dating and Post-glacial vegetational history: Scaleby Moss', *Proc. Roy. Soc.*, B 147 (1957), pp. 352–66

Gray, J. M., and Lowe, J. J. (eds.) *Studies in the Scottish Lateglacial Environment* (Oxford, 1977)

Jardine, W. G. 'Letters to the Editor: the "Perth" re-advance', *Scot. Journ. Geol.*, 4 (1968), pp. 185–6

—— and Peacock, J. D. 'Scotland' in G. F. Mitchell *et al., A Correlation of Quaternary deposits in the British Isles, Geol. Soc. London, Special Report No. 4* (1973), pp. 53–9

Kerney, M. P. 'Interglacial deposits in Barnfield Pit, Swanscombe, and their molluscan fauna', *Journ. Geol. Soc. London*, 127 (1971), pp. 69–86

Koenigswald, W. von 'Veränderungen in der Kleinsäugerfauna von Mitteleuropa zwischen Cromer und Eem (Pleistozän)', *Eiszeitalter und Gegenwart*, 23–4 (1973), pp. 159–67

Manley, G. 'The range of variation of the British climate', *Geogr. Journ.*, 117 (1951), pp. 43–68

Mitchell, G. F., Penny, L. F., Shotton, F. W., and West, R. G. *A Correlation of Quaternary deposits in the British Isles, Geol. Soc. London, Special Report No. 4* (1973)

—— and West, R. G. (eds.) 'The changing environmental conditions in Great Britain and Ireland during the Devensian (Last) Cold Stage', *Phil. Trans. Roy. Soc.*, B 280 (1977), pp. 103–374

Moore, P. D. 'When the ice age seemed to end', *Nature*, 251 (1974), pp. 185–6

Morgan, A. 'Late Pleistocene environmental changes indicated by fossil insect faunas of the English Midlands', *Boreas*, 2 (1973), pp. 173–212

Morgan, A. V. 'The Pleistocene geology of the area north and west of Wolverhampton, Staffordshire, England', *Phil. Trans. Roy. Soc.*, B 265 (1973), pp. 233–97

Norton, P. E. P. 'Marine molluscan assemblages in the early Pleistocene of Sidestrand, Bramerton and the Royal Society borehole at Ludham, Norfolk', *Phil. Trans. Roy. Soc.*, B 253 (1967), pp. 161–200

Paterson, I. B. 'The supposed Perth Re-advance in the Perth district', *Scot. Journ. Geol.*, 10 (1974), pp. 53–66

Pearson, R. G. 'The Coleoptera from a detritus deposit of full-glacial age at Colney Heath, near St. Albans', *Proc. Linnaean Soc. London*, 173 (1962), pp. 37–55

Pennington, W. *The History of British Vegetation* (London, 1969)

——, 'A chronostratigraphic comparison of Late-Weichselian and Late-Devensian subdivisions, illustrated by two radiocarbon-dated profiles from western Britain', *Boreas*, 4 (1975), pp. 157–71

—— and Bonny, A. P. 'Absolute pollen diagram from the British Late-glacial', *Nature*, 226 (1970), pp. 871–3

Price, R. J. 'The glaciation of West Central Scotland – a review', *Scot. Geogr. Mag.*, 91 (1975), pp. 134–45

Reid, E. M. 'The late-glacial flora of the Lea Valley', *New Phytologist*, 48 (1949), pp. 245–52

Shotton, F. W. 'Large scale patterned ground in the valley of the Worcestershire Avon', *Geol. Mag.*, 97 (1960), pp. 404–8

——, 'Some recent advances in British Pleistocene stratigraphy' in M. Ters (ed.), *Etudes sur le Quaternaire dans le monde, Proc. VIIIth Congr. INQUA, Paris, 1969*, pp. 527–9

—— (ed.) *British Quaternary Studies* (Oxford, 1977a)

——, 'British dating work with radioactive isotopes' in F. W. Shotton (ed.), *British Quaternary Studies*, pp. 17–30 (Oxford, 1977b)

——, 'The Devensian Stage: its development, limits and substages' in G. F. Mitchell and R. G. West (eds.), 'The changing environmental conditions in Great Britain and Ireland during the Devensian (Last) Cold Stage', *Phil. Trans. Roy. Soc.*, B 280 (1977c), pp. 107–18

Simpson, I. M., and West, R. G. 'On the stratigraphy and palaeobotany of a late-Pleistocene organic deposit at Chelford, Cheshire', *New Phytologist*, 57 (1958), pp. 239–50

Sissons, J. B. 'The Perth Re-advance in Central Scotland', *Scot. Geogr. Mag.*, 79 (1963), pp. 151–63

——, 'The Perth Re-advance in Central Scotland, Part II', *Scot. Geogr. Mag.*, 80 (1964), pp. 28–36

——, *The Evolution of Scotland's Scenery* (Edinburgh, 1967a)

——, 'Glacial stages and radiocarbon dates in Scotland', *Scot. Journ. Geol.*, 3 (1967b), pp. 375–81

——, 'The Quaternary in Scotland: a review', *Scot. Journ. Geol.*, 10 (1974), pp. 311–37

——, *Scotland* (Geomorphology of the British Isles series) (London, 1976)

——, Lowe, J. J., Thompson, K. S. R., and Walker, M. J. C. 'The Loch Lomond Re-advance in the Grampian Highlands of Scotland', *Nature Phys. Sci.*, 244 (1973), pp. 75–7

Sparks, B. W. 'The ecological interpretation of Quaternary non-marine mollusca', *Proc. Linnaean Soc. London*, 172 (1961), pp. 71–80

——, 'Non-marine mollusca and Quaternary ecology', *Journ. Ecol.*, 52 (Supplement) (1964), pp. 87–98

—— and West, R. G. *The Ice Age in Britain* (London, 1972)

Stuart, A. J. 'Pleistocene history of the British vertebrate fauna', *Biological Review*, 49 (1974), pp. 225–66

——, 'British Quaternary vertebrates' in F. W. Shotton (ed.), *British Quaternary Studies*, pp. 69–82 (Oxford, 1977)

—— and West, R. G. 'Late Cromerian fauna and flora at Ostend, Norfolk', *Geol. Mag.*, 113 (1976), pp. 469–73

Turner, C. 'The Middle Pleistocene deposits at Marks Tey, Essex', *Phil. Trans. Roy. Soc.*, B 257 (1970), pp. 373–437

—— and West, R. G. 'The subdivision and zonation of interglacial periods', *Eiszeitalter und Gegenwart*, 19 (1968), pp. 93–101

Walker, D. 'A Late-glacial deposit at St. Bees, Cumberland', *Quart. Journ. Geol. Soc.*, 112 (1956), p. 93

West, R. G. 'The Quaternary deposits at Hoxne, Suffolk', *Phil. Trans. Roy. Soc.*, B 239 (1956), pp. 265–356

——, 'The Quaternary of the British Isles' in K. Rankama (ed.), *The Quaternary*, Vol. 2, pp. 1–87 (New York, 1967)

——, 'Pleistocene history of British flora' in D. Walker and R. G. West (eds.), *Studies in the Vegetational History of the British Isles*, pp. 1–11 (Cambridge, 1970)

——, Dickson, C. A., Catt, J. A., Weir, A. H., and Sparks, B. W. 'Late Pleistocene deposits at Wretton, Norfolk. II. Devensian deposits', *Phil. Trans. Roy. Soc.*, B 267 (1974), pp. 337–420

Human Biological Development

In recent times, publication and classification in this field of study have usually been overtaken by the rapidity and quantity of new discoveries of early hominid remains, particularly from Africa, so that any attempt at a complete or comprehensive coverage would soon be outdated. New discoveries and theories can best be studied in the journals, particularly *Nature*, but there are catalogues, especially those of Oakley and Campbell (1967) and Oakley, Campbell and Molleson (1971), which present standardised details of discoveries and are therefore most useful as reference works.

Adam, K. D. 'Die mittlelpleistozänen Faunen von Steinheim an der Murr (Württemberg)', *Quaternaria*, 1 (1954), pp. 131–44

Bergman, R. A. M., and Karsten, P. 'The fluorine content of *Pithecanthropus* and of other specimens from the Trinil fauna', *Proc. Kon. Akad. Wetensch. Amsterdam*, 55 (1952), p. 151

Bishop, W. W., and Clark, J. D. *Background to Evolution in Africa* (Chicago, 1967)

—— and Chapman, G. R. 'Early Pliocene sediments and fossils from the Northern Kenya Rift Valley', *Nature*, 226 (1970), pp. 914–18

—— and Miller, J. A. *Calibration of Hominoid Evolution* (Edinburgh, 1972)

Boule, M. 'L'homme fossile de la Chapelle-aux-Saints', *Annales de Paléontologie*, VI/VIII (1911–13)

—— and Vallois, H. V. *Fossil Men* (New York, 1957)

Brace, C. L. 'The fate of the "Classic" Neanderthals: a consideration of hominid catastrophism', *Current Anthropology*, 5 (1964), pp. 3–19

——, *The Stages of Human Evolution* (New Jersey, 1967)

——, Nelson, H., and Korn, N. *Atlas of Fossil Man* (New York, 1971)

Briggs, L. C. 'Hominid evolution in north-west Africa and the question of the North African Neanderthals', *Amer. Journ. Phys. Anthrop*, 29 (1968), pp. 377–85

Brothwell, D. R. 'The people of Mount Carmel', *Proc. Prehist. Soc.*, 27 (1961), pp. 155–9

Campbell, B. G. 'The nomenclature of the hominids', *Roy. Anthrop. Inst., Occasional Paper*, no. 22 (1965)

Coon, C. *The Origin of Races* (New York, 1962)

Dart, R. A. '*Australopithecus africanus:* the man-ape of South Africa', *Nature*, 115 (1925), pp. 195–9

——, 'The osteodontokeratic culture of *Australopithecus prometheus*', *Transvaal Museum Memoirs*, no. 10 (1957)

Day, M. H. *Guide to Fossil Man* (London, 1965)

Dubois, E. '*Pithecanthropus erectus*, eine menschenaehnliche Übergangsform aus Java' (Batavia, 1894)

Garn, S. M. 'The improper use of fossil nomenclature', *Amer. Journ. Phys. Anthrop.*, 35 (1971), p. 217

Harrison, G. A., and Weiner, J. S. 'Some considerations in the formulation of theories of human phylogeny' in S. L. Washburn (ed.), *Classification and Human Evolution*, pp. 75–84 (New York, 1963)

Heberer, G. *Moderne Anthropologie* (Hamburg, 1973)

Howell, F. C. 'Observations on the earlier phases of the European Lower Palaeolithic', *American Anthropologist*, 68 (1966), pp. 88–201

——, *Early Man* (New York, 1970)

Howells, W. W. 'Homo erectus', *Scientific American*, 215 (May 1966), pp. 46–53

Isaac, G. L., and McCown, E. R. (eds.) *Human Origins: Louis Leakey and the East African Evidence* (California, 1976)

Jelinek, J. 'Neanderthal Man and *Homo sapiens* in Central Europe', *Current Anthropology*, 10 (1969), pp. 475–503

Kurtén, B. *Not from the Apes* (London, 1973)

Leakey, L. S. B. 'A new fossil skull from Olduvai', *Nature*, 184 (1959), pp. 491–3

——, 'A preliminary report on the geology and fauna, 1951–1961', *Olduvai Gorge*, Vol. I (Cambridge, 1965)

——, 'Bone smashing by late Miocene Hominidae', *Nature*, 218 (1968), pp. 528–30

——, Tobias, P. V., and Napier, J. R. 'A new species of the genus Homo from Olduvai Gorge', *Nature*, 202 (1964), pp. 7–9

Leakey, M. D. 'Early artefacts from the Koobi Fora area', *Nature*, 226 (1970), pp. 228–30

——, 'Excavations in Beds I and II, 1960–63', *Olduvai Gorge*, Vol. 3 (Cambridge, 1971)

——, 'The early stone industries of Olduvai Gorge' in J. D. Clark and G. L. Isaac (eds.), *The Earlier Industries of Africa*, Colloque V, IXe Congrès de l'Union Internationale des Sciences Préhistoriques et Protohistoriques, pp. 24–41 (Nice, 1976)

Leakey, R. E. F. 'Evidence for an advanced Plio-Pleistocene hominid from East Rudolf, Kenya', *Nature*, 242 (1973a), pp. 447–50

——, 'Australopithecines and Hominines: a summary on the evidence from the early Pleistocene of Eastern Africa' in S. Zuckerman (ed.), *The Concepts of Human Evolution*, Zool. Soc. London Symposium No. 33, pp. 53–69 (1973b)

Le Gros Clark, W. E. *History of the Primates* (London, 1958)
——, *Man-apes or Ape-men?* (New York, 1967)
——, *The Fossil Evidence for Human Evolution* (Chicago, 1969)
Lumley, H. de 'Découverte d'habitats de l'Acheuléen ancien dans des dépôts mindéliens sur le site de Terra Amata (Nice)', *Comptes Rendues de l'Acad. Sci.*, 264 (1967), pp. 801–4
——, 'Une cabane acheuléenne dans la Grotte du Lazaret (Nice), *Mémoires de la Société Préhistorique Française*, 7 (1969a), pp. 1–235
——, 'A Palaeolithic camp at Nice', *Scientific American*, 220 (May 1969b), pp. 42–50
McBurney, C. B. M. 'Evidence for the distribution in space and time of Neanderthaloid and allied strains in northern Africa' in G. H. R. von Koenigswald (ed.), *Hundert Jahre Neanderthaler*, pp. 253–64 (Utrecht, 1958)
McKern, T. W. *The Search for Man's Origins*, Addison-Wesley Module in Anthropology, No. 53 (Reading, Massachusetts, 1974)
Molleson, T. 'Skeletal remains of man in the British Quaternary' in F. W. Shotton (ed.), *British Quaternary Studies*, pp. 83–92 (Oxford, 1977)
Napier, J. R., and Weiner, J. S. 'Olduvai Gorge and human origins', *Antiquity*, 36 (1962), pp. 41–7
Oakley, K. P. 'Man the skilled toolmaker', *Antiquity*, 43 (1969), pp. 222–4
—— and Campbell, B. G. *Catalogue of Fossil Hominids: Part 1, Africa*, Brit. Mus. (Natur. Hist.) (London, 1967)
——, Campbell, B. G., and Molleson, T. *Catalogue of Fossil Hominids: Part 2, Europe*, Brit. Mus. (Natur. Hist.) (London, 1971)
Ovey, C. D. (ed.) *The Swanscombe Skull* (Roy. Anthrop. Inst., London, 1964)
Patterson, B., Behrensmeyer, A. K., and Sill, W. D. 'Geology and fauna of a new Pliocene locality in northwestern Kenya', *Nature*, 226 (1970), pp. 918–21
Pfeiffer, J. E. *The Emergence of Man* (London, 1973)
Pilbeam, D. 'Man's earliest ancestors', *Scientific Journ.*, 3 (1967), p. 47
——, 'Tertiary Pongidae of East Africa', *Peabody Mus. Natur. Hist. Bull.* no. 31 (1969)
——, *The Ascent of Man* (New York, 1972)
Poirier, F. E. *Fossil Man: an Evolutionary Journey* (St Louis, 1973)
——, *Fossil Evidence: the Human Evolutionary Journey* (St Louis, 1977)
Robinson, J. T. 'Further remarks on the relationship between *Meganthropus* and Australopithecines', *Amer. Journ. Phys. Anthrop.*, 13 (1955), pp. 429–46
——, '*Homo habilis* and the Australopithecines', *Nature*, 205 (1965), pp. 121–4
Simons, E. L. 'The phyletic position of *Ramapithecus. Postilla*' (Peabody Museum, Yale University), No. 57 (1961)
——, 'Some fallacies in the study of human phylogeny', *Science*, 141 (1963), p. 879
——, 'On the mandible of *Ramapithecus*', *Proc. Nat. Acad. Sci.*, 51 (1964), p. 528
——, 'The earliest apes', *Scientific American*, 217 (Dec. 1967), pp. 28–35
——, 'A source for dental comparison of *Ramapithecus* with *Australopithecus* and *Homo*', *South African Journ. Sci.*, 64 (1968), pp. 92–112
——, 'Ramapithecus', *Scientific American*, 236, no. 5 (1977), pp. 28–35
Solecki, R. *Shanidar: the First Flower People* (New York, 1971)
Thoma, A. 'L'occipital de l'homme Mindélien de Vertesszöllös', *Anthropologie*, 70 (1966), pp. 495–553
Tobias, P. V. 'Fossil hominid remains from Ubeidiya, Israel', *Nature*, 211 (1966), p. 130
——, 'The cranium and maxillary dentition of *Australopithecus (Zinjanthropus) boisei*', *Olduvai Gorge*, Vol. 2 (Cambridge, 1967)
——, *The Brain in Hominid Evolution* (New York and London, 1971)
—— and Koenigswald, G. H. R. von 'Comparison between the Olduvai hominines and those of Java and some implications for hominid phylogeny', *Nature*, 204 (1964), p. 515
Vallois, H 'The Fontéchevade fossil man', *Amer. Journ. Phys. Anthrop.*, 7 (1949), pp. 339–62
——, 'La mandibule humaine prémoustérienne de Montmaurin (Haute Garonne)', *Comptes Rendues de l'Acad. Sci.*, 240 (1955), pp. 1577–9
Weidenreich, F. 'Morphology of Solo man', *Anthrop. Papers Amer. Mus. Natur. Hist.*, 43 (1951), pp. 205–90
Weiner, J. S. *The Piltdown Forgery* (London, 1955)
—— 'The pattern of evolutionary development of the genus *Homo*', *South African Journ. Med. Sci.*, 23 (1958), pp. 111–20

Palaeolithic – General and European

There are few general studies of the Palaeolithic period in English. Burkitt (1963) and Breuil and Lantier (1965) are still useful, but to a great extent outdated. Clark (1967) and Bordes (1968b) have good but brief coverage, Coles and Higgs (1969) have summaries of developments in the main world regions and Müller–Karpe's (1966) Handbook has general discussion, distribution maps, bibliographies and a large detailed catalogue of the major sites. Apart from a recent catalogue of Palaeolithic sites in Europe (Bhattacharya, 1977), the reader who wants more than a general introduction must turn to regional studies and languages other than English.

Bhattacharya, D. K. *Palaeolithic Europe* (Atlantic Highlands, New Jersey, 1977)
Biberson, P. 'Les plus anciennes industries du Maroc' in J. D. Clark and G. L. Isaac (eds.), *The Earlier Industries of Africa*, Colloque V, IXe Congrès de l'Union Internationale des Sciences Préhistoriques et Protohistoriques (Nice, 1976), pp. 118–39
Bohmers, A. 'Die Höhlen von Mauern', *Palaeohistoria*, 1 (1951), pp. 1–107
Bordes, F. 'Some observations on the Pleistocene succession in the Somme Valley', *Proc. Prehist. Soc.*, 22 (1956), pp. 1–5
——. *Typologie du Paléolithique ancien et moyen* (Bordeaux, 1961)
—— (ed.) *La Préhistoire, Problèmes et Tendances* (Paris, 1968a)
——, *The Old Stone Age* (London, 1968b)
—— and Thibault, C. 'Thoughts on the initial adaptation of hominids to European glacial climates', *Quaternary Research*, 8 (1977), pp. 115–27
Breuil, H. 'The Pleistocene succession in the Somme Valley', *Proc. Prehist. Soc.*, 5 (1939), pp. 33–8
—— and Koslowski, L. 'Etudes de stratigraphie paléolithique dans le nord de la France, la Belgique et l'Angleterre', *L'Anthropologie*, 41 (1931), pp. 449–88
—— and Lantier, R. *The Men of the Old Stone Age* (London, 1965)
Burkitt, M. *The Old Stone Age* (London, 1963)
Chmielewski, W. *Civilisation de Jerzmanowice* (Warsaw, 1961)
——, 'The continuity and discontinuity of the evolution of archaeological cultures in Central and Eastern Europe between the 55th and 25th millenaries B.C.' in F. Bordes (ed.), *The Origin of* Homo sapiens, *Ecology and Conservation*, pp. 173–9 (UNESCO, Paris, 1972)
Clark, J. G. D. 'The reindeer-hunting tribes of Northern Europe', *Antiquity*, 12 (1938), pp. 154–71
——, *The Stone Age Hunters* (London, 1967)
Cole, S. *The Prehistory of East Africa* (New York, 1965)
Coles, J. M. 'Ancient man in Europe' in J. M. Coles and D. D. A. Simpson (eds.), *Studies in Ancient Europe*, pp. 17–43 (Leicester, 1968)
—— and Higgs, E. S. *The Archaeology of Early Man* (London, 1969)
Collins, D. *The Human Revolution: from Ape to Artist* (London, 1976)
Coppens, Y., Howell, F. C., Isaac, G. L., and Leakey, R. E. F. (eds.) *Earliest Man and Environments in the Lake Rudolf Basin* (Chicago, 1976)
Davidson, I. 'Radiocarbon dates for the Spanish Solutrean', *Antiquity*, 48 (1974), pp. 63–5
Drack, W. *Ur- and Frühgeschichtliche Archäologie der Schweiz. Band I, Die Ältere und Mittlere Steinzeit* (Basel, 1968)
Freund, G. *Die Blattspitzen des Paläolithikums in Europa* (Bonn, 1952)
Howell, F. C. 'Observations on the earlier phases of the European Lower Palaeolithic' in J. D. Clark and F. C. Howell (eds.), *Recent Studies in Palaeoanthropology*, American Anthropologist Special Publication, 68 (1966), pp. 88–201
Isaac, G. L. 'Chronology and the tempo of cultural change during the Pleistocene' in W. W. Bishop and J. A. Miller (eds.), *Calibration of Hominoid Evolution*, pp. 381–430 (Edinburgh, 1972)
——, 'Stratigraphy and patterns of cultural change in the Middle Pleistocene', *Current Anthropology*, 15 (1974), pp. 508–14
Klein, R. G. 'The Mousterian of European Russia', *Proc. Prehist. Soc.*, 35 (1969), pp. 77–111
——, *Ice-age Hunters of the Ukraine* (Chicago, 1973)
Leroi-Gourhan, A. *The Art of Prehistoric Man in Western Europe* (London, 1968)
—— and Brézillon, M. *Fouilles de Pincevent* (7e supplément à *Gallia Préhistoire*) (Paris, 1972)

Lumley, H. de 'A Palaeolithic camp at Nice', *Scientific American*, 220 (May 1969), pp. 42–50
——, 'Les premières industries humaines en Provence' in H. de Lumley (ed.), 'Les civilisations Paléolithiques et Mésolithiques de la France, Tome I/2, *La Préhistoire Française*, IXe Congrès UISPP, pp. 765–94 (Nice, 1976)
McBurney, C. B. M. 'From the beginnings of man to *c.* 33,000 B.C.' in S. Piggott, G. Daniel and McBurney (eds.), *France Before the Romans* (London, 1974)
Marshack, A. 'Cognitive aspects of Upper Palaeolithic engraving', *Current Anthropology*, 13 (1972a), pp. 445–77
——, *The Roots of Civilisation* (London, 1972b)
—— and Rosenfeld, A. 'Palaeolithic notation', *Antiquity*, 46 (1972c), pp. 63–5
Müller-Beck, H. 'Palaeohunters in America: origins and diffusion', *Science*, 152 (1966), pp. 1191–210
Müller-Karpe, H. *Handbuch der Vorgeschichte*, Band I, Altsteinzeit (Munich, 1966)
——, *Geschichte der Steinzeit* (Munich, 1974)
Narr, K. J. (ed.) *Handbuch der Urgeschichte*, I. Ältere und Mittlere Steinzeit (Munich, 1966)
Otto, K. H. 'Zur Chronologie der Ilsenhöhle in Ranis, Kr. Ziegenrück', *Jahresschrift Mitteldeutsche Vorgeschichte*, 35 (1951), pp. 8–15
Rust, A. *Das eiszeitliche Rentierjägerlager Meiendorf* (Neumünster, 1937)
——, *Die alt- und mittelsteinzeitliche Funde von Stellmoor* (Neumünster, 1943)
——, *Vor 20,000 Jahren* (Neumünster, 1962)
Sahlins, M. *Stone Age Economics* (Chicago, 1972)
Schwabedissen, H. *Die Federmessergruppen des nordwesteuropäischen Flachlandes* (Neumünster, 1954)
——, 'Northern continental Europe' in R. J. Braidwood and G. R. Willey (eds.), *Courses Toward Urban Life* (Edinburgh, 1962)
Sonneville-Bordes, D. de 'The Upper Palaeolithic, *c.* 33,000–10,000 B.C.' in S. Piggott, G. Daniel and C. B. M. McBurney (eds.), *France Before the Romans*, pp. 30–60 (London, 1974)
Tode, A. *et al.* 'Die Untersuchung der paläolithischen Freilandstation von Salzgitter-Lebenstedt', *Eiszeitalter und Gegenwart*, 3 (1953), pp. 144–220
Tschumi, O. *Urgeschichte der Schweiz* (Frauenfeld, 1949)
Vallois, H. 'The social life of early man: the evidence of skeletons', *Viking Fund Publications in Anthropology*, 31 (1961), pp. 214–35
Valoch, K. 'Evolution of the Palaeolithic in Central and Eastern Europe', *Current Anthropology*, 9 (1968), pp. 351–90
—— (ed.) *Les premières industries de l'Europe*, Colloque VIII, IXe Congrès de l'Union Internationale des Sciences Préhistoriques et Protohistoriques (Nice, 1976)
Vértes, L. 'Neuere Ausgrabungen und paläolithische Funde in der Höhle von Istállóskö, *Acta Archaeologica* (Acad. Scient. Hungaricae), 5 (1955), pp. 111–31
——, 'Problemkreis des Szeletien', *Slovenská Archeológia*, 4 (1956), pp. 318–40
——, 'Beiträge zur Abstammung des ungarischen Szeletien', *Folia Archaeologica*, 10 (1959), pp. 3–15
Zotz, L. F. *Altsteinzeitkunde Mitteleuropas* (Stuttgart, 1951)
——, *Das Paläolithikum in den Weinberghöhlen bei Mauern* (Bonn, 1955)
——, 'Die Forschungen des Instituts für Urgeschichte der Universität Erlangen im Altmühltal', *Prähistorische Zeitschrift*, 39 (1960)

Palaeolithic – British Isles

There has never been a definitive study of the whole of the British Palaeolithic period and it is likely that most workers in this field of study would dispute the value of any single-handed attempt to be comprehensive in an area which requires the multidisciplinary approach to a greater degree than perhaps any other prehistoric period. The Lower and Middle Palaeolithic have had recent coverage in the gazeteer by Roe (1968b) and a study by Wymer (1968) which deals mainly with the Thames Valley but relates generally to the rest of England. For the Upper Palaeolithic the general work has long been the book by Dorothy Garrod (1926) and there is now a 2-volume modern survey by Campbell (1977). Any detailed work involves the use of the journals – archaeological, geological, botanical, zoological, etc., and for many sites the authoritative reports are still those published in the early twentieth or late nineteenth centuries.

Alabaster, C., and Straw, A. 'The Pleistocene context of faunal remains and artifacts discovered at Welton-le-Wold, Lincolnshire', *Proc. Yorks. Geol. Soc.*, 41 (1976), pp. 75–94

Ap Simon, A. M. 'A view of the early prehistory of Wales' in G. C. Boon and J. M. Lewis (eds.), *Welsh Antiquity*, pp. 37–53 (Cardiff, 1976)

Armstrong, A. L. 'Pin Hole Cave excavations, Creswell Crags, Derbyshire; discovery of an engraved drawing of a masked human figure', *Proc. Prehist. Soc. East Anglia*, 6 (1928), pp. 27–9

——, 'Excavations in the Pinhole Cave, Creswell Crags, Derbyshire', *Proc. Prehist. Soc. East Anglia*, 6 (1931), pp. 330–4

Barnes, A. S. 'The differences between natural and human flaking on prehistoric flint implements', *American Anthropologist*, 41 (1939a), pp. 99–112

——, 'De la manière dont la nature imite le travail humain dans l'éclatement du silex', *Bulletin de la Société Préhistorique Française*, 1 (1939b), pp. 1–16

Barnes, B., Edwards, B. J. N., Hallam, J. S., and Stuart, A. J. 'The skeleton of a Late-glacial elk associated with barbed points from Poulton-le-Fylde, Lancashire', *Nature*, 232 (1971), pp. 488–9

Bishop, M. J. 'A preliminary report on the Middle Pleistocene mammal-bearing deposits of Westbury-sub-Mendip, Somerset', *Proc. Univ. Bristol Spelaeol. Soc.*, 13 (1974), pp. 301–18

——, 'Earliest record of man's presence in Britain', *Nature*, 253 (1975), pp. 95–7

Bohmers, A. 'Statistics and graphs in the study of flint assemblages', *Palaeohistoria*, 5 (1956), pp. 1–25

Bowen, D. Q. 'The palaeoenvironment of the "Red Lady" of Paviland', *Antiquity*, 44 (1970), pp. 134–6

——, 'Further comment on the "Red Lady" of Paviland and related matters', *Antiquity*, 46 (1972)

Bramwell, D. 'The excavations at Elder Bush Cave, Wetton, Staffordshire', *North Staffordshire Journ. Field Studies*, 4 (1964), pp. 46–60

——, 'Excavations at Fox Hole Cave, High Wheeldon, 1961–1970', *Derbyshire Archaeol. Journ.*, 91 (1971), pp. 1–19

Breuil, H. 'Les industries à éclats du paléolithique ancien', *Préhistoire*, 1 (1932), pp. 125–90

Buckland, P. C. 'The use of insect remains in the interpretation of archaeological environments' in D. A. Davidson and M. L. Shackley (eds.), *Geoarchaeology*, pp. 369–96 (London, 1976)

Buckland, W. *Reliquiae Diluvianae: or Observations on the organic Remains Contained in Caves, Fissures, and Diluvial Gravel and on Other Geological Phenomena Attesting the Action of an Universal Deluge* (London, 1823)

Calkin, J. B. 'Implements from the higher raised beaches of Sussex', *Proc. Prehist. Soc. East Anglia*, 7 (1934), pp. 333–47

—— and Green, J. F. N. 'Palaeoliths and terraces near Bournemouth', *Proc. Prehist. Soc.*, 15 (1949), pp. 21–37

Campbell, J. B. 'Excavations at Creswell Crags: preliminary report', *Derbyshire Archaeol. Journ.*, 89 (1969), pp. 47–58

——, 'The Upper Palaeolithic period' in J. B. Campbell, D. Elkington, P. Fowler and L. Grinsell, *The Mendip Hills in Prehistoric and Roman Times*, Bristol Archaeol. Research Group Special Publication, No. 1 (1970)

——, *The Upper Palaeolithic of Britain: a Study of Man and Nature in the Late Ice Age* (2 vols., Oxford, 1977)

—— and Sampson, C. G. *A New Analysis of Kent's Cavern, Devonshire, England*, Univ. Oregon Anthropol. Papers No. 3 (1971)

Clark, J. G. D. 'Reindeer hunters' summer camps in Britain?' *Proc. Prehist. Soc.*, 4 (1938), p. 229

Clifford, E. M., Garrod, D. A. E., and Gracie, H. S. 'Flint implements from Gloucestershire', *Antiq. Journ.*, 34 (1954), pp. 178–83

Collins, D. 'Culture traditions and environment of early man', *Current Anthropology*, 10 (1969), pp. 267–316

—— and Collins, A. 'Cultural evidence from Oldbury' (1970), *Univ. London Inst. Archaeol. Bulletin*, 8–9 (1968–9), pp. 151–76

Davidson, I. 'Radiocarbon dates for the Spanish Solutrean', *Antiquity*, 48 (1974), pp. 63–5

Dines, H. G. 'The flint industries of Bapchild', *Proc. Prehist. Soc. East Anglia*, 6 (1929), pp. 12–26

Garrod, D. A. E. *The Upper Palaeolithic Age in Britain* (Oxford, 1926)

Grimes, W. F. *The Prehistory of Wales* (Palaeolithic period, 1–8) (Cardiff, 1951)

—— and Cowley, L. F. 'Coygan Cave, Llansadyrnin, Carmarthenshire', *Archaeologia Cambrensis*, 90 (1935), pp. 95–111

Hallam, J. S., Edwards, B. J. N., Barnes, B., and Stuart, A. J. 'The remains of a Late Glacial elk associated with barbed points from High Furlong, near Blackpool, Lancashire', *Proc. Prehist. Soc.*, 39 (1973), pp. 100–28

Hawkes, C. J., Tratman, E. K., and Powers, R. 'Decorated piece of rib bone from the Palaeolithic levels at Gough's Cave, Cheddar, Somerset', *Proc. Univ. Bristol Spelaeol. Soc.*, 12 (1970), pp. 137–42

Howell, F. C. 'Observations on the earlier phases of the European Lower Palaeolithic' in J. D. Clark and F. C. Howell (eds.), *Recent Studies in Palaeoanthropology*, American Anthropologist Special Publication, 68 (1966), pp. 88–201

Hubbard, R. N. L. B. 'The chronology of the Lower Palaeolithic in southern Britain', *Abstracts Xth INQUA Congress, Birmingham, 1977*, p. 216

Jackson, J. W. 'The Creswell Caves', *Cave Science: Journ. Brit. Spelaeol. Assoc.*, 6 (1967), pp. 8–23

John, B. S. 'The "Red Lady" of Paviland: a comment', *Antiquity*, 45 (1971), pp. 141–4

Kendall, H. G. O. 'Investigations at Knowle Farm Pit', *Wiltshire Archaeol. Natur. Hist. Mag.*, 34 (1906), pp. 299–307

Kitching, J. W. *Bone, Tooth and Horn Tools of Palaeolithic Man: an Account of the Osteodontokeratic Discoveries in Pin Hole Cave, Derbyshire* (Manchester, 1963)

Lacaille, A. D. 'The palaeoliths from the gravels of the Lower Boyn Hill Terrace around Maidenhead', *Antiq. Journ.*, 20 (1940), pp. 245–71

——, 'Some Wiltshire palaeoliths' in G. Sieveking (ed.), *Prehistoric and Roman Studies*, pp. 69–87 (London, 1971)

—— and Grimes, W. F. 'The prehistory of Caldey', *Archaeologia Cambrensis*, 104 (1955), pp. 85–165

Layard, N. F. 'Solutrean blades from South-eastern England', *Proc. Prehist. Soc. East Anglia*, 6 (1932), p. 55

McBurney, C. B. M. 'First season's fieldwork on British Upper Palaeolithic cave deposits', *Proc. Prehist. Soc.*, 25 (1959), pp. 260–9

——, 'The Old Stone Age in Wales' in I. L. Foster and G. Daniel (eds.), *Prehistoric and Early Wales*, pp. 17–34 (London, 1965)

Mace, A. 'An Upper Palaeolithic open site at Hengistbury Head, Christchurch, Hants.,' *Proc. Prehist. Soc.*, 25 (1959), pp. 233–59

Mellars, P. A. 'Radiocarbon dates for a new Creswellian site', *Antiquity*, 43 (1969), pp. 308–10

——, 'The Palaeolithic and Mesolithic' in C. Renfrew (ed.), *British Prehistory*, pp. 41–99 (London, 1974)

Moir, J. R. 'Four Suffolk flint implements', *Antiq. Journ.*, 2 (1922), pp. 114–17

——, 'A series of Solutré blades from Suffolk and Cambridgeshire', *Proc. Prehist. Soc. East Anglia*, 4 (1923), pp. 71–81

——, 'Ancient man in the Gipping-Orwell Valley, Suffolk', *Proc. Prehist. Soc. East Anglia*, 6 (1932a), pp. 182–222

——, 'Further Solutré implements from Suffolk', *Antiq. Journ.*, 12 (1932b), pp. 257–61

——, 'Ancient man in Devon (Part I)', *Proc. Devon. Archaeol. Explor. Soc.*, 2 (1936), pp. 264–75

——, 'Four flint implements', *Antiq. Journ.*, 18 (1938), pp. 258–61

—— and Hopwood, A. T. 'Excavations at Brundon, Suffolk (1935–37)', *Proc. Prehist. Soc.*, 5 (1939), pp. 1–32

Molleson, T. 'Remains of Pleistocene man in Paviland and Pontnewydd Caves, Wales', *Brit. Cave Research Assoc. Trans.*, 3 (1976), pp. 112–16

—— and Burleigh, R. 'A new date for Goat's Hole Cave', *Antiquity*, 52 (1978), pp. 143–5

Moore, J. W. 'Excavations at Flixton, Site 2' in J. G. D. Clark, *Excavations at Star Carr*, Appendix, pp. 192–4 (Cambridge, 1954)

Nedervelde, J. van, Davies, M., and John, B. 'Radiocarbon dating from Ogof-yr-Ychen, a new Pleistocene site, West Wales', *Nature*, 245 (1973), pp. 453–5

Oakley, K. P. 'Geology and Palaeolithic studies' in K. P. Oakley *et al.*, *A Survey of the Prehistory of the Farnham District (Surrey)*, pp. 3–58 (Surrey Archaeol. Soc., 1939)

——, 'The date of the "Red Lady" of Paviland', *Antiquity*, 42 (1968), pp. 306–7

——, *Man the Toolmaker*, 6th edn (London, 1972)

—— and Leakey, M. 'Report on excavations at Jaywick Sands, Essex (1934)', *Proc. Prehist. Soc.*, 3 (1937), pp. 217–60

——, Campbell, B. G., and Molleson, T. *Catalogue of Fossil Hominids: Part 2, Europe*, Brit. Mus. (Natur. Hist.) (London, 1971)

——, Andrews, P., Keeley, L. H., and Clark, J. D. 'A reappraisal of the Clacton spearpoint', *Proc. Prehist. Soc.*, 43 (1977), pp. 13–30

Ovey, C. D. (ed.) *The Swanscombe Skull* (Roy. Anthropol. Soc., London, 1964)

Paterson, T. T. 'Studies in the Palaeolithic succession in England, I. The Barnham sequence', *Proc. Prehist. Soc.*, 3 (1937), pp. 87–135

——, 'Core, culture and complex in the Old Stone Age', *Proc. Prehist. Soc.*, 11 (1945), pp. 1–19

—— and Fagg, B. E. B. 'Studies in the Palaeolithic succession in England, II. The Upper Brecklandian Acheul (Elveden)', *Proc. Prehist. Soc.*, 6 (1940), pp. 1–29

—— and Tebbutt, C. F. 'Studies in the Palaeolithic succession in England, III, Palaeoliths from St. Neots, Huntingdonshire', *Proc. Prehist. Soc.*, 13 (1947), pp. 37–46

Poole, H. F. 'Palaeoliths from Great Pan Farm, Isle of Wight', *Pap. Proc. Hampshire Field Club*, 9 (1924), pp. 305–19

Posnansky, M. 'The Lower and Middle Palaeolithic industries of the English East Midlands', *Proc. Prehist. Soc.*, 29 (1963), pp. 357–94

Pyddoke, E. 'An Acheulian implement from Slindon', *Univ. London Inst. Archaeol. 6th Ann. Report* (1950), pp. 30–3

Roe, D. A. 'The British Lower and Middle Palaeolithic: some problems, methods of study and preliminary results', *Proc. Prehist. Soc.*, 30 (1964), pp. 245–67

——, 'British Lower and Middle Palaeolithic hand-axe groups', *Proc. Prehist. Soc.*, 34 (1968a), pp. 1–82

——, *A Gazeteer of British Lower and Middle Palaeolithic Sites*, Council Brit. Archaeol. Research Report No. 8 (London, 1968b)

——, 'Some Hampshire and Dorset hand-axes and the question of "Early Acheulian" in Britain', *Proc. Prehist. Soc.*, 41 (1975), pp. 1–9

——, 'The earliest industries in Britain' in K. Valoch (ed.), *Les premières industries de l'Europe*, Colloque VIII, IXe Congrès de l'Union Internationale des Sciences Préhistoriques et Protohistoriques (Nice, 1976), pp. 76–95

——, 'The evolution of the Acheulian in Britain' in J. Combier (ed.), *L'évolution de l'acheuléen en Europe*, Collogue X, IXe Congrès de l'Union Internationale des Sciences Préhistoriques et Protohistoriques (Nice, 1976), pp. 31–46

Rowlands, B. M. 'Radiocarbon evidence of the age of an Irish Sea Glaciation in the Vale of Clwyd', *Nature*, 230 (1971), pp. 9–11

Sainty, J. E. 'An Acheulian Palaeolithic workshop site at Whitlingham', *Proc. Prehist. Soc. East Anglia*, 5 (1925), pp. 177–213

——, 'Three Combe-Capelle hand-axes from Norfolk', *Proc. Prehist. Soc.*, 1 (1935), pp. 98–100

Sandford, K. S. 'The river gravels of the Oxford district', *Quart. Journ. Geol. Soc.*, 80 (1924), pp. 113–79

Savory, H. N. 'Excavations at the Hoyle, Tenby, in 1968', *Archaeologia Cambrensis*, 122 (1973), pp. 18–34

Shackley, M. L. 'A contextual study of the Mousterian industry from Great Pan Farm, Newport, Isle of Wight', *Proc. Isle of Wight Natur. Hist. Archaeol. Soc.*, 6 (1973), pp. 542–54

Singer, R., Wymer, J., Gladfelter, B. G., and Wolff, R. G. 'Excavation of the Clactonian industry at the Golf Course, Clacton-on-Sea, Essex', *Proc. Prehist. Soc.*, 39 (1973), pp. 6–74

—— and Wymer, J. 'The sequence of Acheulian industries at Hoxne, Suffolk' in J. Combier (ed.), *L'évolution de l'acheuléen en Europe*, Colloque VIII, IXe Congrès de l'Union Internationale des Sciences Préhistoriques et Protohistoriques (Nice, 1976), pp. 14–30

Smith, R. A. 'A Palaeolithic industry at Northfleet, Kent', *Archaeologia*, 62 (1911), pp. 515–32

——, 'Implements from high-level gravel near Canterbury', *Proc. Prehist. Soc. East Anglia*, 7 (1933), pp. 165–70

Smith, W. G. *Man the Primeval Savage* (London, 1894)

——, 'Notes on the Palaeolithic floor near Caddington', *Archaeologia* (1916), pp. 49–74

Snelling, A. J. R. 'Excavations at the Globe Pit, Little Thurrock, Grays, Essex, 1961', *Essex Naturalist*, 31 (1964), pp. 199–208

Sollas, W. 'Paviland Cave: an Aurignacian station in Wales', *Journ. Roy. Anthropol. Inst.*, 43 (1913), pp. 325–74

Solomon, J. D. 'The implementiferous gravels of Warren Hill', *Journ. Roy. Anthropol. Inst.*, 63 (1933), pp. 101–10

Straw, A. 'Sediments, fossils and geomorphology – a Lincolnshire situation' in D. A. Davidson and M. L. Shackley (eds.), *Geoarchaeology* (London, 1976), pp. 317–26

Szabo, B. J., and Collins, D. 'Ages of fossil bones from British interglacial sites', *Nature*, 254 (1975), pp. 680–2

Taylor, H. 'King Arthur's Cave, near Whitchurch, Ross-on-Wye', *Proc. Univ. Bristol Spelaeol. Soc.*, 3 (1928), pp. 59–83

Tebbutt, C. F. *et al.* 'Palaeolithic industries from the Great Ouse gravels at and near St. Neots', *Proc. Prehist. Soc. East Anglia*, 5 (1927), pp. 166–73

Tester, P. J. 'Palaeolithic flint implements from the Bowman's Lodge Gravel Pit, Dartford Heath', *Archaeologia Cantiana*, 63 (1950), pp. 122–34

——, 'An Acheulian site at Cuxton', *Archaeologia Cantiana*, 80 (1965), pp. 30–60

——, 'Further consideration of the Bowman's Lodge industry', *Archaeologia Cantiana*, 91 (1975), pp. 29–39

Tratman, E. K. 'Second report on the excavations at Sun Hole, Cheddar – the Pleistocene levels', *Proc. Univ. Bristol Spelaeol. Soc.*, 7 (1955), pp. 61–75

——, 'Picken's Hole, Crook Peak, Somerset; a Pleistocene site: preliminary note', *Proc. Univ. Bristol Spelaeol. Soc.*, 10 (1964), pp. 112–15

——, 'Problems of "the Cheddar Man", Gough's Cave, Somerset', *Proc. Univ. Bristol Spelaeol. Soc.*, 14 (1975), pp. 7–23

——, 'A late Upper Palaeolithic calculator (?), Gough's Cave, Cheddar, Somerset', *Proc. Univ. Bristol Spelaeol. Soc.*, 14 (1976), pp. 123–9

——, Donovan, D. T., and Campbell, J. B. 'The Hyaena Den (Wookey Hole), Mendip Hills, Somerset', *Proc. Univ. Bristol Spelaeol. Soc.*, 12 (1971), pp. 245–79

Treacher, M. S. *et al.* 'On the ancient channel between Caversham and Henley, Oxfordshire, and its contained flint implements', *Proc. Prehist. Soc.*, 14 (1948), pp. 126–54

Waechter, J.d'A. 'Swanscombe, 1968', *Proc. Roy. Anthropol. Inst. 1968* (1969), pp. 53–61

—— *et al.* 'Swanscombe, 1969', *Proc. Roy. Anthropol. Inst. 1969* (1970), pp. 83–93

—— *et al.* 'Swanscombe, 1970', *Proc. Roy. Anthropol. Inst. 1970* (1971), pp. 43–64

—— *et al.* 'Swanscombe, 1971', *Proc. Roy. Anthropol. Inst. 1971* (1972), pp. 73–85

Warren, S. H. 'Palaeolithic wooden spear from Clacton', *Quart. Journ. Geol. Soc.*, (1911), p. 67

—, 'The Mesvinian industry of Clacton-on-Sea', *Proc. Prehist. Soc. East Anglia*, 3 (1922), pp. 597–602

——, 'The Clacton flint industry: a new interpretation', *Proc. Geologists' Assoc.*, 62 (1951), pp. 107–35

——, 'The Clacton flint industry: a supplementary note', *Proc. Geologists' Assoc.*, 69 (1958), pp. 123–9

Watson, W. *Flint Implements*, 3rd edn (London, 1968)

West, R. G., and McBurney, C. B. M. 'The Quaternary deposits at Hoxne, Suffolk, and their archaeology', *Proc. Prehist. Soc.*, 20 (1954), pp. 131–54

Wymer, J. J. 'Palaeoliths from the gravel of the ancient channel between Caversham and Henley at Highlands, near Henley', *Proc. Prehist. Soc.*, 22 (1956), pp. 29–36

——, 'A Clactonian flint industry at Little Thurrock, Grays, Essex', *Proc. Geologists' Assoc.*, 68 (1957), pp. 159–77

——, 'The Lower Palaeolithic succession in the Thames Valley and the date of the ancient channel between Caversham and Henley, Oxfordshire', *Proc. Prehist. Soc.*, 27 (1961), pp. 1–27

——, 'Excavations at Barnfield Pit, 1955–60' in C. D. Ovey (ed.), *The Swanscombe Skull* (Roy. Anthropol. Soc., London, 1964), pp. 10–60

——, *Lower Palaeolithic Archaeology in Britain as Represented by the Thames Valley* (London, 1968)

——, 'A possibly Late Upper Palaeolithic site at Cranwich, Norfolk', *Norfolk Archaeol.*, 35 (1971), pp. 259–63

——, 'Flint collecting and the distribution of Palaeolithic and Mesolithic sites' in E. Fowler (ed.), *Field Survey in British Archaeology*, pp. 26–8 (Council Brit. Archaeol., London, 1972)

——, 'Clactonian and Acheulian industries in Britain – their chronology and significance', *Proc. Geologists' Assoc.*, 85 (1974), pp. 391–421

——, 'The interpretation of Palaeolithic cultural and faunal material found in Pleistocene sediments' in D. A. Davidson and M. L. Shackley (eds.) *Geoarchaeology* (London, 1976), pp. 327–34

——, 'The archaeology of man in the British Quaternary' in F. W. Shotton (ed.), *British Quaternary Studies* (Oxford, 1977), pp. 93–106

—— and Singer, R. 'First season of excavations at Clacton-on-Sea, Essex, England: a brief report', *World Archaeology*, 2 (1970), pp. 12–16

——, ——, 'Hoxne: Palaeolithic man's environment', *The Times*, 27 May 1975

—— and Straw, A. 'Hand-axes from beneath glacial till at Welton-le-Wold, Lincolnshire and the distribution of palaeoliths in Britain', *Proc. Prehist. Soc.*, 43 (1977), pp. 355–60

—— and Bonsall, C. J. *Gazeteer of Mesolithic Sites in England and Wales, with a Gazeteer of Upper Palaeolithic Sites in England and Wales*, Council Brit. Archaeol. Research Report No. 20 (London, 1977)

——, Jacobi, R. M., and Rose, J. 'Late Devensian and early Flandrian barbed points from Sproughton, Suffolk', *Proc. Prehist. Soc.*, 41 (1975), pp. 235–41

—— and Rose, J. 'A long blade industry from Sproughton, Suffolk, and the date of the buried channel deposits at Sproughton', *East Anglian Archaeology*, Report No. 3 (1976), pp. 1–15

Palaeolithic Artifacts and Analysis

Bohmers, A., and Wouters, A. 'Statistics and graphs in the study of flint assemblages', *Palaeohistoria*, 5 (1956), pp. 1–39

Bordes, F., and Sonneville-Bordes, D. de 'The significance of variability in Palaeolithic assemblages', *World Archaeology*, 2 (1970), pp. 61–73

Collins, D. 'The recognition of traditions and phases in culture from quantitative studies of stone technology', *Actes VIIᵉ Congrès de l'Union Internationale des Sciences Préhistoriques et Protohistoriques, Prague, 1966*, pp. 301–5

——, 'Stone artefact analysis and the recognition of culture traditions', *World Archaeology*, 2 (1970b), pp. 17–27

Feustel, R. *Technik der Steinzeit* (Weimar, 1973)

Graham, J. M., and Roe, D. A. 'Discrimination of British Lower and Middle Palaeolithic hand-axe groups using canonical variates' (1970), *World Archaeology*, 1 (1969–70), pp. 321–42

Keeley, L. H. 'The functions of Palaeolithic flint tools', *Scientific American*, 237, no. 5 (1977), pp. 108–26

Kleindienst, M. R., and Keller, C. M. 'Towards a functional analysis of hand-axes and cleavers: the evidence from East Africa', *Man*, 11 (1976), pp. 176–87

Knowles, F. H. S. *Stone-worker's Progress*, Pitt-Rivers Museum Occasional Papers on Technology, no. 6 (1953)

Mellars, P. 'Some comments on the notion of "functional variability" in stone tool assemblages', *World Archaeology*, 2 (1970), pp. 74–89

Newcomer, M. H. 'Some quantitative experiments in hand-axe manufacture', *World Archaeology*, 3 (1971), pp. 85–94

Oakley, K. P. *Man the Toolmaker*, 6th edn (London, 1972)

Roe, D. A. 'Typology and the trouble with hand-axes' in G. de G. Sieveking *et al.* (eds.), *Problems in Economic and Social Archaeology*, pp. 61–70 (London, 1976)

Rosenfeld, A. 'The examination of use marks on some Magdalenian end scrapers' in G. de G. Sieveking (ed.), *Prehistoric and Roman Studies*, pp. 176–82 (London, 1971)

Semenov, S. A. *Prehistoric Technology* (London, 1964)

——, 'The forms and functions of the oldest tools (a reply to Prof. F. Bordes)', *Quartär*, 21 (1970), pp. 1–20

Shackley, M. L. 'Stream abrasion of flint implements', *Nature*, 248 (1974), pp. 501–2

Sheets, P. D., and Muto, G. R. 'Pressure blades and total cutting edge: an experiment in lithic technology', *Science*, 175 (1972), pp. 632–4

Sheperd, W. *Flint – its Origins, Properties and Uses* (London, 1972)

Siiriänen, A. 'Pieces in vertical movement – model for rock-shelter archaeology', *Proc. Prehist. Soc.*, 43 (1977), pp. 349–53

Watson, W. *Flint Implements*, 3rd edn (London, 1968)

Post-glacial Environment – Land- and Sea-level Changes

Binns, R. E. 'Flandrian strandline chronology for the British Isles and correlation of some European post-glacial strandlines', *Nature*, 235 (1972), pp. 206–10

Bishop, W. W., and Dickson, J. H. 'Radiocarbon dates related to the Scottish Late-glacial sea in the Firth of Clyde', *Nature*, 227 (1970), pp. 480–2

Churchill, D. M. 'The displacement of deposits formed at sea level 6500 years ago in Southern Britain', *Quaternaria*, 7 (1965), pp. 239–49

Clapham, A. R., and Godwin, H. 'Studies of the Post-glacial history of British vegetation. VIII, Swamping surfaces in the peats of the Somerset Levels', *Phil. Trans. Roy. Soc.*, B 233 (1948), pp. 233–73

Craig, G. Y. (ed.) *The Geology of Scotland* (Edinburgh, 1965)

Dinham, C. H. 'The geology of the Stirling district', *Proc. Geol. Assoc.*, 38 (1927), pp. 470–94

Donner, J. J. 'The Late- and Post-glacial raised beaches in Scotland, I', *Ann. Acad. Sci. Fennicae*, AIII, 53 (1959), pp. 1–25

——, 'The Late- and Post-glacial raised beaches in Scotland, II', *Ann. Acad. Sci. Fennicae*, AIII, 68 (1963), pp. 1–13

——, 'Land/sea level changes in Scotland' in D. Walker and R. G. West (eds.), *Studies in the Vegetational History of the British Isles* (Cambridge, 1970), pp. 23–40

Dunham, K. C., and Gray, D. A. 'A discussion on problems associated with the subsidence of South-east England', *Phil. Trans. Roy. Soc.*, A 272 (1972), pp. 79–274

Fairbridge, R. W. 'Eustatic changes in sea level', *Physics and Chemistry of the Earth*, 4 (1961), pp. 99–185

Godwin, H. 'Coastal peat beds of the British Isles and North Sea', *Journ. Ecol.*, 31 (1943), p. 199

——, 'Coastal peat beds of the North Sea region, as indices of land- and sea-level changes', *New Phytologist*, 44 (1945), pp. 29–69

——, Suggate, R. P., and Willis, E. H. 'Radiocarbon dating of the eustatic rise in ocean level', *Nature*, 181 (1958), pp. 1518–19

Hawkins, A. B. 'The late Weichselian and Flandrian transgressions of south-west Britain', *Quaternaria*, 14 (1971), pp. 115–30

Jamieson, T. F. 'On the history of the last geological changes in Scotland', *Quart. Journ. Geol. Soc. London*, 21 (1865), pp. 161–203

Jardine, W. G. 'Post-glacial sediments at Girvan, Ayrshire', *Trans. Geol. Soc. Glasgow*, 24 (1962), pp. 262–78

——, 'Post-glacial sea levels in South-west Scotland', *Scot. Geogr. Mag.*, 80 (1964), pp. 5–11

——, 'Sediments of the Flandrian transgression in south-west Scotland: terminology and criteria for facies determination', *Scot. Journ. Geol.*, 3 (1967), pp. 221–6

——, 'Form and age of late Quaternary shorelines and coastal deposits of south-west Scotland: critical data', *Quaternaria*, 14 (1971), pp. 103–14

——, 'Chronology of marine transgression and regression in south-western Scotland', *Boreas*, 4 (1975), pp. 173–96

——, 'Location and age of Mesolithic coastal occupation sites on Oronsay, Inner Hebrides', *Nature*, 267 (1977a), pp. 138–40

——, 'The Quaternary marine record in south-west Scotland and the Scottish Hebrides' in C. Kidson and M. J. Tooley (eds.), *The Quaternary History of the Irish Sea, Geol. Journ. Special Issue No. 7* (1977b), pp. 99–118

——, 'Radiocarbon ages of raised-beach shells from Oronsay, Inner Hebrides, Scotland: a lesson in interpretation', *Boreas*, 7 (1978), pp. 183–96

—— and Morrison, A. 'The archaeological significance of Holocene coastal deposits in south-western Scotland' in D. A. Davidson and M. L. Shackley (eds.), *Geoarchaeology*, pp. 175–95 (London, 1976)

Jelgersma, S. 'Sea-level changes during the last 10,000 years' in J. S. Sawyer (ed.), *World Climate from 8000 to 0 B.C.*, pp. 54–71 (Roy. Meteorological Soc., London, 1966)

Kidson, C., and Tooley, M. J. *The Quaternary History of the Irish Sea, Geol. Journ. Special Issue No. 7* (London, 1977)

Mörner, N.-A. 'Eustatic changes during the last 20,000 years and a method of separating the isostatic and eustatic factors in an uplifted area', *Palaeogeography, Palaeoclimatology, Palaeoecology*, 9 (1971), pp. 153–81

Morrison, I. A. 'Comparative stratigraphy and radiocarbon chronology of Holocene marine changes on the western seaboard of Europe' in D. A. Davidson and M. L. Shackley (eds.), *Geoarchaeology*, pp. 159–75 (London, 1975)

Morrison, M. E. S., and Stephens, N. 'Stratigraphy and pollen analysis of raised beach deposits at Ballyhalbert, Co. Down, Northern Ireland', *New Phytologist*, 59 (1960), pp. 153–62

Newey, W. W. 'Pollen analysis of sub-carse peats of the Forth Valley', *Trans. Inst. Brit. Geogr.*, 39 (1966), pp. 53–9

Peacock, J. D. 'Marine shell radiocarbon dates and the chronology of deglaciation in western Scotland', *Nature*, 230 (1971), pp. 43–5

Ritchie, W., and Crofts, R. *The Beaches of Islay, Jura and Colonsay* (University of Aberdeen, 1974)

Sissons, J. B. 'A re-interpretation of the literature of Late-glacial shorelines in Scotland with particular reference to the Forth area', *Trans. Edinburgh Geol. Soc.*, 19 (1962), pp. 83–99

——, 'The Perth Re-advance in Central Scotland', *Scot. Geogr. Mag.*, 80 (1964a), pp. 28–36

——, 'The Glacial Period' in J. W. Watson and J. B. Sissons (eds.), *The British Isles: a Systematic Geography*, pp. 131–51 (London, 1964b)

——, 'Relative sea-level changes between 10,300 and 8300 B.P. in part of the Carse of Stirling', *Trans. Inst. Brit. Geogr.*, 39 (1966), pp. 19–29

——, 'The Quaternary in Scotland: a review', *Scot. Journ. Geol.*, 10 (1974), pp. 34–7

——, *Scotland* (The Geomorphology of the British Isles) (London, 1976)

—— and Smith, D. E. 'Peat bogs in a Post-glacial sea and a buried raised beach in the western part of the Carse of Stirling', *Scot. Journ. Geol.*, 1 (1965a), pp. 247–55

Steers, J. A. 'The changing coastline', *Science Journ.*, 1 (1965), pp. 66–73

Stephens, N. 'Late-glacial and Post-glacial shorelines in Ireland and South-west Scotland' in R. B. Morrison and H. E. Wright, Jr. (eds.), 'Means of Correlation of Quaternary Successions', *Proc. VIIth Congress INQUA, Colorado, 1965*, Vol. 8 (University of Utah Press, 1968)

—— and Synge, F. 'Pleistocene shorelines' in G. H. Dury (ed.), *Geomorphological Essays*, pp. 1–51 (London, 1966)

Tooley, M. J. 'Sea-level changes during the last 9000 years in north-west England', *Geogr. Journ.*, 140 (1974), pp. 18–42

West, R. G. 'Relative land- sea-level changes in south-eastern England during the Pleistocene', *Phil. Trans. Roy. Soc.*, A 272 (1972), pp. 87–98

Willis, E. H. 'Marine transgression sequences in the English Fenlands', *Ann. New York Acad. Sci.*, 95 (1961), pp. 368–76

Post-glacial Environment – Climate and Vegetation

There is no single comprehensive survey of the Post-glacial environment of Britain and Ireland, but the major developments have been covered in other more general works, such as Pennington (1969), West (1968), Walker and West (1970), Evans (1975), Evans *et al.* (1975) and Limbrey and Evans (1978). British flora has been studied in detail by Godwin (1956 and 1975). A standard textbook for pollen analysis is Faegri and Iversen (1975), and there is a useful brief introduction to the subject by West (1971). A recent study of environmental change in general is that of Goudie (1977).

Blytt, A. *Essay on the Immigration of the Norwegian Flora During Alternating Rainy and Dry Periods* (Christiania, 1876)

Dimbleby, G. W. 'The ancient forest of Blackamore', *Antiquity*, 35 (1961), pp. 123–8

——, *The Development of British Heathlands and Their Soils*, Oxford Forestry Memoirs, No. 23 (1962)

——, *Plants and Archaeology* (London, 1967)

——, 'Archaeological evidence of environmental change', *Nature*, 256 (1975), pp. 265–7

Donner, J. J. 'The geology and vegetation of Late-glacial retreat stages in Scotland', *Trans. Roy. Soc. Edinburgh*, 63 (1957), pp. 221–64

Durno, S. E. 'Pollen analysis of peat deposits in Scotland', *Scot. Geogr. Mag.*, 72 (1956), pp. 177–87

Erdtman, G. 'Studies in the postarctic history of the forests of North-western Europe. I, Investigations in the British Isles', *Geol. Fören, Stockholm Förh.*, 50 (1928), p. 123

Evans, J. G. *The Environment of Early Man in the British Isles* (London, 1975)

——, Limbrey, S., and Cleere, H. (eds.) *The Effect of Man on the Landscape: the Highland Zone*, Council Brit. Archaeol. Research Report No. 11 (London, 1975)

Faegri, K., and Iversen, J. *Textbook of Pollen Analysis*, 2nd edn (Copenhagen, 1975)

Frenzel, B. 'Climatic change in the Atlantic/Sub-Boreal transition in the Northern Hemisphere: botanical evidence' in J. S. Sawyer (ed.), *World Climate from 8000 to 0 B.C.* (Roy. Meteorological Soc., London, 1966)

Geer, G. de 'A geochronology of the last 12,000 years', *Proc. 11th Int. Geol. Congr. (Stockholm)* (1912), pp. 241–58

Godwin, H. 'Pollen analysis and forest history of England and Wales', *New Phytologist*, 39 (1940a), p. 370

——, 'Studies of the Post-glacial history of British vegetation. III, Fenland pollen diagrams. IV, Post-glacial changes of relative land- and sea-level in the English Fenland', *Phil. Trans. Roy. Soc.* B 230 (1940b), pp. 239–303

——, 'Studies of the Post-glacial history of British vegetation. VI, Correlations in the Somerset Levels', *New Phytologist*, 40 (1941), pp. 108–32

——, 'Studies of the Post-glacial history of British vegetation. X, Correlations between climate, forest composition, prehistoric agriculture and peat stratigraphy in Sub-Boreal and Sub-Atlantic peats of the Somerset Levels', *Phil. Trans. Roy. Soc.*, B 233 (1948), p. 275

——, *The History of the British Flora* (Cambridge, 1956 and 1975)

——, 'Radiocarbon dating and Quaternary history in Britain', *Proc. Roy. Soc.*, B 153 (1960), pp. 287–320

—— and Clifford, M. H. 'Studies of the Post-glacial history of British vegetation. I, Origin and stratigraphy of Fenland deposits near Woodwalton, Hunts. II, Origin and stratigraphy of deposits in Southern Fenland', *Phil. Trans. Roy. Soc.*, B 229 (1938), pp. 323–406

—— and Tallantire, P. A. 'Studies of the Post-glacial history of British vegetation. XII, Hockham Mere, Norfolk', *Journ. Ecol.*, 39 (1951), pp. 285–307

——, Walker, D., and Willis, E. H. 'Radiocarbon dating and Post-glacial vegetational history: Scaleby Moss', *Proc. Roy. Soc.*, B 147 (1957), pp. 352–66

Goudie, A. S. *Environmental Change* (Oxford, 1977)

Grahmann, R. 'Das Eiszeitalter und der Übergang zur Gegenwart', *Erdkundliches Wissen*, 1 (4. Aufl.) (1965)

Hibbert, F. A., Switsur, V. R., and West, R. G. 'Radiocarbon dating of pollen zones at Red Moss, Lancashire', *Proc. Roy. Soc.*, B 177 (1971), pp. 161–76

Iversen, J. 'The influence of prehistoric man on vegetation', *Danm. Geol. Unders.*, IV R, no. 6 (1949), pp. 1–25

Jessen, K. 'Studies in late Quaternary deposits and floral-history of Ireland', *Proc. Roy. Irish Acad.*, B 52 (1949), pp. 85–290

Jones, R. L. 'The activities of Mesolithic man: further palaeobotanical evidence from north-east Yorkshire' in D. A. Davidson and M. L. Shackley (eds.), *Geoarchaeology* (London, 1976), pp. 355–67

Lamb, H. H., Lewis, R. P. W., and Woodruffe, A. 'Atmospheric circulation and the main climatic variables between 8000 and 0 B.C.: meteorological evidence' in J. S. Sawyer (ed.), *World Climate from 8000 to 0 B.C.*, pp. 174–217 (Roy. Meteorological Soc., London, 1966)

Limbrey, S., and Evans, J. G. *The Effect of Man on the Landscape: the Lowland Zone*, Council Brit. Archaeol. Research Report No. 11 (London, 1978)

Manley, G. 'Evolution of the climatic environment' in J. W. Watson and J. B. Sissons (eds.), *The British Isles: a Systematic Geography*, pp. 152–76 (London, 1964)

——, 'Possible climatic agencies in the development of Post-glacial habitats', *Proc. Roy. Soc.*, B 161 (1965), pp. 363–75

Mitchell, G. F. 'Studies in Irish Quaternary deposits. No. 7', *Proc. Roy. Irish Acad.*, B 53 (1951), pp. 111–206

——, 'Post-Boreal pollen diagrams from Irish raised bogs', *Proc. Roy. Irish Acad.*, B 57 (1956), pp. 185–251

——, 'Radiocarbon dates and pollen zones in Ireland', *Journ. Roy. Soc. Antiq. Ireland*, 88 (1958), pp. 49–56

Moore, P. D. 'The influence of prehistoric cultures upon the initiation and spread of blanket bog in upland Wales', *Nature*, 241 (1972), pp. 350–3

——, 'Origin of blanket mires', *Nature*, 256 (1975), pp. 267–9

Nichols, H. 'Vegetational change, shoreline displacement and the human factor in the late Quaternary history of South-west Scotland', *Trans. Roy. Soc. Edinburgh*, 67 (1967), pp. 145–87

Osborne, P. J. 'Evidence from the insects of climatic variation during the Flandrian period: a preliminary note', *World Archaeology*, 8 (1976), pp. 150–8
——, 'Insect evidence for the effect of man on the lowland landscape' in S. Limbrey and J. G. Evans (eds.), *The Effect of Man on the Landscape: the Lowland Zone*, Council Brit. Archaeol. Research Report No. 21 (1978), pp. 32–4
Pennington, W. *The History of British Vegetation* (London, 1969)
Post, L. von 'Om skogsträd pollen i sydsvenska torfmosselagerfolijder (föredragsreferat)', *Geol. För. Stockh. Förh.*, 38 (1916), p. 384
Sernander, R. 'On the evidence of Post-glacial changes of climate furnished by the peat mosses of northern Europe', *Geol. För. Stockh. Förh.*, 30 (1908), pp. 465–78
Simmons, I. G. 'Pollen diagrams from Dartmoor', *New Phytologist*, 63 (1964), pp. 165–80
——, 'Pollen diagrams from the N. York Moors', *New Phytologist*, 68 (1969a), pp. 807–27
——, 'Evidence for vegetation changes associated with Mesolithic man in Britain, in G. W. Dimbleby and P. Ucko (eds.), *The Domestication and Exploitation of Plants and Animals*, pp. 111–19 (London, 1969b)
——, 'Environment and early man on Dartmoor, Devon, England', *Proc. Prehist. Soc.*, 35 (1969c), pp. 203–19
——, 'The ecological setting of Mesolithic man in the Highland Zone' in J. G. Evans, S. Limbrey and H. Cleere (eds.), *The Effect of Man on the Landscape: the Highland Zone*, Council Brit. Archaeol. Research Report No. 11 (1975a), pp. 57–63
——, 'Towards an ecology of Mesolithic man in the uplands of Great Britain', *Journ. Archaeol. Science*, 2 (1975b), pp. 1–15
—— and Dimbleby, G. W. 'The possible role of ivy (*Hedera helix L.*) in the Mesolithic economy of western Europe', *Journ. Archaeol. Science*, 1 (1974), pp. 291–6
—— and Cundill, P. R. 'Late Quaternary vegetational history of the North York Moors. I, pollen analyses of blanket peats', *Journ. Biogeography*, 1 (1974), pp. 159–69
Sims, R. E. 'The anthropogenic factor in East Anglian vegetational history: an approach using A. P. F. techniques' in H. J. B. Birks and R. G. West (eds.), *Quaternary Plant Ecology*, pp. 223–36 (London, 1973)
Smith, A. G. 'Problems of inertia and threshold related to post-glacial habitat changes', *Proc. Roy. Soc.*, B 161 (1965), pp. 331–42
——, 'Late- and Post-glacial vegetational and climatic history of Ireland: a review' in N. Stephens and R. E. Glasscock (eds.), *Irish Geographical Studies* (1970a), pp. 65–88
——, 'The influence of Mesolithic and Neolithic man on British vegetation' in D. Walker and R. G. West (eds.), *Studies in the Vegetational History of the British Isles*, pp. 81–96 (Cambridge, 1970b)
—— and Pilcher, J. R. 'Radiocarbon dates and vegetational history of the British Isles', *New Phytologist*, 72 (1973), pp. 903–14
Spencer, P. J. 'Habitat change in coastal sand-dune areas: the molluscan evidence' in J. G. Evans, S. Limbrey, and H. Cleere (eds.), *The Effect of Man on the Landscape: the Highland Zone*, Council Brit. Archaeol. Research Report No. 11 (1975), pp. 96–103
Spratt, D. A., and Simmons, I. G. 'Prehistoric activity and environment on the North York Moors', *Journ. Archaeol. Science*, 3 (1976), pp. 193–210
Stewart, O. C. 'Fire as the first great force employed by man' in W. L. Thomas (ed.), *Man's Role in Changing the Face of the Earth*, pp. 115–33 (Chicago, 1956)
Tallantire, P. A. 'Studies of the Post-glacial history of British vegetation. XIII, Lopham Little Fen, a Late-glacial site in central East Anglia', *Journ. Ecol.*, 41 (1953), p. 361
Taylor, J. A. 'Chronometers and chronicles: a study of the palaeo-environments of West Central Wales', *Progress in Geography*, 5 (1973), pp. 248–334
——, 'The role of climatic factors in environmental and cultural changes in prehistoric times' in J. G. Evans, S. Limbrey, and H. Cleere (eds.), *The Effect of Man on the Landscape: the Highland Zone*, Council Brit. Archaeol. Research Report No. 11 (1975), pp. 6–19
Troels-Smith, J. 'The Muldbjerg dwelling-place: an early Neolithic archaeological site in the Aamosen Bog, West Zealand, Denmark', *The Smithsonian Report for 1959* (1960), pp. 577–601
Turner, J. 'A contribution to the history of forest clearance', *Proc. Roy. Soc.*, B 161 (1965), pp. 343–53
Walker, D., and West, R. G. *Studies in the Vegetational History of the British Isles* (Cambridge, 1970)

West, R. G. *Pleistocene Geology and Biology* (London, 1968)
——, 'Pollen zones in the Pleistocene of Great Britain and their correlation', *New Phytologist*, 69 (1970), pp. 1179–83
——, *Studying the Past by Pollen Analysis* (Oxford, 1971)
Zeuner, F. E. *Dating the Past* (London, 1958)

Mesolithic – General and Europe

There is no study of the Mesolithic period in Europe as a whole, but there are good studies of particular regions, e.g. Clark (1936, 1975) and summaries of recent work and research, e.g. Kozlowski (1973). Although this book deals with the cultures of Britain and Ireland, some important references to European areas have been given, apart from those mentioned in the text.

Albrethsen, S. E. and Brinch Petersen, E. 'Excavation of a Mesolithic cemetery at Vedbaek, Denmark', *Acta Archaeologica*, 47 (1976), pp. 1–28
Bandi, H.-G. 'Die mittlere Steinzeit Europas' in K. J. Narr (ed.), *Handbuch der Urgeschichte*, Band I – Ältere und Mittlere Steinzeit, pp. 321–46 (Bern, 1966)
Binford, L. R. 'Post-Pleistocene adaptations' in S. R. and L. R. Binford (eds.), *New Perspectives in Archaeology*, pp. 313–41 (Chicago, 1968)
Bokelmann, K. 'Duvensee, ein Wohnplatz des Mesolithikums in Schleswig-Holstein, und die Duvenseegruppe (Köln, 1969)', *Archäologische Informationen*, 1 (1972), pp. 92–3
Braidwood, R. J., and Willey, G. R. 'Conclusions and afterthoughts' in R. J. Braidwood and G. R. Willey (eds.), *Courses Toward Urban Life*, pp. 330–59 (Edinburgh, 1962)
Breuil, H., and Lantier R. *Les Hommes de la Pierre Ancienne* (Paris, 1951)
Brinch Petersen, E. 'A survey of the late Palaeolithic and of the Mesolithic in Denmark' in S. K. Kozlowski (ed.), *The Mesolithic in Europe*, pp. 77–127 (Warsaw, 1973)
Campbell, J. 'Territoriality among ancient hunters: interpretations from ethnography and nature', *Anthropological Archaeology in the Americas* (Anthropological Society of Washington, 1971)
Cartailhac, E. *La France Préhistorique* (Paris, 1889)
Childe, V. G. 'The Forest Cultures of Northern Europe: a study in evolution and diffusion', *Journ. Roy. Anthropol. Inst. Gr. Brit. Ireland*, 61 (1931), pp. 325–48
——, 'Adaptation to the Post-glacial forest on the north Eurasiatic plain' in G. C. MacCurdy (ed.), *Early Man*, pp. 233–42 (Philadelphia, 1937)
——, *Prehistoric Migrations in Europe* (Oslo, 1950)
Clark, J. G. D. *The Mesolithic Settlement of Northern Europe* (Cambridge, 1936)
——, 'Whales as an economic factor in prehistoric Europe', *Antiquity*, 21 (1947), pp. 84–104
——, 'Fowling in prehistoric Europe', *Antiquity*, 22 (1948), pp. 116–30
——, 'The development of fishing in prehistoric Europe', *Ant. Journ.*, 28 (1948), pp. 44–85
——, 'The earliest settlement of the West Baltic area in the light of recent research', *Proc. Prehist. Soc.*, 16 (1950), pp. 87–100
——, *Prehistoric Europe: the Economic Basis* (London, 1952)
——, 'The economic approach to prehistory (Albert Reckitt Archaeological Lecture)', *Proc. Brit. Academy*, 39 (1953), pp. 215–38
——, *Archaeology and Society*, 3rd edn (London, 1957)
——, 'Blade and trapeze industries of the European stone age', *Proc. Prehist. Soc.*, 24 (1958), pp. 24–52
——, 'A survey of the Mesolithic phase in the prehistory of Europe and South-west Asia', *Atti VI Congresso Internazionale Scienze Preistoriche e Protostoriche, Rome, 1962. I – Relazioni Generale*, pp. 97–111 (1962)
——, 'The economic impact of the change from late-glacial to post-glacial conditions in Northern Europe', *Proc. VIIIth International Congress of Anthropological and Ethnological Sciences, Tokyo and Kyoto, 1968*, vol. 3, pp. 241–4 (1968)
——, 'The archaeology of Stone Age settlement', *Ulster Journ. Archaeol.*, 35 (1972), pp. 3–16
——, 'Prehistoric Europe: the economic basis' in G. R. Willey (ed.), *Archaeological Researches in Retrospect*, pp. 33–57 (Cambridge, Massachusetts, 1974)
——, *The Earlier Stone Age Settlement of Scandinavia* (Cambridge, 1975)

Clarke, D. L. 'Mesolithic Europe: the economic basis' in G. Sieveking, I. H. Longworth, and K. E. Wilson (eds.), *Problems in Economic and Social Archaeology*, pp. 449–82 (London, 1976)

Degerbøl, M. 'Some remarks on Late- and Post-glacial vertebrate fauna and its ecological relations in Northern Europe', *Journ. Animal Ecology*, 33 (Supplement) (1964), pp. 71–85

Ducos, P. 'Le gisement de Châteauneuf-les-Martigues (Bouches du Rhône). Les mammifères et les problèmes de domestication', *Bull. Musée d'Anthropologie Préhistorique de Monaco*, 5 (1958), pp. 119–33

Escalon de Fonton, M. 'Origine et développement des civilisations néolithiques méditerranéennes en Europe occidentale', *Palaeohistoria*, 12 (1967), pp. 209–48

———, 'From the end of the Ice Age to the first agriculturalists' in S. Piggott, G. Daniel and C. B. M. McBurney (eds.), *France Before the Romans*, pp. 61–101 (London, 1974)

Gabel, W. C. 'The Mesolithic continuum in Western Europe', *American Anthropologist*, 60 (1958), pp. 658–67

Gramsch, B. *Das Mesolithikum im Flachland zwischen Elbe und Oder*, Veröffentlichungen des Museums für Ur- und Frühgeschichte, Band 7 (Potsdam, 1973)

Hodges, H. *Artifacts* (London, 1964)

Kozlowski, S. K. (ed.) *The Mesolithic in Europe* (1st International Symposium on the Mesolithic in Europe (Warsaw, 1973a)

———, 'Introduction to the history of Europe in the early Holocene' in S. K. Kozlowski (ed.), *The Mesolithic in Europe*, pp. 331–66 (Warsaw, 1973b)

———, *Les civilisations du 8e au 5e millénaire avant notre ère en Europe*, Colloque XIX, IXe Congrès de l'Union Internationale des Sciences Préhistoriques et Protohistoriques (Nice, 1976a)

———, 'Les courants interculturels dans le Mésolithique de l'Europe occidentale' in S. K. Kozlowski (ed.), *Les civilisations du 8e au 5e millénaire avant notre ère en Europe*, Colloque XIX, IXe Congrès Internationale des Sciences Préhistoriques et Protohistoriques (Nice, 1976b), pp. 135–60

———, 'Studies on the European Mesolithic, II – rectangles, rhomboids and trapezoids in North-western Europe', *Helinium*, 16 (1976c), pp. 43–54

Lee, R. B., and de Vore, I. (eds.) *Man the Hunter* (Chicago, 1968)

Louwe Kooijmans, L. P. 'Mesolithic bone and antler implements from the North Sea and from the Netherlands' (1970), *Ber. Rijksdienst Oudheidkundig. Bodemonderz.*, 20–21 (1970–1), pp. 27–73

Lumley, H. de (ed.) 'Les civilisations de l'épipaléolithique et du mésolithique', *La Préhistoire Française*, vol. I/2, pp. 1365–495 (Paris, 1976)

MacCurdy, G. G. *The Coming of Man* (London, 1935)

Mathiassen, T., Degerbøl, M., and Troels-Smith, J. 'Dyrholmen. En Stenalderboplads paa Djursland', *Det Kongelige Danske Videnskabernes Selskab. Arkaeologisk-Kunsthistoriske Skrifter*, I/1 (1942)

Moberg, C. A. 'The Mesolithic', *Antiquity*, 33 (1959), pp. 220–1

Mortillet, G. de *Le Préhistorique: Antiquité de l'Homme* (Paris, 1883)

Müller-Karpe, H. *Geschichte der Steinzeit* (Munich, 1974)

Munro, R. 'On the transition between the Palaeolithic and Neolithic civilisations in Europe', *Archaeol. Journ.*, 65 (1908), pp. 205–44

Newell, R. R. 'The Post-glacial adaptations of the indigenous population of the North-west European Plain' in S. K. Kozlowski (ed.), *The Mesolithic in Europe*, pp. 399–440 (Warsaw, 1973)

Piette, E. 'L'époque de transition intermédiare entre l'âge du renne et l'époque de la pierre polie', *Comptes Rendus Xeme Session, Congrès International d'Anthropologie et Archéologie Préhistoriques, Paris* (1889), p. 203

———, 'Hiatus et lacune. Vestiges de la période de transition dans la grotte du Mas d'Azil', *Bull. Soc. d'Anthropol. de Paris* (1895), pp. 27–8

Piggott, S. *Ancient Europe* (Edinburgh, 1965)

Richter, M. 'Die jüngere Altsteinzeit im Ostthüringer Orlagau', *Alt-Thüringen*, 1 (Weimar, 1955)

Roux, I., and Leroi-Gourhan, A. 'Les défrichements de la période atlantique', *Bull. Soc. Préhist. Française*, 61 (1964), pp. 309–15

Rozoy, J.-G. 'The Franco-Belgian Epipaleolithic. Current problems' in S. K. Kozlowski (ed.), *The Mesolithic in Europe*, pp. 503–30 (Warsaw, 1973)

——, *Les Derniers Chasseurs* (3 vols., Charleville-Mézierès, 1978)

Sarauw, G. F. L. 'En stenalders Boplads i Maglemose ved Mullerup, sammenholdt med beslaegtede Fund', *Aarbøger* (1903), pp. 148–315

Schlette, F. 'Die ältesten Haus- und Siedlungsformen des Menschen', *Ethnographisch-Archäologische Forschungen*, 5 (1958)

Schuldt, E. *Hohen Viecheln. Ein mittelsteinzeitlicher Wohnplatz in Mecklenburg* (Berlin, 1961)

Schwabedissen, H. *Die mittlere Steinzeit im westlichen Norddeutschland unter besonderer Berücksichtigung der Feuersteinwerkzeuge* (Neumünster, 1944)

Smith, M. A. 'The Mesolithic in the south of France: a critical analysis', *Proc. Prehist. Soc.*, 18 (1952), pp. 103–20

Tauber, H. 'Radiocarbon chronology of the Danish Mesolithic and Neolithic', *Antiquity*, 46 (1972), pp. 106–10

Troels-Smith, J. 'The Ertebølle culture and its background', *Palaeohistoria*, 12 (1966), pp. 505–28

Waterbolk, H. T. 'The Lower Rhine Basin' in R. J. Braidwood and G. R. Willey (eds.), *Courses Toward Urban Life*, pp. 227–53 (Edinburgh, 1962)

——, 'Food production in prehistoric Europe', *Science*, 162 (1968), pp. 1093–102

Wilkins, J. 'The Mesolithic', *Antiquity*, 33 (1959), pp. 130–1

Mesolithic – Britain and Ireland (General)

Bonsall, C. 'British Antiquity, 1974–75. Review of Palaeolithic/Mesolithic publications', *Archaeol. Journ.*, 132 (1975), pp. 302–9

Bradley, R. *The Prehistoric Settlement of Britain* (London, 1978)

Burkitt, M. C. 'The transition between Palaeolithic and Neolithic times, i.e. the Mesolithic period', *Proc. Prehist. Soc. East Anglia*, 5 (1925), pp. 16–33

Clark, J. G. D. *The Mesolithic Age in Britain* (Cambridge, 1932)

——, 'The separation of Britain from the continent', *Proc. Prehist. Soc.*, 2 (1936), p. 238

Evans, P. 'The intimate relationship: an hypothesis concerning pre-Neolithic land use' in J. G. Evans, S. Limbrey and H. Cleere (eds.), *The Effect of Man on the Landscape: the Highland Zone*, Council Brit. Archaeol. Research Report No. 11 (London, 1975), pp. 43–8

Higgs, E. S., and Vita-Finzi, C. 'Prehistoric economics: a territorial approach' in E. S. Higgs (ed.), *Papers in Economic Prehistory*, pp. 27–36 (London, 1972)

Jacobi, R. M. 'Aspects of the "Mesolithic Age" in Great Britain' in S. K. Kozlowski (ed.), *The Mesolithic in Europe*, pp. 237–65 (Warsaw, 1973)

——, 'Britain inside and outside Mesolithic Europe', *Proc. Prehist. Soc.*, 42 (1976), pp. 67–84

Kozlowski, S. K. 'Studies on the European Mesolithic: local and foreign elements in the British Mesolithic', *Wiadomości Archeologniczne*, 42 (1977), pp. 111–16

Mellars, P. A. 'The Palaeolithic and Mesolithic' in C. Renfrew (ed.), *British Prehistory: a New Outline*, pp. 41–99 (London, 1974)

——, 'Ungulate populations, economic patterns and the Mesolithic landscape' in J. G. Evans, S. Limbrey, and H. Cleere (eds.), *The Effect of Man on the Landscape: the Highland Zone*, Council Brit. Archaeol. Research Report No. 11 (London, 1975), pp. 49–56

——, 'The appearance of "Narrow Blade" microlithic industries in Britain: the radiocarbon evidence' in S. K. Kozlowski (ed.), *Les Civilisations de 8e au 5e millénaire avant notre ère en Europe*, Colloque XIX, IXe Congrès Internationale des Sciences Préhistoriques et Protohistoriques (Nice, 1976), pp. 166–74

——, 'Fire ecology, animal populations and man: a study of some ecological relationships in prehistory', *Proc. Prehist. Soc.*, 42 (1976b), pp. 15–45

——, 'Settlement patterns and industrial variability in the British Mesolithic' in G. de G. Sieveking, I. H. Longworth and K. Wilson (eds.), *Problems in Economic and Social Archaeology*, pp. 375–99 (London, 1976c)

Palmer, S. *Mesolithic Cultures of Britain* (Poole, 1977)

Wymer, J. J., and Bonsall, C. J. *Gazeteer of Mesolithic Sites in England and Wales with a Gazeteer of Upper Palaeolithic Sites in England and Wales*, Council Brit. Archaeol. Research Report No. 20 (London, 1977)

Mesolithic – England and Wales

Armstrong, A. L. 'Two East Yorkshire bone harpoons', *Man*, 75 (1922), pp. 130–1

——, 'The Maglemose remains of Holderness and their Baltic counterparts', *Proc. Prehist. Soc. East Anglia*, 4 (1923), pp. 57–70

——, 'A late Upper Aurignacian station in North Lincolnshire', *Proc. Prehist. Soc. East Anglia*, 6 (1931), pp. 335–9

Bonsall, C. J. 'Monk Moors, Eskmeals', *Dept. of Environment, Archaeological Excavations, 1975* (1976), p. 35

——, 'The coastal factor in the Mesolithic settlement of north-west England', 2nd International Symposium, *The Mesolithic in Europe* (Potsdam, 1978; in press)

Bradley, R. 'A Mesolithic assemblage from East Sussex [Belle Tout]', *Sussex Archaeol. Soc. Occasional Paper No. 2* (1970)

—— and Lewis, E. 'A Mesolithic site at Wakefords Copse, Havant', *Rescue Archaeology in Hampshire*, 2 (1974), pp. 5–18

Bramwell, D. 'The excavation of Dowel Cave, Earl Sterndale, 1958–59', *Derbyshire Archaeol. Journ.*, 33 (1959), pp. 97–109

Buckland, P. C., and Dolby, M. J. 'Mesolithic and later material from Misterton Carr, Notts – an interim report', *Trans. Thoroton Soc. Nottinghamshire*, 77 (1973), pp. 5–33

Buckley, F. *A Microlithic Industry, Marsden, Yorkshire* (privately printed, 1921)

——, *A Microlithic Industry of the Pennine Chain, related to the Tardenois of Belgium* (privately printed, 1924)

——, 'The microlithic industries of Northumberland', *Archaeologia Aeliana*, 4th ser., 1 (1925), pp. 42–7

Burchell, J. P. T. 'A final account of the investigations carried out at Lower Halstow, Kent', *Proc. Prehist. Soc. East Anglia*, 5 (1928), pp. 288–96

Calkin, J. B. 'Pygmy and other flint implements found at Peacehaven', *Sussex Archaeol. Coll.*, 65 (1924), pp. 224–41

Carter, H. H. 'Fauna of an area of Mesolithic occupation in the Kennet valley considered in relation to contemporary eating habits', *Berkshire Archaeol. Journ.*, 68 (1976), pp. 1–3

Cherry, J. 'Eskmeals sand-dunes occupation sites', *Trans. Cumberland Westmorland Antiq. Archaeol. Soc.*, 63 (1963), pp. 31–52

——, 'Early Neolithic sites at Eskmeals', *Trans. Cumberland Westmorland Antiq. Archaeol. Soc.*, 69 (1969), pp. 40–53

—— and P. J. 'Mesolithic habitation sites at St. Bees, Cumberland', *Trans. Cumberland Westmorland Antiq. Archaeol. Soc.*, 73 (1973), pp. 47–66

—— and Pennington, W. 'Flint-chipping sites at Drigg', *Trans. Cumberland Westmorland Antiq. Archaeol. Soc.*, 65 (1965), pp. 66–85

Churchill, D. M. 'The stratigraphy of the Mesolithic sites III and V at Thatcham, Berkshire', *Proc. Prehist. Soc.*, 28 (1962), pp. 362–70

—— and Wymer, J. J. 'The kitchen midden site at Westward Ho!, Devon, England: ecology, age and relation to changes in land and sea level', *Proc. Prehist. Soc.*, 31 (1965), pp. 74–84

Clark, J. G. D. 'The classification of a microlithic culture: the Tardenoisian of Horsham', *Archaeol. Journ.*, 90 (1934a), pp. 52–77

——, 'A late Mesolithic settlement at Selmeston, Sussex', *Antiquaries Journ.*, 14 (1934b), pp. 134–58

——, 'The prehistory of the Isle of Man', *Proc. Prehist. Soc.*, 1 (1935), pp. 70–92

——, 'Microlithic industries from the tufa deposits at Prestatyn, Flintshire and Blashenwell, Dorset', *Proc. Prehist. Soc.*, 4 (1938), pp. 330–4

——, 'A further note on the tufa deposit at Prestatyn, Flintshire', *Proc. Prehist. Soc.*, 5 (1939), pp. 201–2

——, *Excavations at Star Carr* (Cambridge, 1954)

——, 'A microlithic industry from the Cambridgeshire Fenland and other industries of Sauveterrian affinities from Britain', *Proc. Prehist. Soc.*, 21 (1955), pp. 3–20

——, *Star Carr: a Case Study in Bioarchaeology* (Reading, Mass., 1972)

——, Godwin, H., Godwin, M. E., and Clifford, M. H. 'Report on recent excavations at Peacock's Farm, Shippea Hill, Cambridgeshire', *Antiquaries Journ.*, 15 (1935), pp. 284–319

—— and Rankine, W. F. 'Excavations at Farnham, Surrey, 1937–38', *Proc. Prehist. Soc.*, 5 (1939), pp. 61–118

—— and Thompson, M. W. 'The groove and splinter technique of working antler in Upper Palaeolithic and Mesolithic Europe', *Proc. Prehist. Soc.*, 19 (1953), pp. 148–60

—— and Godwin, H. 'A Maglemosian site at Brandesburton, Holderness, Yorkshire', *Proc. Prehist. Soc.*, 22 (1956), pp. 6–22

—— and Godwin, H. 'The Neolithic in the Cambridgeshire fens', *Antiquity*, 36 (1962), pp. 10–21

Corcoran, J. X. W. P. 'Excavation of the bell barrow in Deerleap Wood, Wotton', *Surrey Archaeol. Coll.*, 60 (1963), pp. 1–18

Coupland, G. *A Mesolithic industry at 'The Beacon' S.E. Durham.* (privately printed, Gloucester, 1948)

Cowling, E. T., and Mellars, P. A. 'A Mesolithic flint site: the Sandbeds, Otley, Yorkshire. The affinities of the Sandbeds Mesolithic site', *Yorkshire Archaeol. Journ.*, 45 (1973), pp. 1–18

Crawford, O. G. S., and Peake, H. J. E. 'A flint factory at Thatcham, Berkshire', *Proc. Prehist. Soc. East Anglia*, 3 (1922), pp. 499–514

Davies, J. 'A Mesolithic site on Blubberhouses Moor, Wharfedale, West Riding of Yorkshire', *Yorkshire Archaeol. Journ.*, 41 (1963), pp. 60–70

—— and Rankine, W. F. 'Mesolithic flint axes from the West Riding of Yorkshire', *Yorkshire Archaeol. Journ.*, 40 (1960), pp. 209–14

Degerbøl, M. 'On a find of a Preboreal domestic dog (*Canis familiaris L.*) from Star Carr, Yorkshire, with remarks on other Mesolithic dogs', *Proc. Prehist. Soc.*, 27 (1961), pp. 35–55

Dimbleby, G. W. 'The ancient forest of Blackamore', *Antiquity*, 35 (1961), pp. 123–8

Elgee, F. *Early Man in North-East Yorkshire* (Gloucester, 1930)

Froom, F. R. *Wawcott III: A Stratified Mesolithic Succession*, Brit. Archaeol. Report No. 27 (1976)

Godwin, H., and Godwin, M. E. 'British Maglemose harpoon sites', *Antiquity*, 7 (1933), pp. 36–48

Gordon-Williams, J. P. 'The Nab Head chipping floor', *Archaeologia Cambrensis*, 81 (1926), pp. 86–110

Grimes, W. F. *The Prehistory of Wales* (Cardiff, 1951)

Higgs, E. 'Excavations at a Mesolithic site at Downton, near Salisbury, Wiltshire', *Proc. Prehist. Soc.*, 25 (1959), pp. 209–32

Jacobi, R. M. 'Britain inside and outside Mesolithic Europe', *Proc. Prehist. Soc.*, 42 (1976), pp. 67–84

——, Tallis, J. H., and Mellars, P. A. 'The Southern Pennine Mesolithic and the ecological record', *Journ. Archaeol. Science*, 3 (1976), pp. 307–20

Keef, P. A. M., Wymer, J. J., and Dimbleby, G. W. 'A Mesolithic site on Iping Common, Sussex, England', *Proc. Prehist. Soc.*, 31 (1965), pp. 85–92

Kelly, J. H. 'The excavation of Wetton Mill rock shelter, Manifold Valley, Staffs.', *Stoke-on-Trent Museum Archaeol. Soc.*, 9 (1976), pp. 1–99

Lacaille, A. D. 'Mesolithic industries beside Colne waters in Iver and Denham, Buckinghamshire', *Records of Buckinghamshire*, 17 (1964), pp. 148–64

—— and Grimes, W. F. 'The prehistory of Caldey', *Archaeologia Cambrensis*, 104 (1955), pp. 85–165

Layard, N. 'A late Palaeolithic settlement in the Colne Valley, Essex', *Antiquaries Journ.*, 7 (1927), pp. 500–14

Leakey, L. S. B. 'Preliminary excavations of a Mesolithic site at Abinger Common, Surrey', *Surrey Archaeol. Soc. Research Paper No. 3* (1951)

Livens, R. G. 'The Irish Sea element in the Welsh Mesolithic cultures' in F. Lynch and C. Burgess (eds.), *Prehistoric Man in Wales and the West*, pp. 19–29 (Bath, 1972)

Lynch, F., and Allen, D. 'Brenig Valley excavations, 1974', *Trans. Denbighshire Hist. Soc.*, 24 (1975), pp. 13–37

McBurney, C. B. M. 'The Old Stone Age in Wales' in I.Ll. Foster and G. Daniel (eds.), *Prehistoric and Early Wales*, pp. 17–34 (London, 1965)

Manby, T. G. 'A Creswellian site at Brigham, East Yorkshire', *Antiquaries Journ.*, 46 (1966), pp. 211–28

Mellars, P. A. 'An antler harpoon-head of "Obanian" affinities from Whitburn, County Durham', *Archaeologia Aeliana*, 48 (1970), pp. 337–46

Miles, H. 'Excavations at Rhuddlan, 1969–71: interim report', *Journ. Flintshire Hist. Soc.*, 25 (1972), pp. 1–18

Money, J. H. 'Excavations at High Rocks, Tunbridge Wells, 1954–1956', *Sussex Archaeol. Coll.*, 98 (1960), pp. 173–221

——, 'Excavations in the Iron Age hill-fort at High Rocks, near Tunbridge Wells, 1957–1961', *Sussex Archaeol. Coll.*, 106 (1968), pp. 158–205

Moore, J. W. 'Mesolithic sites in the neighbourhood of Flixton, North-East Yorkshire', *Proc. Prehist. Soc.*, 16 (1950), pp. 101–8

Nickson, D., and MacDonald, J. H. 'A preliminary report on a microlithic site at Drigg, Cumberland', *Trans. Cumberland Westmorland Antiq. Archaeol. Soc.*, 55 (1955), pp. 17–29

Noe-Nygaard, N. 'Two shoulder blades with healed lesions from Star Carr', *Proc. Prehist. Soc.*, 41 (1975), pp. 10–16

Norman, C. 'Four Mesolithic assemblages from West Somerset', *Somerset Archaeol. Natur. Hist. Soc.*, 119 (1975), pp. 26–37

O'Malley, M. 'Broom Hill, Braishfield, Hampshire', *Dept. of Environment, Archaeological Excavations, 1975* (1976), pp. 37–8

——, 'Broom Hill, Braishfield. Mesolithic dwelling', *Current Archaeology*, no. 63 (1978), pp. 117–20

Palmer, S. 'The Stone Age industries of the Isle of Portland, Dorset, and the utilisation of Portland chert as artefact material in Southern England', *Proc. Prehist. Soc.*, 36 (1970), pp. 82–115

——, 'The Mesolithic habitation site at Culver Well, Portland, Dorset: interim note', *Proc. Prehist. Soc.*, 42 (1976), pp. 324–7

Peake, A. E. 'A prehistoric site at Kimble, South Buckinghamshire', *Proc. Prehist. Soc. East Anglia*, 2 (1918), pp. 437–58

Petch, J. A. *Early Man in the Huddersfield District*, Tolson Memorial Museum, Huddersfield, Publication no. 3 (1924)

Radley, J. 'Excavations at a rock shelter at Whaley, Derbyshire', *Derbyshire Archaeol. Journ.*, 87 (1967), pp. 1–17

——, 'A Mesolithic structure at Sheldon, with a note on chert as a raw material on Mesolithic sites in the southern Pennines', *Derbyshire Archaeol. Journ.*, 88 (1968), pp. 26–36

——, 'An archaeological survey and policy for Wiltshire: Part II, the Mesolithic', *Wiltshire Archaeol. Mag.*, 64 (1969a), pp. 18–20

——, 'A note on four Maglemosian bone points from Brandesburton, and a flint site at Brigham, Yorkshire', *Antiquaries Journ.*, 49 (1969b), pp. 377–8

——, 'The Mesolithic period in north-east Yorkshire', *Yorkshire Archaeol. Journ.*, 42 (1969c), pp. 314–27

—— and Marshall, G. 'Mesolithic sites in south-west Yorkshire', *Yorkshire Archaeol. Journ.*, 41 (1963), pp. 81–97

—— and Mellars, P. A. 'A Mesolithic structure at Deepcar, Yorkshire, and the affinities of its associated flint industries', *Proc. Prehist. Soc.*, 30 (1964), pp. 1–24

—— and Marshall, G. 'Maglemosian sites in the Pennines', *Yorkshire Archaeol. Journ.*, 41 (1965), pp. 394–402

——, Tallis, J. H., and Switsur, V. R. (ed. P. A. Mellars) 'The excavation of three "Narrow Blade" Mesolithic sites in the Southern Pennines, England', *Proc. Prehist. Soc.*, 40 (1974), pp. 1–19

Raistrick, A. 'Mesolithic sites of the North-East coast of England', *Proc. Prehist. Soc. East Anglia*, 7 (1933), pp. 188–98

Rankine, W. F. 'A Mesolithic site at Farnham', *Surrey Archaeol. Coll.*, 44 (1936), pp. 24–46

——, 'Stone "maceheads" with Mesolithic associations from south-eastern England', *Proc. Prehist. Soc.*, 15 (1949a), pp. 70–6

——, 'A Mesolithic Survey of the West Surrey Greensand', *Surrey Archaeol. Soc. Research Paper No. 2* (1949b)

——, 'A Mesolithic chipping floor at the Warren, Oakhanger, Selborne, Hants.', *Proc. Prehist. Soc.*, 18 (1952a), pp. 21–35

——, 'Implements of coloured flint in Britain. Their distribution and derivation of raw material', *Archaeol. Newsletter*, 4 (1952b), pp. 145–9

——, 'Mesolithic research in southern England', *Archaeol. Newsletter*, 5 (1954), pp. 37–41

——, 'The Mesolithic of Southern England', *Surrey Archaeol. Soc. Research Paper No. 4* (1956)

——, 'Further excavations at Oakhanger, Selborne, Hants. Site VIII', *Wealden Mesolithic Research Bulletin* (Privately printed, 1961), pp. 1–6

——, Rankine, W. M, and Dimbleby, G. W. 'Further excavations at a Mesolithic site at Oakhanger, Selborne, Hants.', *Proc. Prehist. Soc.*, 26 (1960), pp. 246–62

Sainty, J. E. 'A flaking site on Kelling Heath, Norfolk', *Proc. Prehist. Soc. East Anglia*, 4 (1924), pp. 165–75

Sheridan, R., Sheridan, P., and Hassen, P. 'Rescue excavation of a Mesolithic site at Greenham Dairy Farm, Newbury, 1963', *Trans. Newbury District Field Club*, 11 (1967), pp. 66–73

Spratt, D. A., Goddard, R. E., and Brown, D. R. 'Mesolithic settlement sites at Upleatham, Cleveland', *Yorkshire Archaeol. Journ.*, 48 (1976), pp. 19–26

Switsur, V. R., and Jacobi, R. M. 'Radiocarbon dates for the Pennine Mesolithic', *Nature*, 256 (1975), pp. 32–4

Trechmann, C. T. 'Mesolithic flints from the submerged forest at West Hartlepool', *Proc. Prehist. Soc.*, 2 (1936), pp. 161–8

Wainwright, G. J. 'The excavation of a Mesolithic site at Freshwater West, Pembrokeshire', *Bull. Board Celtic Studies*, 18 (1959), pp. 196–205

——, 'Three microlithic industries from South-west England and their affinities', *Proc. Prehist. Soc.*, 26 (1960a), pp. 193–201

——, 'The re-examination of a chipping floor at Frainslake, Pembrokeshire and its affiliated sites', *Bull. Board Celtic Studies*, 19 (1960b), pp. 49–56

——, 'A re-interpretation of the microlithic industries of Wales', *Proc. Prehist. Soc.*, 29 (1963), pp. 99–132

Walker, D. 'A site at Stump Cross, near Grassington, Yorkshire and the age of the Pennine microlithic industry', *Proc. Prehist. Soc.*, 22 (1956), pp. 23–8

Warren, S. H., Clark, J. G. D., Godwin, H., Godwin, M. E., and MacFadyen, W. A. 'An early Mesolithic site at Broxbourne sealed under Boreal peat', *Journ. Roy. Anthropol. Inst.*, 64 (1934), pp. 101–28

Wheeler, A. 'Why were there no fish remains at Star Carr?' *Journ. Archaeol. Science*, 5 (1978), pp. 85–9

White, R. B. 'Excavations at Trwyn Du, Aberffraw, Anglesey', *Archaeology in Wales*, 15 (1975), p. 25

Woodcock, A. G. *The nature of the Horsham Industry and its place within the British Mesolithic*, Chichester Museum Occasional Paper No. 1 (1973)

Woodman, P. C. 'A re-appraisal of the Manx Mesolithic' in P. Davey (ed.), *Man and Environment in the Isle of Man*, pp. 119–39, Brit. Archaeol. Report (Brit. series), No. 54 (1978) (i–ii)

Wymer, J. J. 'Excavations at the Maglemosian sites at Thatcham, Berkshire', *Proc. Prehist. Soc.*, 28 (1962), pp. 329–61

——, Jacobi, R. M., and Rose, J. 'Late Devensian and early Flandrian barbed points from Sproughton, Suffolk', *Proc. Prehist. Soc.*, 41 (1975), pp. 235–41

—— and Bonsall, C. J. *Gazeteer of Mesolithic Sites in England and Wales with a Gazeteer of Upper Palaeolithic Sites in England and Wales*, Council Brit. Archaeol. Research Report No. 20 (1977)

Mesolithic – Ireland

Addyman, P. V. and Vernon, P. D. 'A beach pebble industry from Dunaff Bay, Inishowen, Co. Donegal', *Ulster Journ. Archaeol.*, 29 (1966), pp. 6–15

Ap Simon, A. 'Ballynagilly and the beginning and end of the Irish Neolithic' in S. J. de Laet (ed.), *Acculturation and Continuity in Atlantic Europe* (4th Atlantic Colloquium, Ghent, 1975), pp. 15–30 (Brugge, 1976)

Burchell, J. P. T. 'Some littoral sites of early Post-glacial times, located in Northern Ireland', *Proc. Prehist. Soc. East Anglia*, 7 (1934), pp. 366–72

Cross, R. E. 'Lough Gara: a preliminary survey', *Journ. Roy. Soc. Antiq. Ireland*, 83 (1953), pp. 93–6

Herity, M. 'The early prehistoric period around the Irish Sea' in D. Moore (ed.), *The Irish Sea Province in Archaeology and History*, pp. 29–37 (Cambrian Archaeol. Assoc., Cardiff, 1970)

Hodges, H. W. M. 'Some observations on the Mesolithic period in Ireland', *Ulster Journ. Archaeol.*, 16 (1953), pp. 25–30

Liversage, G. D. 'A note on the occurrence of Larnian flints on the Leinster coast', *Journ. Roy. Soc. Antiq. Ireland*, 91 (1961), pp. 109–16

——, 'Excavations at Dalkey Island, Co. Dublin', *Proc. Roy. Irish Acad.*, C 66 (1968), pp. 53–233

Mitchell, G. F. 'An early kitchen-midden in Co. Louth', *Journ. Co. Louth Archaeol. Soc.*, 11 (1947), pp. 169–74

——, 'The "Larnian" culture: a review', *Journ. Roy. Soc. Antiq. Ireland*, 79 (1949a), pp. 170–81

——, 'Further kitchen-middens in Co. Louth', *Journ. Co. Louth Archaeol. Soc.*, 12 (1949b), pp. 14–20

——, 'The Mesolithic site at Toome Bay, Co. Londonderry', *Ulster Journ. Archaeol.*, 18 (1955), pp. 1–16

——, 'An early kitchen-midden site at Sutton, Co. Dublin', *Journ. Roy. Soc. Antiq. Ireland*, 86 (1956), pp. 1–26

——, 'Some chronological implications of the Irish Mesolithic', *Ulster Journ. Archaeol.*, 33 (1970), pp. 3–14

——, 'The Larnian culture: a minimal view', *Proc. Prehist. Soc.*, 37 (1971), pp. 274–83

——, 'Further excavations of the early kitchen-midden site at Sutton, Co. Dublin', *Journ. Roy. Soc. Antiq. Ireland*, 102 (1972a), pp. 151–9

——, 'Some Ultimate Larnian sites at Lake Derravaragh, Co. Westmeath., *Journ. Roy. Soc. Antiq. Ireland*, 102 (1972b), pp. 160–73

——, *The Irish Landscape* (London, 1976)

Morrison, M. E. S. 'The palynology of Ringneill Quay, a new Mesolithic site in Co. Down, Northern Ireland', *Proc. Roy. Irish Acad.*, C 61 (1960), pp. 171–82

Movius, H. L. 'A Neolithic site on the River Bann', *Proc. Roy. Irish Acad.*, C 43 (1936), pp. 17–40

——, 'A Stone Age site Glenarm, Co. Antrim', *Journ. Roy. Soc. Antiq. Ireland*, 67 (1937), pp. 181–220

——, 'An early Post-glacial archaeological site at Cushendun, Co. Antrim', *Proc. Roy. Irish Acad.*, C 46 (1940a), pp. 1–84

——, 'Report on a Stone Age excavation at Rough Island, Strangford Lough, Co. Down', *Journ. Roy. Soc. Antiq. Ireland*, 70 (1940b), pp. 111–42

——, *The Irish Stone Age* (Cambridge, 1942)

——, 'Curran Point, Larne, Co. Antrim: the type site of the Irish Mesolithic', *Proc. Roy. Irish Acad.*, C 56 (1953), pp. 1–195

Ryan, M. 'Lough Boora excavations', *An Taisce*, 2 (1978), pp. 13–14

Smith, A. G., and Collins, A. E. P. 'The stratigraphy, palynology and archaeology of diatomite deposits at Newferry, Co. Antrim', *Ulster Journ. Archaeol.*, 34 (1971), pp. 3–25

Stephens, N., and Collins, A. E. P. 'The Quaternary deposits at Ringneill Quay and Ardmillan, Co. Down', *Proc. Roy. Irish Acad.*, C 61 (1960), pp. 41–77

Whelan, C. B. 'Studies in the significance of the Irish Stone Age: the cultural sequence', *Proc. Roy. Irish Acad.*, C 44 (1938), pp. 115–38

——, *A Bone Industry from the Lower Bann*, Archaeological Research Publications (Northern Ireland) No. 1 (Belfast, 1952)

Woodman, P. C. 'Some implement types from Glenarm', *Ulster Journ. Archaeol.*, 30 (1967), pp. 3–8

——, 'The chronological position of the latest phases of the Larnian', *Proc. Roy. Irish Acad.*, C 74 (1974a), pp. 237–58

——, 'Settlement patterns of the Irish Mesolithic', (1974b) *Ulster Journ. Archaeol.*, 36–37 (1973–4), pp. 1–16

——, 'Mount Sandel' in T. G. Delaney (ed.), *Excavations 1973. Summary Accounts of Archaeological Work in Ireland*, p. 9 (Belfast, 1974c)

——, 'Mount Sandel' in T. G. Delaney (ed.), *Excavations 1974. Summary Accounts of Archaeological Work in Ireland*, pp. 12–13 (Belfast, 1975)

——, 'The Irish Mesolithic/Neolithic transition' in S. J. de Laet (ed.), *Acculturation and Continuity in Atlantic Europe* (4th Atlantic Colloquium, Ghent, 1975), pp. 296–307 (Brugge, 1976a)

——, 'Early Mesolithic hut sites at Mount Sandel, Co. Derry', *Résumés des Communications, IXe Congrès Internationale des Sciences Préhistoriques et Protohistoriques* (Nice, 1976), p. 256

——, 'Mount Sandel', *Current Archaeology*, 5 (1977a), pp. 372–6

——, 'Recent excavations at Newferry, Co. Antrim', *Proc. Prehist. Soc.*, 43 (1977b), pp. 155–99
——, *The Mesolithic in Ireland*, Brit. Archaeol. Report No. 58 (1978)

Mesolithic – Scotland

Anderson, J. 'Notice of a cave recently discovered at Oban, containing human remains and a refuse-heap of shells and bones of animals, and stone and bone implements' (1895), *Proc. Soc. Antiq. Scot.*, 29 (1894–5), pp. 211–30
——, 'Notes on the contents of a small cave or rock-shelter at Druimvargie, Oban; and of three shell-mounds in Oronsay', *Proc. Soc. Antiq. Scot.*, 32 (1897–8), pp. 298–313
Atkinson, R. J. C. 'Fishermen and farmers' in S. Piggott (ed.), *The Prehistoric Peoples of Scotland*, pp. 1–38 (London, 1962)
Bishop, A. H. 'An Oronsay shell-mound – a Scottish pre-Neolithic site' (1914), *Proc. Soc. Antiq. Scot.*, 48 (1913–14), pp. 52–108
Blackadder, A. 'On the superficial strata of the Forth district', *Memoirs Wernerian Natur. Hist. Soc.*, 5 (1824), pp. 424–41
Breuil, H. 'Observations on the pre-Neolithic industries of Scotland' (1922), *Proc. Soc. Antiq. Scot.*, 56 (1921–2), pp. 261–81
Bryce, T. H. 'On the cairns and tumuli of the Island of Bute' (1904) *Proc. Soc. Antiq. Scot.*, 38 (1903–4), pp. 17–81
Burgess, C. 'An early Bronze Age settlement at Kilellan Farm, Islay, Argyll' in C. Burgess and R. Mikct (eds.), *Settlement and Economy in the Third and Second Millennia B.C.*, Brit. Archaeol. Reports No. 33 (1976), pp. 181–207
Callander, J. G. 'A flint workshop on the Hill of Skares' (1917), *Proc. Soc. Antiq. Scot.*, 51 (1916–17), pp. 117–27
——, 'A collection of Tardenoisian implements from Berwickshire' (1927), *Proc. Soc. Antiq. Scot.*, 61 (1926–7), pp. 318–27
——, 'A collection of stone and flint implements from Airhouse, Parish of Channelkirk, Berwickshire' (1928), *Proc. Soc. Antiq. Scot.*, 62 (1927–8), pp. 166–80
——, 'Land movements in Scotland in prehistoric and recent times' (1929), *Proc. Soc. Antiq. Scot.*, 63 (1928–9), pp. 314–22
Clark, J. G. D. 'Notes on the Obanian with special reference to antler- and bone-work' (1956), *Proc. Soc. Antiq. Scot.*, 89 (1955–6), pp. 91–106
Coles, J. M. 'Kilmelfort Cave', *Discovery and Excavation Scotland* (1959), p. 4
——, 'Tiretigan Cave, near Kilberry', *Discovery and Excavation Scotland* (1961), p. 10
——, 'Cave of the Crags, near Kilmelfort', *Discovery and Excavation Scotland* (1963), p. 9
——, 'New aspects of the Mesolithic settlement of South-west Scotland', *Trans. Dumfriesshire Galloway Natur. Hist. Antiq. Soc.*, 41 (1964), pp. 67–98
——, 'The early settlement of Scotland: excavations at Morton, Fife', *Proc. Prehist. Soc.*, 37 (1971), pp. 284–366
Cormack, W. F. 'A Mesolithic site at Barsalloch, Wigtownshire', *Trans. Dumfriesshire Galloway Natur. Hist. Antiq. Soc.*, 47 (1970), pp. 63–80
—— and Coles, J. M. 'Mesolithic site at Low Clone, Wigtownshire', *Trans. Dumfriesshire Galloway Natur. Hist. Antiq. Soc.*, 45 (1968), pp. 44–72
Corrie, J. M. 'Notes on some stone and flint implements found near Dryburgh in the Parish of Mertoun, Berwickshire' (1916), *Proc. Soc. Antiq. Scot.*, 50 (1915–16), pp. 307–13
Davidson, J. M., Phemister, J., and Lacaille, A. D. 'A stone age site at Woodend Loch, near Coatbridge', *Proc. Soc. Antiq. Scot.*, 83 (1948–9), pp. 77–98
Edgar, W. 'A Tardenoisian site at Ballantrae, Ayrshire' (1940), *Trans. Glasgow Archaeol. Soc.*, 9 (1937–40), pp. 184–8
Ferguson, W. 'Notes on some collections of flint implements from Buchan, Aberdeenshire', (1874) *Proc. Soc. Antiq. Scot.*, 10 (1873–4), pp. 507–18
Geikie, J. 'Discovery of an ancient canoe in the old alluvium of the Tay at Perth', *Scottish Naturalist*, 5 (1880), pp. 1–7
Gray, A. 'Notice of the discovery of a cinerary urn of the Bronze Age, and of worked flints underneath it at Dalaruan; also of an old flint working-place in the 30-foot raised beach at Millknowe, Campbeltown' (1894), *Proc. Soc. Antiq. Scot.*, 28 (1893–4), pp. 263–74

Grieve, D. 'Notes on the shell heaps near Inveravon, Linlithgowshire' (1872), *Proc. Soc. Antiq. Scot.*, 9 (1870–2), pp. 45–52

Grieve, S. *The Great Auk or Garefowl* (London, 1885)

Hutcheson, A. 'Notice of the discovery of a stratum containing worked flints at Broughty Ferry' (1886), *Proc. Soc. Antiq. Scot.*, 20 (1885–6), pp. 166–9

Idle, E. T., and Martin, J. 'The vegetation and land use history of Torrs Warren, Wigtownshire', *Trans. Dumfriesshire Galloway Natur. Hist. Soc.*, 51 (1975), pp. 1–9

Jardine, W. G. 'Location and age of Mesolithic coastal occupation sites on Oronsay, Inner Hebrides', *Nature*, 267 (1977), pp. 138–40

—— and Morrison, A. 'The archaeological significance of Holocene coastal deposits in south-western Scotland' in D. A. Davidson and M. L. Shackley (eds.) *Geoarchaeology*, pp. 175–95 (London, 1976)

Lacaille, A. D. 'Mesolithic implements from Ayrshire' (1930), *Proc. Soc. Antiq. Scot.*, 64 (1929–30), pp. 34–47

——, 'Silex tardenoisiens de Shewalton', *Bull. Soc. Préhist. Française*, 28 (1931), pp. 301–12

——, 'The Tardenoisian micro-burin in Scotland' (1935), *Proc. Soc. Antiq. Scot.*, 69 (1934–5), pp. 443–5

——, 'A barbed point of deer-antler from Shewalton, Ayrshire' (1939), *Proc. Soc. Antiq. Scot.*, 73 (1938–9), pp. 48–50

——, 'The microlithic industries of Scotland' (1940), *Trans. Glasgow Archaeol. Soc.*, 9 (1937–40), pp. 56–74

——, 'Unrecorded microliths from Tentsmuir, Deeside and Culbin' (1944), *Próc. Soc. Antiq. Scot.*, 78 (1943–4), pp. 5–16

——, 'The stone industries associated with the raised beach at Ballantrae', *Proc. Soc. Antiq. Scot.*, 79 (1944–5), pp. 81–106

——, 'A stone industry from Morar, Inverness-shire: its Obanian (Mesolithic) and later affinities', *Archaeologia*, 94 (1951), pp. 103–39

——, *The Stone Age in Scotland* (London, 1954)

Livens, R. G. 'Three tanged flint points from Scotland' (1956), *Proc. Soc. Antiq. Scot.*, 89 (1955–6), pp. 438–43

——, 'Excavations at Terally, Wigtownshire' (1957), *Trans. Dumfriesshire Galloway Natur. Hist. Antiq. Soc.*, 35 (1956–7), pp. 85–102

McCallien, W. J., and Lacaille, A. D. 'The Campbeltown raised beach and its contained stone industry' (1941), *Proc. Soc. Antiq. Scot.*, 75 (1940–1), pp. 55–92

MacDougall, A. J. 'Notice of the excavation of a rock-shelter at Dunollie, Oban' (1907), *Proc. Soc. Antiq. Scot.*, 41 (1906–7), pp. 181–2

MacKie, E. W. 'Radiocarbon dates for two Mesolithic shell heaps and a Neolithic axe factory in Scotland', *Proc. Prehist. Soc.*, 38 (1972), pp. 412–16

Mann, L. McL. 'Oronsay period: discoveries at Risga', *Glasgow Herald*, 21 August 1920

Mapleton, R. J. 'Note of a bone cave at Duntroon' (1874), *Proc. Soc. Antiq. Scot.*, 10 (1872–4), pp. 306–8

Marshall, D. 'A survey of the caves of Bute and Cumbrae', *Trans. Buteshire Natur. Hist. Soc.*, 12 (1938), pp. 113–18

Mason, W. D. 'Prehistoric man at Tweed Bridge, Selkirk', *Proc. Soc. Antiq. Scot.*, 65 (1930–1), p. 414

Masters, L. J., and Langhorne, T. 'A probable Mesolithic hearth at Redkirk Point, Gretna, Dumfriesshire', *Discovery and Excavation Scotland* (1976), pp. 27–8

Mathewson, A. 'Notes on stone cists and an ancient kitchen midden near Dundee' (1879), *Proc. Soc. Antiq. Scot.*, 13 (1878–9), pp. 303–7

Mellars, P. A. 'Excavation and economic analysis of Mesolithic shell-middens on the island of Oronsay' in L. M. Thoms (ed.), 'Early Man in the Scottish Landscape', *Scottish Archaeological Forum*, 9 (1979), pp. 43–61

—— and Payne, S. 'Excavation of two Mesolithic shell middens on the island of Oronsay', *Nature*, 231 (1971), pp. 397–8

Mercer, J. 'Stone tools from a washing-limit deposit of the highest Post-glacial transgression, Lealt Bay, Isle of Jura' (1968), *Proc. Soc. Antiq. Scot.*, 100 (1967–8), pp. 1–46

——, 'Flint tools from the present tidal zone, Lussa Bay, Isle of Jura, Argyll' (1970a), *Proc. Soc. Antiq. Scot.*, 102 (1969–70), pp. 1–30

——, 'The microlithic succession in N. Jura, Argyll, W. Scotland', *Quaternaria*, 13 (1970b), pp. 177–85

——, 'A regression-time stone-workers' camp 33 ft O.D., Lussa River, Isle of Jura' (1971), *Proc. Soc. Antiq. Scot.*, 103 (1970–1), pp. 1–32

——, 'Microlithic and Bronze Age camps, 75–62 ft O.D., N. Carn, Isle of Jura' (1972), *Proc. Soc. Antiq. Scot.*, 104 (1971–2), pp. 1–22

——, 'New C14 dates from the Isle of Jura', *Antiquity*, 48 (1974a), pp. 65–6

——, *Hebridean Islands: Colonsay, Gigha, Jura* (Glasgow, 1974b)

——, 'Glenbatrick Waterhole, a microlithic site on the Isle of Jura' (1974c), *Proc. Soc. Antiq. Scot.*, 105 (1972–4), pp. 9–32

Morris, D. B. 'Whale remains, prehistoric implements, etc., found at Causewayhead' (1898), *Trans. Stirlingshire Natur. Hist. Archaeol. Soc.* (1897–8), pp. 57–61

——, 'The whale remains of the Carse of Stirling', *Scottish Naturalist* (1925), pp. 137–40

Morrison, A. 'The coastal Mesolithic in south-west Scotland', 2nd International Symposium, *The Mesolithic in Europe* (Potsdam, 1978, in press)

—— and Jardine, W. G. 'The coastal environment as a habitat of Mesolithic man, with particular reference to northern Britain', *Actes IX e Congrès Internationale des Sciences Préhistoriques et Protohistoriques* (Nice, 1976, in press)

Mulholland, H. 'The microlithic industries of the Tweed Valley', *Trans. Dumfriesshire Galloway Natur. Hist. Antiq. Soc.*, 47 (1970), pp. 81–110

Munro, R. *Prehistoric Scotland* (Edinburgh, 1899)

——, 'On the transition between the Palaeolithic and Neolithic civilisations in Europe', *Archaeol. Journ.*, 65 (1908), pp. 205–44

Paterson, H. M. L., and Lacaille, A. D. 'Banchory microliths' (1936), *Proc. Soc. Antiq. Scot.*, 70 (1935–6), pp. 419–34

Peach, B. N. 'Explanation of Sheet 31', *Memoirs of the Geological Survey, Scotland* (Edinburgh, 1879)

Smith, J. *Prehistoric Man in Ayrshire* (London, 1895)

Stevenson, R. B. K. 'A shell-heap at Polmonthill, Falkirk' (1946), *Proc. Soc. Antiq. Scot.*, 80 (1945–6), pp. 135–9

Tait, L. 'Notes on the shell-mounds, hut-circles and kist-vaens of Sutherland', *Proc. Soc. Antiq. Scot.*, 7 (1866–8), pp. 525–32

——, 'Note on the shell-mounds of Sutherland' (1870), *Proc. Soc. Antiq. Scot.*, 8 (1868–70), pp. 63–4

Truckell, A. E. 'The Mesolithic in Dumfries and Galloway: recent developments', *Trans. Dumfriesshire Galloway Natur. Hist. Antiq. Soc.*, 40 (1963), pp. 43–7

Turner, W. 'On some implements of stag's horn associated with whales' skeletons found in the Carse of Stirling', *Report British Assoc.* (1889), pp. 789–91

——, 'On human and animal remains found in caves at Oban, Argyllshire' (1895), *Proc. Soc. Antiq. Scot.*, 29 (1894–5), pp. 410–38

INDEX

Aberystwyth 141
Abinger 138
Acheulian industries 45, 49, 54, 59, 60, 66, 70, 72, 74, 75, 81
Aegyptopithecus 39
Ahrensburgian culture 96, 100
Airhouse Farm 171
Airthrey 168
Allerød 21, 22, 91
Altmühl industries 82, 83, 87
Anglian glacial 17; Clactonian industries 56, 70; deposits 72; fauna 24; limits 17
Anston Stones (Dead Man's Cave) 96, 100, 116
Ardeer 155
Aurignacian culture 82, 90
Australopithecus 27, 40–3; *africanus* 41; earliest 40; (*Homo*) *habilis* 41; 'osteodontokeratic' culture 41; *robustus/boisei* 41; '*Zinjanthropus*' (*boisei*) 27
Aveline's Hole 93–5, 100
Azilian culture 114

Badger Hole 87
Baker's Farm 63, 66
Baker's Hole 75
Ballantrae 155, 172
Ballynagilly 172
Banchory 165
Bann, river 130, 148–9, 152
'Bann Flake' 146, 151, 152
Bapchild 75
barbed points, bone or antler: Mesolithic 99, 102, 114, 120, 132, 136, 154, 157–61, 164; Middle Palaeolithic 79; Upper Palaeolithic 85, 93, 97, 99
Barnfield Pit, Swanscombe: Clactonian industries 72; hand-axe industries 61, 70; river terraces 20–1; skull 45, 47, 61; stratification 61–5; uranium series dating 61, 72
Barnham St Gregory 72
Barsalloch 154
'*bâton-de-commandement*' 85, 95
Belle Tout 138
Bench Fissure 87
Biggar 170
Blacklane 112

Blair Drummond 168
'Blattspitzen', leaf points 82–91
boulder clay 17
Bowman's Lodge 66
Bramford Road, Ipswich 90
Brenig Valley 141–3
Broken Hill, Zambia 43
Broom Hill, Braishfield 140
Broome 66
Broomhead Moor 128–9, 134
Broughty Ferry 165, 168
Broxbourne 122, 126
Brundon 77
burin busqué 90
Burry Holms 126

Caddington 74
Cae Gwyn Cave 89–90
Caisteal-nan-Gillean 158
Caldey (Caldy) Island 89, 95–6, 141
Callander 102
Campbeltown 157
Cannoncourt Farm 63–6
Cardross 168
Carse Clays 102, 168
Carstairs 170
Castleroe 146
Cat's Hole (Cat Hole) 95
Causewayhead 168
Charsfield 90
Châteauneuf-les-Martigues 172
'Cheddar Man' 95
Cheddarian industries 93–100 *passim*
'Chellean' 59
Choukoutien, China 43, 45, 70, 74
Christchurch 79
Church Hole 81, 96
Clactonian industries 54, 56, 66, 70–2; classification 70; development 81
Clacton-on-Sea 70–2, 74
Cleveland Hills 112
climatic optimum 22, 24, 110
Clonava Townland 152
Cnoc Coig 158
Cnoc Riach 158
Cnoc Sligeach 158–61
coastal habitat: fauna 161, 167–8; resources 130, 144; seasonal 130, 161; shell middens 141, 149, 151, 155, 157,

158–61, 165; sites 141, 149, 151,
154–69 *passim*
coleoptera: as environmental indicators 26,
83, 91
Colne Valley 122, 126
Colney Heath 93
Colonsay 158, 161
Constantine Road, Ipswich 90
Coralline Crag 17, 32
'core scrapers' 151
Corfe Mullen 60
Cow Cave 87
Coygan Cave 81
Cranwich 97–9
Crayford 77, 85
Creffield Road, Acton 77
Creswell Crags 81, 90, 96,116
Creswellian industries 93–100 *passim*, 116
Cromerian interglacial 38; fauna 56–9;
zonation 58–9
Crossakeel 152
Culbane 149
Culbin Sands 164
Culver Well 141
Cumstoun 154–5
Curran Point 149 51
Cushendun 149
Cuxton 66

Dalkey Island 151, 172
dating techniques: absolute dating 26–7;
dendrochronology 29–30; fluorine
analysis 26, 43, 45; nitrogen analysis 26;
potassium–argon (K/Ar) 27,
30–1;Protoactinium/Thorium
(Pa^{231}/Th^{230}) 30, 35; radiocarbon (C14)
27–30; radiometric dating 27–31;
relative dating 26; uranium analysis 26;
uranium series 30; varves 101
Daylight Rock 141
Deepcar 127
deep-sea cores: dating 30; foraminifera
34–5; micropalaeontology 34; O^{18}/O^{16}
analysis 34–5; palaeomagnetism 34–5;
palaeotemperatures 34–5; uranium
series dating 35
Deerleap Wood 138
dendrochronology 29–30
Devensian glacial: Chelford interstadial 83;
fauna 79, 83, 85–100 *passim*; glacial
maximum 90–1, 93; ice-retreat stages
93, 96–7, 101; Levalloisian industries
77; limits 17; Mousterian industries
79–81; sea-level 102; Upton Warren
interstadial 81, 83, 85; vegetation 22,
91–3
Distillery Cave 157
Doune 102
Downton 140

Dozemare Pool 124
Drigg 144
Druimvargie 157–8, 164
dug-out canoe 168
Dunaff Bay 152
Dunford Bridge 143
Dunollie Cave 157
Duvensee culture 118
Dyrholmen, Denmark 168

Ebbsfleet 77
Eemian interglacial: Neanderthal man 47;
soil development 18
Ehringsdorf, E. Germany 77, 82
Elder Bush Cave 96
Elsterian glacial 17; fauna 24, 58; limits 17
Elveden 66, 70
'eoliths' 40, 55–6
'epi Mesolithic' 172
'epi-Palaeolithic' 100, 114, 115
Ertebølle, Denmark 140, 168
eustasy 18, 101, 144

Farndale Moor 143
Farnham: Lower Palaeolithic 60, 69;
Mesolithic 138
Federmesser cultures 99, 100
Federsee, W. Germany 122
Ffynnon Beuno 90
Filpoke Beacon 146
fire: early use 15, 40, 45, 59, 72–4;
environmental impact 15, 112, 113, 124,
129, 144
Fladbury 81
Flandrian 22; climate 106–12;
environmental changes 101 13; human
influence on environment 112–13, 144;
raised beaches 101–6; sea-levels 101–6,
130, 144, 154–61 *passim*, 167, 168;
vegetation 106–13; *see also* Holocene,
Post-glacial
flint 54
Flixton I 122, 127
Flixton II 97
Fontéchevade, France 45, 47, 77
Fordwich 59, 69
Fort Ternan, Kenya 40
Forth Valley 168–9
Forty Acres Pit 87
Four Ashes 83
Fox Hole Cave 96
Freswick Sands 164
Friarton 168

Gaddesden Row 74
Gasworks Cave 157
geological time scale 15
Gipping Valley 79
Girvan 155–6

glacial period: deposits 91; faunas 24–6; ice-
    retreat stages 93, 96–7; maximum 90–1,
    93; melt-water 101; varves 101;
    vegetation 22, 91–3; *see also* Anglian,
    Devensian, Wolstonian
glaciation, evidence for 17, 101
glaciers 15–18, 93, 96–7, 101
Glecknabae 171–2
Glen Wyllan 138, 146
Glenarm 149
Glenavon 158, 164
Globe Pit 72
Glynn 146
Gough's Cave 95, 100
great auk 161
Great Pan Farm 81
Greenham Dairy Farm 124
Grimston Hall 97
'groove and splinter' technique 85, 118, 120
Grovelands 72
Günz glacial 32

Hackpen Hill 66
Hamburgian culture 95, 96, 99, 100
hand-axes 45, 54, 59; 'bifaces' 79–81, 82;
    bout coupé 79; classification 60–1;
    development 81; evolution 69–70;
    function 66; Levalloisian industries 75;
    Lower Palaeolithic 59–72 *passim*; 'pre-
    Hoxnian' 59–60, 81
Hengistbury Head 99, 100
High Furlong, Poulton-le-Fylde 97, 118
High Lodge 66, 72
Highlands Farm 66
Hilton 67
Hockham Mere 108, 113
Holocene: climate 106–12; environmental
    changes 101–13; human influence on
    environment 112–13, 144; raised
    beaches 101–6; sea-levels 101–6, 130,
    144, 154–61 *passim*, 167, 168; sub-
    division of Quaternary 15; vegetation
    106–13; *see also* Flandrian, Post-glacial
Holsteinian interglacial: duration 38
Homo erectus 26, 41, 43–5, 70, 74
Homo sapiens neanderthalensis 47
Homo sapiens sapiens 49, 53, 82
'Horsham culture' 126, 138
'Horsham point' 138
Hoxne: human activity 47, 72–4; 'Lower
    Industry' 61, 70; 'Upper Industry' 61, 70
Hoxnian interglacial 22; Clactonian
    industries 70–2; duration 38; early
    sapiens 47; fauna 24, 67; hand-axes 60;
    sea-level 66; vegetation 72
Hoyle's Mouth 96
Hyaena Den 81, 87

Icenian Crag 17
Ilsen Cave, E. Germany 82

interglacial: definition 22, 101; faunas 24;
    Flandrian 22; Hoxnian 22; Ipswichian
    22; vegetation 22–4; zonation 22–4, 110
interstadial: Allerød 21, 22, 91; Chelford 83;
    definition 22; Upton Warren 81, 83, 85;
    Windermere 116
Inveravon 169
Iping Common 112, 122–4
Ipswichian interglacial 22; fauna 24, 77;
    hand-axes 66; Levalloisian industries 77;
    Swanscombe 63
Islay 161, 162
Isle of Man 138, 146
isostasy 18, 101, 102
Istállóskö Cave, Hungary 82
Iver 77

Jerzmanowician culture 82
Jura 161, 162–4

Kent's Cavern: Earlier Upper Palaeolithic
    85–7, 91; Later Upper Palaeolithic 93;
    Lower Palaeolithic 59, 69; Mousterian
    industries 79
Kettlebury 140
Kildale Hall 97 (footnote)
Kilellan Farm 162
King Arthur's Cave 87, 95
Kinneil 169
Knowle Farm 66
Kostenki 49

La Chapelle-aux-Saints, France 47, 49
La Ferrassie 49
Lake Rudolf, Kenya 41, 53, 56
Langwith Cave 96
Larne 149–51
'Larnian' 146, 151
Lazaret, France 45
Le Moustier, France 49
Lea Valley 83
Lealt Bay 164
Levalloisian industries 54, 75–81; function
    75; prepared cores 75; 'tortoise cores'
    75, 77
'limpet hammers, limpet punches, limpet
    scoops' 141, 151, 157, 158, 167
Little Paxton 79
Loch Doon 154
Loch Lomond Re-advance 96–7, 116
loess 18
Lominot 127–8
Long Hole 87–9
Lough Allen 152
Lough Beg 148–9
Lough Boora 146
Lough Derravaragh 152
Lough Gara 152
Lough Neagh 149
Low Clone 154

Luce Sands 154, 164, 172
Lussa Bay 162
Lussa River 164
Lussa Wood 162
Lynch Hill Terrace 63
Lyne Hill 144

MacArthur Cave 157–8
Mackay Cave 157
Magdalenian culture 49, 114
Maglemosian culture 97, 126, 158
Makapansgat, Transvaal 41
Malin Head 152
March Hill 143
Marks Tey 38, 72
Marsh Benham 124
Mas d'Azil, France 115
Mauley Cross 143
Meganthropus palaeojavanicus 43
Meiklewood 168–9
Mendips 56–9, 81, 82, 87, 93–5
Mesolithic: beginning 116; 'Broad Blade'
    industries 118, 132, 134–5; concept
    114–15; dwelling structures 124, 130,
    138, 140, 143, 154, 167; earlier 115–33,
    136; later 134–73, 136; 'micro-burin'
    135; microliths 134–6; 'Narrow Blade'
    industries 132, 134–6; population 171,
    173; seasonal activity 120–2, 126–7,
    129, 132, 148–9, 161, 171; transition to
    Neolithic 171–3
Messingham 97
'Mesvinian' 70
'micro-burin' 135
microliths 114, 134–6
Middlezoy 124–6
Mindel glacial: fauna 24
Mindel-Riss interglacial: duration 38; early
    sapiens 47
Miocene period 17, 39, 40
Misterton Carr 129
mollusca, as environmental indicators 26
Molodova, U.S.S.R. 49
Monk Moors, Eskmeals 144–6
Montmaurin 45
moraines 17
Morton 165–8
Mother Grundy's Parlour 96, 116
Mount Sandel 130, 134, 146
Mousehold Heath 79
Mousterian industries 49, 54; Acheulian
    tradition 79–81; classification 77–9
Mousterian of Acheulian tradition 24,
    79–81
Mugharet es-Skhūl, Israel 47, 49
Mugharet et-Tabūn, Israel 47
Muldbjerg, Denmark 112

Nab Head 126, 141
Nana's Cave 96

natural 'artifacts' 55
Neanderthal man 45, 47–9, 74, 77–9, 83
Neasham 97
Neolithic 171–3
Newferry 148–9
Ngandong, Java 43
Nietoperzowa, Poland 82
North Sea:barbed points 102, 132; bone and
    antler objects 102, 118; land-link 118;
    sinking 105, 106, 134, 141
North Yorkshire Moors 143–4
Norwood Lane, Southall 77

Oakhanger 113, 140
Oare 99
Oban 157–8
'Obanian' culture 157, 158, 164, 167
Ogof-yr-Ychen 89
Oldbury 81
Oldowan culture 54, 56
Olduvai Gorge, Tanzania: dating 27, 31;
    hominid remains 53; tools 41, 43, 56, 74
Orlagau, E. Germany 168
Oronsay 158–61
Ostend, Norfolk 59
'osteodontokeratic' culture 41

Palaeolithic (Old Stone Age) 15; 'core
    industries' 54; 'flake industries' 54;
    Lower Palaeolithic, cultural development
    81, cultures 54–74 *passim*, habitations
    74, hominid types 74, human activity
    72–4, 77; Middle Palaeolithic 38, 77–81,
    cultural development 81, human activity
    79–81, industries 77–81, 82,
    Neanderthal man 77, 79; stone-working
    54; tool materials 54, 83–5; Upper
    Palaeolithic, Earlier 82, 83, 85–91,
    habitations 99–100, human activity 91,
    99–100, human remains 91, industries
    49, 54, 82–99 *passim*, 116, Later 83,
    91–100, life expectation 91, population
    90–1, 99–100, quantity of artifacts 90,
    ritual practices 96, stone tool
    classification 85, tool materials 83–5
palaeomagnetic time-scale: construction 31;
    deep-sea cores 31; Pliocene/Pleistocene
    boundary 32; Vallonet 56
Paviland Cave 27, 89, 91, 95
Peacock's Farm 136–8
'Peking Man' 70
'Perth Re-advance' 96
Picken's Hole 85
'Piltdown Man' 26
Pincevent, France 100
Pinhole Cave 81, 90, 96
'pit dwellings' 138
'*Pithecanthropus*': dating 27, 43; *erectus* 43
plant foods: Mesolithic 129–30, 136, 168;
    Palaeolithic 74

Pleistocene: chronology 32–8; climatic
    fluctuations 34–5; dating methods
    26–31; environment 21–6; fauna 24–6;
    glaciations 15–21; raised beaches 18;
    sea-levels 18; sub-division of Quaternary
    15; temperature 21; vegetation 22–4
Pliocene/Pleistocene boundary: deep-sea
    cores 34–5; location of 17, 32–5
pollen analysis, palynology 61, 72, 93, 138;
    diagrams 106–10; vegetation zones
    22–4, 106–13
Polmonthill 169
Pontnewydd 81
Port St Mary 138, 146, 171
Post-glacial 15, 101; climate 106–12; early
    114; environmental changes 101–13;
    human influence on environment
    112–13, 144; raised beaches 101–6; sea-
    levels 101–6, 130, 144, 154–61 *passim*,
    167, 168; vegetation 106–13; *see also*
    Flandrian, Holocene
potassium-argon (K/Ar) dating 27, 30–1,
    38; palaeomagnetic time-scale 31
Předmosti, Czechoslovakia 49
Prestatyn 141
Priory Midden 158
Propliopithecus 39
'proto-Solutrean' 82

Quaternary era: climate 21; sub-divisions 15

radiocarbon (C 14) dating: datable materials
    27; deep-sea cores 35;
    dendrochronological checks 30; half-life
    30; limits 29; Mesolithic dates 30, 116;
    Palaeolithic dates 79, 85–100 *passim*;
    sources of error 29, 169; standard
    deviation 29, 30, 116
Ragunda (Lake), Sweden 101
raised beaches: deposits 102–5, 156–7;
    Holocene 101–6; Pleistocene 18
Ramapithecus 39–40
Reculver 60
Red Crag 17, 32
red deer (*Cervus elaphus*) 122, 126–7, 129,
    152
'Red Lady' of Paviland 27, 89
Rhuddlan 126
Rickson's Pit 72
Ringneill Quay 151
Risga 161–2
Riss glacial: fauna 24; loess deposits 18
Riss-Würm interglacial: Neanderthal man
    47; soil development 18
river terraces: as chronological indicators
    20–1; formation of 18–20; *thalassostatic*
    18–20; Thames terraces 20–1, 45
Robin Hood's Cave 81, 90, 91, 96
Rocher Moss 143

Rockmarshall 151
Rough Island 151
Round Green 74

Saalian glacial: fauna 24; loess deposits 18
St Bees 97, 144
St Catherine's Hill 60
Salzgitter-Lebenstedt, W. Germany:
    environment and fauna 24; human
    activity 79; Neanderthal man 49, 79
Salzofenhöhle, Austria 83
Sandbeds 122
Sangiran, Java 43
Scaleby Moss 97, 108
sea-levels: Holocene 101–6, 130, 144,
    154–61 *passim*, 167, 168; Hoxnian 66;
    Pleistocene 18
Selmeston 138
Shanidar, Iraq 47, 49
Shapwick 124, 126
Shewalton 155, 157, 164, 172
Sidi Abderrahman, Morocco 74
'site-catchment area': Mesolithic 130, 144;
    Star Carr 120; Upper Palaeolithic 85–7,
    91, 97
Slindon 66
Soldier's Hole 87, 91
Solutrean culture 54, 82
Solway Firth 105, 154–5
Southacre 72
Southwold 90
Sproughton 99, 118
stadial, stade 22; Lowestoft 17
Stairhaven 154
Stannergate 165, 168
Star Carr 97, 108, 113, 116, 118–22, 124,
    127, 129, 143, 144, 171
Steinheim skull 45, 47, 74
Stoke Newington 74
Stony Low 118
stratigraphy: biostratigraphy 32, 38, 56–9,
    91, 110, 111; chronostratigraphy 32;
    climatostratigraphy 32; lithostratigraphy
    17, 32, 38, 56–9, 91
Sun Hole 95
Sutton 151, 172
Svaerdborg, Denmark 140
Swanscombe skull, 45, 47, 61, 74
Szeleta Cave, Hungary 82
Szeletian culture 82

Tarnflat 144
Tautavel, France 45
Tell Ubeidiya, Israel 43
Ternifine, Algeria 43, 74
Terra Amata, France 45, 74
Tertiary era 15, 18
Teshik-Tash, U.S.S.R. 49
Thatcham 124, 126

Thorpe Common 143
Tjörnes, Iceland 32–3
tool-making and tool-using 55
Toome Bay 149
Tornewton Cave 87
Torralba/Ambrona, Spain 45, 72, 74
Trinil, Java 26, 27, 43
Trwyn Du, Aberffraw 126
Tweed Valley 154, 170–1

Uphill Cave 87
Upleatham Hills 144
uranium series dating: Clacton-on-Sea 72;
    deep-sea cores 35; Swanscombe 61, 72;
    technique 30
Urstromtäler 18
Ursus deningeri 58
Ursus spelaeus, cave bear 49, 58, 59

Vallonet, France 56
varves 101
Vértesszöllös, Hungary 43, 45, 70, 74
Villafranchian: fauna 17, 24, 32, 34, 38;
    Lower 34; type-sites 32; Upper
    34, 56

Wakefords Copse 140
Wangford 99
Warcock Hill 127–8
Warren Hill 60, 69
Weichselian glacial: Late 91; limits 17; loess
    deposits 18
Weinberg caves, Mauern, Bavaria 82, 87
Welton-le-Wold 67
West Drayton 77
Westbury sub-Mendip 56–9
Westward Ho! 141
whale remains 168
Whitburn 158
White Gill 143
White Hill 136
Whitlingham 66
Willington 67
Windy Hill 127
Winfrith Heath 113
Wolstonian glacial: deposits 59; fauna 24;
    hand-axes 66; Levalloisian industries 75;
    Swanscombe 61–3
Wolvercote 66, 70
Woodend Loch 169
Wookey Hole 81, 82, 87
Würm glacial: limits 17; loess deposits 18